THE POLITICS OF THE IND

CONTEMPORARY HISTORY IN CONTEXT
Published in association with the Institute of Contemporary British History

General Editor: Peter Catterall, Director, Institute of Contemporary British History

Titles include:

Contemporary History in Context
Series Standing Order ISBN 0–333–71470–9
(*outside North America only*)

You can receive future titles in this series as they are published by placing a standing order. Please contact your bookseller or, in case of difficulty, write to us at the address below with your name and address, the title of the series and the ISBN quoted above.

Customer Services Department, Macmillan Distribution Ltd
Houndmills, Basingstoke, Hampshire RG21 6XS, England

The Politics of the Independence of Kenya

Keith Kyle
Visiting Professor of History
University of Ulster
Northern Ireland

in association with
INSTITUTE OF CONTEMPORARY BRITISH HISTORY ICBH

First published in Great Britain 1999 by
MACMILLAN PRESS LTD
Houndmills, Basingstoke, Hampshire RG21 6XS and London
Companies and representatives throughout the world

A catalogue record for this book is available from the British Library.

ISBN 0–333–72008–3 hardcover
ISBN 0–333–76098–0 paperback

First published in the United States of America 1999 by
ST. MARTIN'S PRESS, INC.,
Scholarly and Reference Division,
175 Fifth Avenue, New York, N.Y. 10010

ISBN 0–312–22201–7

Library of Congress Cataloging-in-Publication Data
Kyle, Keith.
The politics of the independence of Kenya / Keith Kyle.
p.   cm. — (Contemporary history in context)
Includes bibliographical references and index.
ISBN 0–312–22201–7 (cloth)
1.Kenya—Politics and government—To 1963.   2.Kenya—History–
–Autonomy and independence movements.   I. Title.   II. Series:
Contemporary history in context series.
DT433.575.K95   1999
967.62'03—dc21   98–50837
                                                                    CIP

This book is printed on paper suitable for recycling and made from fully managed and sustained forest sources.

10   9   8   7   6   5   4   3   2   1
08   07   06   05   04   03   02   01   00   99

Printed and bound in Great Britain by
Antony Rowe Ltd, Chippenham, Wiltshire

For Suzy, her Kenya book

Contents

General Editor's Preface

After the elapse of some 30 years it is easy to forget how much time and energy the demission of the British empire absorbed in the late 1950s and early 1960s. It is a truism that this was disproportionately the case in the settler colonies, such as Southern Rhodesia or Kenya. However, the presence of white settlers, as Keith Kyle shows, was by no means the only problem in Kenya. The richest and most populous of the East African colonies, it was nevertheless the last to achieve independence. No doubt this had much to do with the presence of settlers, and not only in terms of the political and electoral pressures from the Poujadist tendencies of which Harold Macmillan complained in his diary in the wake of the 1962 Orpington by-election disaster. Attempts to safeguard settlers were also a complicating factor in a succession of constitutions, each of which rapidly proved unworkable. At the same time, however, these compounded existing inter-tribal difficulties and contributed towards the intensity of political conflict in Kenya. The result was that progress towards independence was anything but smooth. There was dissension over the future governance of Kenya, exemplified by the conflict between KADU and KANU. Meanwhile, in their attempts to achieve a peaceful transition to a legally constituted, secure and pro-western independent Kenya, the British had to bear in mind not only the cold war dimension to the politics of independence, but also the need to avoid the example of the Congo.

Keith Kyle is particularly well-placed to tell this story. As a young journalist in Nairobi he was an inside observer of the politics of Kenyan independence. His account of key events in this story is enlivened by personal recollection of, for instance, the release of Jomo Kenyatta, and has been enriched by his own collection of papers and archives. But this is not a memoir, nor is it told from a particular standpoint. It provides a detailed and authoritative assessment not only of political developments in Kenya but also of the course of colonial policy in London. Instead of focusing on one or the other Kyle skilfully interweaves both, in the process showing how they interacted and impacted upon each other. Neither operated in a vacuum; just as the successive constitutional settlements

played a part in structuring Kenyan politics so the political realities of Kenya forced themselves upon Colonial Office policy, not
least in prompting the change in policy towards Kenyatta that forms
an important part of this account. This marked a dramatic shift in
the British attitude to the man who they had so demonized at the
time of the Mau Mau Emergency. In a sense, however, it was a
purely pragmatic reaction to the pressures building up in Kenya,
which were in turn driven in part by the rather negative fact that
the desirability of Kenyatta's release was the one thing most African politicians could agree on. The British attitude was to change
much more dramatically thereafter. As Keith Kyle shows, Kenyatta
was redefined by the colonial power, and indeed by settlers, from
being central to the problem to being central to the solution. Despite his age, he provided the figure around which Kenyan politics
could coalesce in the run-up to independence. Kenyatta was thus
able to reconcile many of the tensions in Kenyan political life. But
he was perhaps too central, obscuring the degree to which the flaws
in the politics of Kenya's independence remained unresolved; flaws
which would however become increasingly apparent under his
successor.

PETER CATTERALL

Preface

One day shortly after the independence of Kenya I was walking through the streets of Fort Hall (as Marang'a was still named) with two veterans of the independence struggle, Jesse Kariuki and James Beauttah. Kariuki suddenly produced out of his pocket a small, leather-bound notebook in which were handwritten in English a few outstanding dates, including his own computed year of birth and the (subsequent) arrival of the white man. He asked me how long the Romans had been in Britain. I told him about four hundred years. 'Ah!' he said with great satisfaction, snapping the notebook shut. The lesson was plain. He had seen the British in and he had seen the British out.

Part I of this book is an abbreviated, and necessarily selective, historical introduction to Britain's brief association with Kenya (as it was known after 1920) from the time the British arrived in the 1890s until the beginning of Harold Macmillan's Premiership in 1957. The core of the book is contained in Part II and deals with the political events that brought Kenya to independence. During the first part of that period I was the political and parliamentary correspondent of *The Economist*. From 1961 to 1964 I worked for BBC television in East and Central Africa, appearing regularly on the nightly *Tonight* programme. I also wrote for various British and American papers including the *Spectator, Time and Tide, Forum Service, Reynolds News, Christian Science Monitor,* and *Atlantic Monthly.* My main base was Nairobi. I was therefore a witness of many of the events I describe in the latter part of the book. On occasion I have quoted directly from what I wrote at the time.

While I was living in Nairobi I assembled a sizeable archive of documents and interview notes with a view to publishing a book soon after independence. I made some use of this material in published articles and when I was teaching a course in African politics as a Fellow of the Institute of Politics, the John F. Kennedy School of Government, Harvard, but the project, though started, was never finished. After a thirty-year break I took up the subject again when I was invited to contribute a paper to the Institute of Contemporary British History's 1995 conference. This has subsequently appeared in *Contemporary British History* (vol. 11, no. 4, Winter 1997) under the same title as this book. The lapse of time has meant that British documents have become available under the Thirty-Year Rule at the Public Record Office at Kew, as have rich sources in the Rhodes House branch of the Bodleian Library at Oxford. I have also had the advantage of being able to interview some of the surviving British Ministers involved, especially the Duke of Devonshire and the Earl of Perth, and some of the retired civil servants who held key positions in the Colonial Office during the approach to independence.

KEITH KYLE

Acknowledgements

As already implied the research for this book was done in two periods, separated by more than thirty years. In the 1960s I interviewed the following, some now deceased, to all of whom I wish to express gratitude:

Iain Macleod, Reginald Maudling, T. J. Mboya, Oginga Odinga, Daniel arap Moi, Sir Derek Erskine, Sir Walter Coutts, Sir Eric Griffith-Jones, Luke Obok, Omolo Agar, Charles Njonjo, Dr Mungai Njoroge, Dr Julius Kiano, W. W. W. Awori, James Gichuru, Bildad Kaggia, Ronald Ngala, Mwai Kibaki, Peter Okondo, Dick Oloo, Rhoderick Macleod, Patrick Ooko, Masinde Muliro, Clement Argwings-Kodhek, J. D. Otiende, Leslie Brown, Chanan Singh, Musa Amalemba, Josef Mathenge, Sir Michael Blundell, Sir Humphrey Slade, Fitz de Souza, Sir Ralph Windham.

I am especially grateful to the memory of Tom Mboya for giving me free access to many of his files, which are here quoted as 'Mboya Papers', and to Rhoderick Macleod, executive officer of KADU, who gave me similar access to files in his possession, cited as 'KADU Papers'. Ambu Patel gave me the complete run of his remarkable literary and pictorial collection of material on the history of African nationalism in Kenya.

I acknowledge with gratitude the decision of Alasdair Milne, the editor of the BBC's *Tonight* programme, to employ me as a resident correspondent in Nairobi from 1961 to 1964, and the invitation from the late Sir Bernard de Bunsen, Vice-Chancellor of the University of East Africa, to spend a term as scholar-in-residence at Makerere College, Kampala. Dame Margery Perham of St Antony's College, Oxford, willingly gave me her advice and guidance in the 1960s. For the Director and Fellows of the Institute of Politics at Harvard, this, belatedly, is the book I feel I owe them.

I thank the Macmillan Trustees for permission to quote from the unpublished diaries of Harold Macmillan, Earl of Stockton, now accessible in the Bodleian Library.

Finally, I cannot depart from the 1960s scene without expressing my warm feelings for A. J. Hughes, who was my friend, adviser and landlord in Nairobi, and for those remarkable sisters, Jean Wacira (later Cliffe) and Charity Waciuma.

In the 1990s I am grateful for assistance from the Duke of Devonshire, the Earl of Perth, Sir Peter Kitcatt, Ian Buist and Henry Steel.

The Kenya National Archives in Nairobi, the Public Record Office at Kew, the Bodleian Library at Oxford, both in its Rhodes House and Modern Mss manifestations, the British Library (Newspaper Section) at Colindale, the London Library and Chatham House Library have all given admirable support.

Dr John Lonsdale of Trinity College, Cambridge, Professor T. G. Fraser of the University of Ulster, Dr Philip Murphy of Reading University and Colin Legum, former Africa Editor of *The Observer*, have most kindly read the text in typescript and made valuable suggestions. Sole responsibility for the content, however, is my own.

My wife, Susan, has been of tremendous help in every possible way.

KEITH KYLE

A Note on Kenya

Since 1924 when a slice of Jubaland in the east was ceded by Britain to Italian Somalia, Kenya has contained just under a quarter of a million square miles (582,646 sq.km), of which the northern half is extremely arid and very lightly populated by nomadic pastoralists. In the south, the land rises from a low coastal plain to a broad plateau of 3,000 to 10,000 feet above sea level, cut through by the Rift Valley, 30 to 40 miles wide. In the west, Kenya borders on the Kavirondo Gulf of Lake Victoria Nyanza. The Equator bisects the country almost precisely and runs seven miles north of the 17,040 ft. summit of Mount Kenya, Africa's second highest mountain. There are dense forests on the slopes of Mount Kenya and on the Aberdare range, whose highest peak is over 13,000 ft.

Administratively, Kenya was, by the time covered by Part II of this book, divided into six provinces and the Nairobi extra-provincial district. Outside the enormous empty Northern Province, these were the Coast Province, Southern Province, Central Province (including the three Kikuyu districts of Kiambu, Fort Hall and Nyeri), Rift Valley and Nyanza Province (the home of the Luo and the Luhya). Ethnically the Africans were divided between the Bantu-speaking majority to be found in the central areas (Kikuyu, Kamba, Meru and Embu), in the west (Luhya) and in the coastal region (Giriama, Duruma, Pokomo); the Nilotic Luo in the west; the Nilo-Hamitic cattle-owners (Maasai and the Kalenjin group including Nandi, Kipsigis, Tugen, Pokot and Marakwet) in the Rift Valley and Southern Province as well as the Turkana and Samburu in Northern Province; and the Hamites (Somalis and Boran) in the eastern parts of the Northern Province. The largest tribes according to the 1962 census were the Kikuyu with 1,642,000 (19.6 per cent), the Luo with 1,148,000 (13.7 per cent), the Luhya with 1,086,000 (12.9 per cent) and the Kamba with 933,000 (11.1 per cent). The total population at that date was found to be 8,366,000, a million more than had previously been estimated. In 1994 it was estimated to be 26,017,000, the annual rate of increase being a little under 3 per cent.

A Word on Pronunciation

On the insistence of its first Governor, General Northey, Kenya was pronounced during the period of colonial rule as 'Keenya'. Since independence it has been pronounced with a short 'e'.

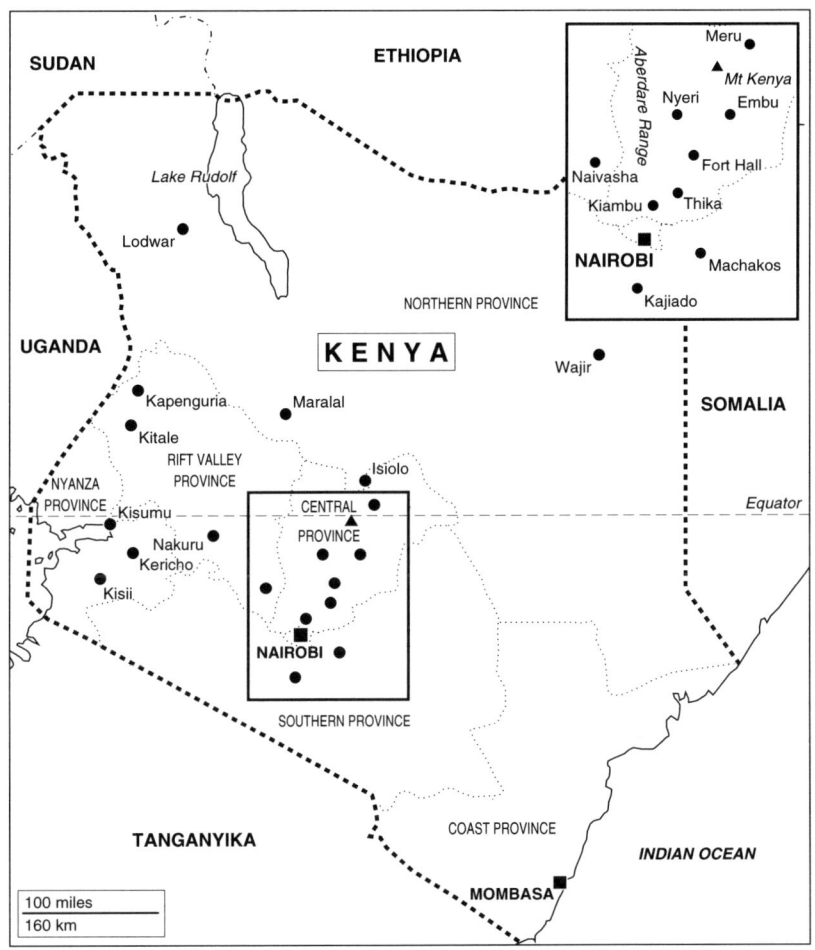

Kenya in 1960

List of Abbreviations

AEMs	African Elected Members
AEMO	African Elected Members' Organization
AFL-CIO	American Federation of Labour and Congress of Industrial Organizations
APP	African People's Party
CEMO	Constituency Elected Members' Organization
CPC	Colonial Policy Committee
CRO	Commonwealth Relations Office
EACSO	East African Common Services Organization
EAP	East African Protectorate
GAG	Ginger Action Group
GSU	Government Services Unit
ICFTU	International Confederation of Free Trade Unions
KADU	Kenya African Democratic Union
KANU	Kenya African National Union
KAR	King's African Rifles
KASU	Kenya African Studies Union
KAU	Kenya African Union
KCA	Kikuyu Central Association
KFL	Kenya Federation of Labour
KFRTU	Kenya Federation of Registered Trade Unions
KIM	Kenya Independence Movement
KNFU	Kenya National Farmers' Union
KNP	Kenya National Party
KPA	Kalenjin Political Alliance
KPU	Kenya People's Union
Legco	Legislative Council
LNCs	Local Native Councils
MLCs	Members of Legco
NDAC	Nairobi District African Congress
NFD	Northern Frontier District
NKG	New Kenya Group
NKP	New Kenya Party
NPCP	Nairobi People's Convention Party
NPPPP	Northern Province People's Progressive Party
WFTU	World Federation of Trade Unions

Part I

An Historical Introduction 1895–1957

1 The Foundation of Kenya Colony

'You are getting . . . white landlords occupying the higher posts of the country; you are getting a middle-class of clerks, engine drivers, guards, stationmasters, all Indians; and you are preventing the African native from rising from a proletariat position at all.'
(William Ormsby-Gore, Conservative MP, later Colonial Under-Secretary)

The British colony of Kenya was born by decree of the King's Most Excellent Majesty in Council on 11 June 1920 annexing and adding to His Majesty's Dominions most, though not all, of the territory of the East African Protectorate. It named the territory after its most celebrated physical feature, Mount Kenya, whose three snow-capped peaks, the tallest 17,058 ft above sea level, are almost on the Equator.[1] Forty-three years later on the eve of Kenya's independence, Jomo Kenyatta, her first Prime Minister, was to tell the Governor that his only objection to Queen Elizabeth becoming the country's head of state lay in three words – the Queen's Dominions. He had respect and liking for the person of the Queen, he said, but it would embarrass him politically in front of African VIPs to be regarded as part of her property.[2]

Kenya's annexation, said an article in *The Times* on 9 July 1920, 'will have come as a surprise to those, probably the majority of Britons, who supposed that the country was [already] British in fact as well as in name.' The principal reason of the home government was financial: to allow the territory's government to raise a substantial loan, mainly to lay railways where white farmers really wanted them, as opposed to the existing line which was a route for explorers and missionaries to travel to Lake Victoria.[3] The *Daily Sketch* was particularly cutting about the new colony's name. 'Nobody seems to be pleased with Kenia [*sic*] Colony,' it wrote. 'Tanganyika may well stand for the old German East Africa as a new name was really needed but why change the name of a colony which had always been British? . . . And why Kenya, unless by some sort of physical rivalry, one [Tanganyika] being a lake, the other must be a mountain?'[4]

3

The new status was announced to everyone's surprise in Nairobi on 5 July by the High Commissioner, General Sir Edward Northey, who had just come back after a long absence caused by a polo accident that had cost him the sight of one eye. The change was hailed by the *East African Standard*, the principal settler paper, as 'the greatest event in [our] history so far'. There were at this date no organs of African opinion, though two were started on a small scale in the following year,[5] but among those Africans who were literate in English there was a very real fear that 'protection' of their rights was being formally superseded in the English King's priorities by the policy of colonization by white settlers.[6] This conclusion was perfectly reasonable, though lawyers had twenty years before given advice that the previous status of Protectorate offered Africans no legal protection whatsoever.[7] As the Native Affairs Department created under the new colonial setup remarked sardonically in its initial report, 'The "sovereign tribes" of legal fiction with whom the great British Government made solemn treaties have for better, for worse, become citizens of the British Empire.'[8]

That part of the old East African Protectorate which had been excluded from the colony amounted to a ten-mile-wide coastal strip and its associated offshore islands, including Mombasa and Lamu, which were subject to the shadowy sovereignty of the Sultan of Zanzibar. The Sultan had been asked if he minded giving this up. He is recorded as receiving the proposal 'complacently', replying that, as 'he was the child of HMG', he would do whatever was required of him. But for Treaty reasons the French had to be consulted and, when they began to hint that there would be a price, it was decided not to bother. The strip therefore remained known as the Kenya Protectorate and was administered, except in form, as though it were part of the colony.[9]

'White settlers are in a better position as citizens of a British colony,' explained *The Times*, 'than as dwellers in a land over which rights of protection alone are claimed. . . . The change in status . . . will certainly be regarded as a step towards giving the settler a further voice in the control of public affairs, notably in respect of the vexed question of Indian immigration.'[10]

According to the census of 1921 the European population (and this was one context in which Englishmen had no objection to being called Europeans) totalled less than ten thousand. 'Thus,' wrote Norman Leys, a former civil servant, 'the whole European colony is no more than equal to the population of a large street in a European city.'[11] Of these, 1,893 were in some way connected to the land. Forty years later Iain Macleod, as Colonial Secretary, reported to the Cabinet that 'rather surprisingly, only 3,500 of the Europeans are farmers'.[12] In the 1921 census the African population was reckoned at two-and-a-third million, which was almost certainly an underestimate.[13] Against the 9,651 Europeans there were 22,822 Indians and 10,102 Arabs. When the issue of immigration became the hottest political item in the 1920s it was Indian immigration that was meant.

India, which had for generations supplied pioneering merchants along the coast – forming indeed much the greater part of the so-called British community in Zanzibar[14] and supplying East Africa with 25,000 indentured labourers to build the Uganda Railway into the interior,[15] with troops to fight off the threat from German East Africa and with traders, clerks, builders and artisans to promote commercial life and staff the lower ranks of the administration – considered that Kenya should be treated as an Indian colony just as much as a British colony.[16] After all, the currency (until after the First World War) had been the Indian rupee, and the criminal code was that of India. 'The East African Protectorate is governed as if it were a province of India,' complained the (European) Colonists' Association to the Colonial Secretary in 1905; 'East African colonists object altogether to adultery or "taking away a married woman" being subject to criminal law.'[17]

HOW THE WHITES CAME

In the latter part of the nineteenth century the future Kenya Colony had been thought of by the British as the space that needed to be crossed between the Indian Ocean seaboard and Uganda. Uganda had the double attraction of being the source of the Nile and of having, in the Kabaka of Buganda, his court, his hereditary office-holders and his Parliament (the Great Lukiiko), a political system which, even given its traditions of random cruelty on a sometimes terrifying scale, bore sufficient resemblance to European institutions to invite expectations of rapid conversion to Christianity and modern commerce. There were also two lesser neighbouring kingdoms, Bunyoro and Toro. By contrast in the area between the Kabaka's realms and those of the Sultan of Zanzibar there seemed to untutored Western eyes to be no structure whatever.

The problem about Lake Victoria and its adjacent kingdoms was how to get there routinely from the territories of the Sultan of Zanzibar which formed Britain's base on the east coast. The standard nineteenth-century answer was to build a railway.[18] Would such a project, however convenient it might be for Christian missionaries and helpful for the strategic control of the Upper Nile and in the suppression of the slave trade (always since the Congress of Vienna a standard objective of British foreign policy), be commercially worthwhile? The Imperial British East Africa Company was given a charter and allowed to try its own hand, in the East India Company tradition, at building a railway between Mombasa and Lake Victoria, whereupon it soon got bogged down in local politics and civil war in Buganda and ran out of money. Amid much controversy, the Foreign Office assumed the task of building the railway itself.[19]

The Uganda Protectorate was established on 12 April 1894. In 1900 a Treaty was signed with the Kabaka that incorporated his dominions as a province of the much larger territory of the Protectorate, but with considerable autonomy. To look after whatever lay between the Uganda Protectorate[20] and the islands of Zanzibar and Pemba, the British Consul-General in Zanzibar proclaimed the East African Protectorate (EAP) in Mombasa on 15 June 1895. The Powers were officially notified by the Foreign Office the following year.

In three and a half years, the rails rose from the hot coastal plain to the temperate climate of Nairobi, 5,500 feet above sea level. On 30 May 1899 they actually reached the site of the future capital, selected solely to suit the purposes of railway administration, since it was a large flat area at the entrance to the Highlands. It was 'villainously constructed', according to Sir Charles Eliot, the second Commissioner of the EAP.[21] In picking a site no regard had been paid to such factors as its inadequate drainage, while 'the Nairobi river flows through a swamp for two miles in the middle of the township'. In the opinion of a senior administrator, 'it will never be a healthy place and will never be free from the possibility of a recurrence of plague'.[22] Herbert Samuel, who had been there, told the House of Commons that the Protectorate's capital would 'have to be removed from a site which ought never to have been chosen'.[23]

Work on the line from coast to lake was not completed until 1903. Now, at very considerable expense (just under £8 million of taxpayers' money) the British Government were in possession of what Eliot described as 'a backbone without a body'[24] and satirical critics termed 'the lunatic line'. A visitor could expect to travel from Mombasa to what was, a little fancifully, termed 'the heart of Africa' and back again in five days.

The railway had not been built or the protectorates proclaimed with white settlement in mind but it was soon apparent that the economic advantages of opening up Uganda and the Lake region had, as the anti-imperialist Harry Labouchère forcefully pointed out at the time, been greatly exaggerated,[25] so that the existence of the railway and the need to justify retrospectively the expense of having built it made white settlement *en route* essential. 'The increase of [rail] traffic. . . . is likely to depend entirely on the encouragement given by Government to European settlement and colonization . . . because the native element is small and shows no inclination to use European goods,' wrote Sir Charles Eliot.[26]

Some white civilians like Lord Delamere had been coming to the Protectorates since 1897. By 1903 there were nearly a hundred white settlers in or near Nairobi, which was described as 'a straggling settlement of corrugated iron somewhat resembling a West American mining town'.[27] On a trip to Nairobi to offer the settlers Government assistance, Arthur Marsden, who among many other offices held that of Collector of Customs in Mombasa, found that it was race week, with the result that 'it was difficult to obtain that attention to business matters which could have been possible in a less exciting period'.[28] However, he went on to South Africa, where he stimulated numbers of Boers to come.

The first settlers were a very mixed crowd, usually foregathering round Wood's Hotel, the only one then in existence. A few had enough capital and agricultural skills to make good, others had not. 'What little money they have,' according to Frederick Jackson, Eliot's Deputy Commissioner but no admirer of his or his pro-settler policy, 'they spend at Wood's Hotel and try and breed discontent amongst the few *bona fide* settlers there are . . . Yet Eliot Kow-tows to them to an extent that disgusts everyone . . . he is afraid of "public opinion" as occasionally expressed by Mrs [Olive] Gray of the Mombasa "Rag" [the Australian editor of the Protectorate's first newspaper, the *East Africa and Uganda Mail* and author of the first East African novel, *The Phenomenal Rise of a Rat*][29]. . . . but what can you expect from a man who excluded several *bona fide* settlers from the lunch to [Joseph] Chamberlain at Nairobi

and insisted on asking a well-known drunkard. . . . For the lunch at
Mombasa he asked Mrs Gray, who lives with a black man.'[30]

A few years later, in 1907, Winston Churchill, visiting East Africa
as Colonial Under-Secretary, wrote famously, 'Every white man in
Nairobi is a politician and most of them are leaders of parties.'[31]
But the dominant tone was described two decades later by Norman
Leys, who had served in the early years of the protectorate as a
young medical officer:

> The public school and ex-officer type impart the pepper and gin-
> ger which form so large an ingredient in colonial politics. This
> kind of man is the lineal descendant of the old gentlemen ad-
> venturers who colonized Virginia, singed the King of Spain's beard,
> exacted homage from those people who are compendiously called
> 'natives' and ended their careers, some in Westminster Abbey,
> some at a yard-arm.[32]

It was Margery Perham[33] who remarked of the Baron von Blixen,
a Swedish settler, in 1930, 'He told me that he was absolutely broke.
It doesn't seem to matter much going broke in Kenya, you still
have motor-cars and drink.'[34] From Churchill onwards most British politicians and governors who had to deal with the Kenya settlers
speculated on the possible link between the altitude and the complete absence of restraint with which political views were habitually
expressed.[35]

THE WHITE HIGHLANDS

It was against the Indians not the Africans that the whiteness of
the White Highlands was originally asserted. No one suggested that
these temperate and fertile zones of astonishing physical beauty
astride the Equator should be owned by Africans. For one thing,
the militarily dominant Maasai, whose renown as warriors normally
kept other tribes like the Kikuyu at bay in steep ridges and forest
clearings, had at that time not recovered from a multiplicity of
disasters, some natural, others self-inflicted. A disastrous rinderpest
epidemic and the combined outcome of famine, drought, smallpox
and vicious civil wars among the Maasai seemed to offer up these
beautiful, cool, and fertile Highlands to the adventurous newcomer.
'We have in East Africa the rare experience of dealing with a *tabula*

rasa, an almost untouched and sparsely inhabited country, where we can do as we will, regulate immigration and open or close the door as seems best,' wrote Eliot.[36]

In 1908 the Earl of Elgin, the Colonial Secretary, defined the European monopoly in a statement which is a classic text of British hypocrisy. 'It is not consonant with the views of HMG to impose legal restrictions on any particular section of the community,' he asserted. 'But as a matter of administrative convenience grants in the upland area should not be made to Indians.' It was later argued that to have Indians on the Highlands would amount to racial discrimination against the whites since it was well known that white families could only live year-round at a high altitude while the Indian metabolism was accustomed to more sultry climates.

What upset settlers and administrators alike was any need to bring in more Indians or Goans at higher pay to fill vacancies. It was for this reason that the Nairobi Postmaster-General asked for five female telephone operators and a supervisor (with extra pay as matron) to be sent out from Britain. 'The dangers of sex will be raised but conditions in Nairobi are not so favourable to any such tendency as they are at home. . . . It may perhaps be desirable that the Imperial Post Office should see that the persons sent out are not too attractive.'[37]

COLONISTS AND TRIBESMEN

British officials were able to negotiate two formal treaties in 1904 and 1911 with the Maasai, by which the tribe, with the cattle which provided their sole source of wealth, moved out of the Rift Valley, which had been identified as 'God's own [and, therefore, white man's own] country' and settled in two reserves further south. The operation was not flawless – a law court subsequently found that because their agreement had the status of a treaty between allies the Maasai had no standing in a lawsuit they had brought alleging that they were being cheated of what they had been promised.[38] But this once formidable tribe, who wanted to live their own lives without contact with modernity, was effectively removed from the political scene, leaving the Maasai Treaties as a complication to be unscrambled during the preparation for the independence for Kenya half a century later.

Apart from some Maasai, the Africans with whom most early

settlers had to deal were the Kikuyu whose lands bordered on Nairobi. They were thought of as a people of the forest but they were really de-foresters, cultivators of the soil in forest clearings[39] who had a long love–hate relationship with the pastoral and belligerent Maasai, with whom they sometimes intermarried but against whose superior warlike traditions they had learnt to refine their own qualities of intelligence, secrecy, cunning and enterprise. Although much of the Highlands were virtually empty when the whites arrived this was not so of the area along the line of rail where most of the earliest contacts took place between the settlers and black Africans. These contacts were mainly with the Kikuyu and their ethnic cousins the Kamba. Various transactions occurred early between settlers and Kikuyu, often based on misconceptions about the nature of African land tenure which, contrary to self-serving white assumptions, involved quite sophisticated notions of ownership.[40] These resulted in the long-running grievances about land which fuelled the beginnings of nationalist politics.

As epidemics and natural disasters had led to the Kikuyus having withdrawn for the time being from much of their land, the treatment by the newcomers of all unused land as 'Crown land' eligible to be leased out for 99 years or in some cases 999 years threatened their ability to recoup what in some cases, at least, had definitely belonged to them.[41] But lest anyone suppose that it was only unused land that was under threat, the Crown Lands Ordinance of 1915 completed the process by providing in effect that all Africans were Crown tenants at will and that land reserved for tribal use could at any time be taken out of that category and be alienated to settlers.[42]

In the southern part of Kiambu district, the Kikuyu district closest to Nairobi, Eliot allowed Europeans to acquire 60,000 acres containing 11,000 of the tribe. The white settlements began in the areas around Nairobi and then moved northwest into the Rift Valley and northeast to Nyeri and then beyond the Kikuyu reserve to the rangelands above Mount Kenya. All did not go well with the settlers' first efforts at tropical agriculture. In 1908–9 the majority of them were facing bankruptcy. They were saved partly by a sharp increase in the world price of coffee, which with maize and sisal gave the protectorate a basis for its export trade. Under great pressure from the settlers and the local press, the Government banned Africans from growing coffee and sisal and thus from competing with Europeans.[43]

It was often said that Kenya was not a colony of conquest and it was true that there was never any general resistance to the coming of white rule.[44] As the Kikuyu Land Board Association were to put it in a Memorandum to Parliament presented in 1930 by Kenyatta and Parmenas Mockerie,

> It is within the memory of many an old man when the [Europeans] began to visit our Country at short intervals. We looked upon these men as a curious creation of the nature unseen, unknown and unheard of by us . . . Our Land was never won by conquest, by the force of arms . . . We were told that there would, as the result of the new friendship, be no more inter-tribal wars, no raids by slave-traders and that we would enjoy a perfect freedom and peace in our Country.[45]

There were, however, accidents, as when in 1908 a Kikuyu was shot dead by an American missionary 'in mistake for a baboon'.[46] And there were periodic clashes in the early days before the new rules had been firmly grasped when lightly armed young British officers would bring in Maasai auxiliaries to inflict at times brutal punishment on offending Kikuyu. The diary of one such officer, by no means the most callous, shows that if a white man had been murdered a whole village and its inhabitants could be wiped out, the fate of the women being excused on the grounds of their unseemly rejoicing in the white man's death. In a 1904 expedition against the Iraini branch of the Kikuyu, 'we killed about 796 niggers' and against the Embu 'we killed about 250'. 'I was surprised at the ease with which a bayonet goes into a man's body. One scarcely feels it unless it goes in to the hilt,' the same officer noted after a successful ambush had killed all fifty of a party of 'savages'.[47]

In the west the contrast was between the Luo and the Nandi. Whereas the Nandi repeatedly resisted British rule and the laying of the railway, the Luo, the Nilotic tribe on the shores of Lake Victoria and its Kavirondo gulf, offered no general armed resistance to the white newcomers, though a clash with one section of the tribe (at the behest of another section) is recorded in December 1899.[48] On the contrary Luo tribesmen were advised by their spiritual leaders to give Europeans active co-operation. A succession of so-called punitive expeditions – six of them against the Nandi tribe and two against the Kisii, another western tribe – slaughtered quite large numbers of Africans before 'the crushing of the Nandi as a tribe' could be claimed in 1906 following the killing of their spiritual leader. The figures of the casualties – 1,117 tribesmen killed – were deliberately suppressed in the published despatches of the Nandi Field Force. The survivors withdrew into the reserve allotted to them out of the way of the railway track.[49]

Since the end of 1905 a Liberal Government had been in power in London and humanitarian themes were in the ascendant. In January 1908, Churchill, as Colonial Under-Secretary, protested vigorously against the killing of 160 members of the western Kisii tribe without loss to the British on a punitive raid. 'It looks like butchery,' he minuted, 'and if the H. of C. gets hold of it, all our plans in E[ast] A[frican] P[rotectorate] will be under a cloud. Surely it cannot be necessary to go on killing these defenceless people on such an enormous scale.'[50] And, indeed, it was not considered necessary to use force after 1908, except in the isolated instance of the rebellion of the Giriama tribe in the Coast in 1914.[51]

To the European administrator the Africans situated between the Kingdom of Buganda and the Sultanate of Zanzibar lacked polities with recognizable institutions. A tribe like the Kikuyu, as Jomo Kenyatta illustrated and subsequent anthropologists have refined, had its unifying traditions and rituals. Yet there was no central focus and there were distinct differences of behaviour and image that corresponded crudely to the three districts into which British administration divided the Kikuyu reserve – Fort Hall (Murang'a), Nyeri and Kiambu.[52] The Luo tribe, according to Professor Bethwell Ogot, constituted twelve or thirteen independent units, each of which had its own council of clan elders, peacemaker, and war leader, with a structure of sub-chiefs with their councils underneath; and similar observations could have been made of other tribes.[53]

The British, desperately understaffed at the beginning, were faced with the task of imposing some kind of administration on the top of what must have struck them as chaos and anarchy. They applied the Indian system of Provinces and Districts with European officials in charge, but installed African chiefs in Locations and sub-Locations. But as most of the tribes did not have hereditary rulers the individuals chosen for these posts often had little traditional right to claim legitimacy. In the case of the Luo, Ogot has shown that the British did 'somewhat unwittingly' manage to base their chiefly appointments on genuinely indigenous institutions. But even there a centralized system, in which the new chiefs were civil servants appointed by the Provincial Commissioners and paid by the Central Government fitted awkwardly on top of the reality of segmented clans and lineages.[54]

WHITE MAN'S BURDEN

When in 1914 war was declared against Germany the East African Protectorate found itself bordering enemy territory in the colony of German East Africa. This situation had apparently been provided for in Article XI of the Berlin Act of 1885 which had arbitrated the 'scramble for Africa' between the European imperial powers.[55] 'The evils of war,' Bismarck had said, 'would assume a specially fatal character if the natives were led to take sides in disputes between civilized powers.' Accordingly provision was made for the neutralization, in case of war, of the 'Conventional Basin of the Congo,' which included, strangely enough, the British and German spheres in East Africa. Each of the signatories undertook, if occasion arose, to use the channels open to it to obtain such a declaration.

The *East African Standard* was now the principal European organ in the Protectorate.[56] Under the heading 'White Man's Burden' its opening wartime leader argued that, 'The first duty of the three protectorates [two British, one German], now as in the past, is to maintain proper control over the great native area for which they are responsible.' The views of 'a distinguished German minister' were called in aid for the proposition that 'the native mind makes no great distinction between one white man and another'. Hence, 'the native must not be allowed to take any part in the troubles arising between the white men. Whatever their national sentiments may be, the settlers of British East Africa and German East Africa must, during the crisis, continue to carry the white man's burden.' The protectorates 'were not actively at war ... As far as these territories are concerned, the last word will be said not here but in Europe.'[57]

The day after war had been declared and without any regard for 'the white man's burden', the Offensive Sub-Committee of the Committee of Imperial Defence met at Whitehall and resolved to put to immediate use two of Britain's vaunted geo-strategic assets, her ability to deploy the armed forces of India and her command of the seas. It was decided to take German East Africa by sudden sea-borne coup; the original idea was to strike at Dar es-Salaam, the capital, but for no very good reason this was altered to Tanga, which was closer to British East Africa but closer also to the German settler community.

The Indian troops, commanded by British officers, who after several false starts and stops were finally landed on a beachhead one mile from Tanga, were under-trained, under-armed, groggy on their legs after the sea voyage and abysmally generalled. They blundered through the jungle, fell into a machine-gun trap and then fled from the jungle pursued by bees. The aims – of hitting the Germans fast and of 'establish(ing) a territorial connection between the British Protectorates of East Africa and Uganda on the one hand and Rhodesia and the Union of South Africa on the other'[58] – took over four years to accomplish. The brilliant German general and master of bush warfare, Paul von Lettow-Vorbeck, did not surrender until several days after the Armistice in November 1918.[59]

The significant aspect from the viewpoint of this book was the extent to which a white man's war was to involve the Africans. Fighting men were already enlisted in the King's African Rifles (KAR), but tens of thousands of others were recruited from both the British protectorates into the Carrier Corps as porters. The Kikuyu and the Luo, who did not join up in significant numbers in the KAR, were large contributors to the Carrier Corps, whose heavy casualties were almost all due to disease and the failure to maintain proper logistical support. Though technically volunteers, these porters were recruited by very heavy pressure exercised through the government chiefs. According to official figures 42,318 porters from the two Protectorates died on active duties during the war, compared with 7,281 African troops of the 22 battalions of the KAR.

The Kikuyu were badly hit not only by actual war service but by the influenza epidemic which swept the world immediately the war ended. The estimate of a leading missionary, Dr J. W. Arthur, put the combined loss of life among the Kikuyu from these two causes at 120,000, and the Native Affairs Department reckoned to losses to the Kenya Africans as a whole as at least 200,000.[60] The Kikuyu Land Board Association, already quoted, summed it up, 'It is true that the scourge of the inter-tribal warfare and the slave-raiders' invasions have ceased in the sense we knew them before the British advent, but . . . the number of men who have been killed in the Great War in which we were not in the least interested or involved has probably exceeded the number who were killed in the local warfare for a preceding century.'[61]

Wartime conditions both increased the white settlers' hold on government in Nairobi and at the same time, at the level of the Imperial War Conferences, advanced the claims of India to be accorded equality of treatment with the whites throughout the Empire, including East Africa. There had been a Legislative Council ('Legco') since 1907, with five official members and three nominated unofficial Europeans.[62] But in 1915 the settlers took charge of the war effort, led by Lt.-Col. Ewart Grogan, a charismatic figure who had walked from Cape to Cairo and who had only not been included in the first Legco in 1907 because he had publicly flogged three Africans without legal warrant on manifestly inadequate grounds.[63] A War Council was formed for which the settlers were for the first time allowed to hold an election to chose three of the members.[64]

The Africans noticed that while the difficult post-war economic situation would not permit the paying out of promised gratuities to the demobilized carriers and their dependents, the new subsidized settlement schemes for white ex-officers went right ahead. 'There were many thousand of porters who came back from very, very difficult conditions in the East Africa campaign and found that they would not get any gratuity,' wrote Harry Thuku, the first educated African to achieve political prominence. 'Instead the government under General Northey decided that the white soldiers, and especially the officers, should be rewarded.'[65]

WHITE SETTLERS AND THE IMPERIAL FACTOR

Relations between Europeans and Asians had been deteriorating because of demands from India of rights of free entry into East Africa and equal citizenship. If the new notions of a colour-blind Empire, proclaimed at the Imperial War Conference in recognition of India's very substantial contribution to the war effort, meant that for imperial reasons Eastern influences were to be treated on the same footing as Western, the lords of the White Highlands were to be among the earliest of anti-imperialists. In 1919, after General Northey's arrival as Governor, the white settlers obtained for the first time an elected presence of eleven members in the Legco. The Indians wanted to be elected too and on a common franchise with the whites. Offered originally two nominated members of Legco they were then grudgingly to be allowed to elect them but only by communal franchise (Indians voting for Indian candidates). A. M. Jeevanjee, the most prominent member of the Indian community, described this as bearing 'a grossly inferior proportion to that enjoyed by the European community, who are inferior to the Indians in numbers and wealth, whose period of settlement in the country had been infinitely shorter and whose contribution present and past to the economic fabric and prosperity of the Colony does not for a moment bear comparison with that of the Indians who founded the prosperity of the country.'[66]

It soon became apparent that in Kenya both white settlers and Indians intended to play the African card while the spectacle of both brands of 'civilizers' belabouring each other in the press and on the public platform was not liable to redound to the credit of either. Sharp remarks about Indian child marriage and arranged marriages produced a reflection in the Indian paper *The Democrat* of Mombasa on the morals of Englishwomen, most of whom, it said, 'had to procure an abortion before being finally led to the altar'. This observation gave rise to an intense outburst of racial feeling.[67]

The settlers' spokesmen became robust advocates of African advancement, claiming that it was to the African that the Asian offered unfair competition by blocking off such jobs as clerk, artisan, carpenter or mechanic for which he could very well be trained but for which Asians refused to train him. As the new Native Affairs Department argued, 'The Native is everywhere clamouring for education and shows a keenness and intelligence very hopeful for the future. In Kavirondo alone there are now over 600 schools.'[68] In response, the Indians not only pointed out that African agriculture needed the help of the Indian trader to expand and find markets but they also encouraged the first signs of political activity by mission-educated Africans, especially Harry Thuku, a diminutive Kikuyu telephone operator at the Treasury.

THUKU RIOTS AND KIKUYU CHIEFS

The first stirring of modern African politics arose as a response to the pro-settler policies of Sir Edward Northey. A general whose war had been entirely fought in Africa, he was determined to establish Kenya as a colony (insisting as he did so that it be spelt with a 'y' rather than an 'i' as in the then province and pronounced 'Keenya' with a long 'e')[69] and to strengthen the depleted white community by pushing through at top speed the soldier settlement scheme, which was heavily tilted in the direction of the officer class. Public works were to support this objective and to be financed by loans that were possible now that Kenya, as a fully annexed colony, was unambiguously British territory. Africans, including women and children, were to be exposed to 'insistent advocacy' to leave their reserves and work for the settlers. This development had to be driven forward against a background of financial stringency, caused originally by world prices but made worse by a bungled conversion from a currency based on the Indian rupee to one based on the East African shilling.

Since the British Treasury would not wear the territory's huge deficit, higher taxes had to be found and while in principle both Europeans and Africans were to pay them it proved easier to force the chiefs to collect poll tax and a higher hut tax than it was to introduce an off-setting income tax for white farmers.[70] Not only did the income tax take a year longer to be introduced but, when it finally came, it was so effectively sabotaged by the settlers that it had eventually to be withdrawn. The heavier taxes for the Africans had the additional motive of driving them into the monetary economy in order to be able to pay them. African but not other workers were to be disciplined by being obliged to wear an employment record in a metal container strung round their necks (called a *kipande*). This was the most resented item of all. 'If I am a native why should I be registered in my own country and carry a pass or any other thing like a dog which is supposed to go astray?' wrote Z. K. Ssentongo, a Muganda[71] living in Nairobi, to the *East African Standard*. 'Why should I be deprived of my liberty in my native land?'[72]

This was just the moment when white employers decided that, because of hard times, wages for Africans should be cut by a third. On 31 May 1921 the first 'mass meeting' of Africans was called in Nairobi by a High Court interpreter called Ishmael Ithong'o. It resolved that 'if the Europeans did make a reduction in wages, Africans would all return to the reserves'.[73] Ithong'o, threatened with the loss of his plum job, turned over the leadership to Harry Thuku, the Treasury telephonist. On 7 June, Thuku, partly influenced by the substantial number of Baganda at that time in Nairobi who enjoyed prestige as the subjects of an African King, formed the Young Kikuyu Association in imitation of the already existing Young Buganda Association. When Z. K. Ssentongo started a

Luganda newspaper called *Sekanyolya*,[74] Thuku followed suit with a single-sheet newsletter in Swahili entitled *Tangazo*, which did not hesitate to hold up to criticism the Government, the missions and the chiefs.[75]

On 24 June an authorized meeting of the Kikuyu Association, which was an officially sponsored body designed to provide the tribe with a sounding board, was called by the tribe's senior chiefs, who chose Thuku to act as secretary. This meeting adopted resolutions against wage cuts, tax increases and compulsory work for women and in favour of more provision for African education. On 10 July Thuku held another meeting of his own on a sports ground to which he not only put the Kikuyu Association's four resolutions but also four more of his own, which the radical Indian editor M. A. Desai had helped him to draft. They included Africans' right to vote for their own representatives in the Legco and on Municipal Councils and, most controversial of all, the statement that 'next to missionaries, Indians are our best friends'. This was linked to a request that an Indian delegation that was going to London be asked to present African grievances as well. In imitation of the way settlers and Indian politicians behaved, Thuku was authorized by the meeting to cable all resolutions to the Colonial Secretary, Winston Churchill. To make doubly sure, he sent them as well to Lloyd George, the Prime Minister. Kikuyu opinion was split; the chiefs went on complaining for years afterwards that Thuku had 'stolen our resolutions and told lies to the people in England'.

The particular lie that the chiefs had in mind was Thuku's open endorsement of the Indian as the African's friend. Although this brought him political and financial support, it alienated some African opinion. For example, *Sekanyolya* came out with an English edition which said bluntly, 'The Indians have done nothing in the way of native education and though the members of the [Indian] deputation [to London] can be called educated, the mass of Indians are illiterate and inferior in education to the natives.'

Thuku was moving fast. He had grasped that it was unwise to base a nationalist movement on one tribe alone, however prominent. He renamed his association the East African Association, took advice from Gandhi's friend, the Rev. C. F. Andrews, who was visiting Kenya, and travelled around Kenya by car to contact members of other tribes.[76] 'The development of the native peoples in Kenya in one short year is simply past thinking,' wrote the head of the Church of Scotland mission at Kikuyu, Dr J. W. Arthur, on 14

March 1922. 'They are almost now able to safeguard themselves against oppression and exploitation.... This lad Harry Thuku ... likens himself to Ngangi [*sic*] in India.'[77]

Thuku was accused of sedition, a letter having been intercepted in which he had said, 'The D[istrict] C[ommissioner] is nothing to us nor is any European whatever anything to us because we know that all men are subjects of King George and there is no more to be said,' and he was arrested on 14 March 1922. Crowds collected outside the police station in Nairobi where he was detained. They were for some time peaceful but when it was learnt that the King's African Rifles were approaching, the women incited the men to attack.[78] The police opened fire and twenty-five Africans were killed. Thuku was never charged and was released in 1930 after being held in detention in various remote parts of the country. The government chiefs drew what they considered the appropriate moral from his having associated with Indians but among politically conscious Africans his name and legend remained something to be conjured with.

All the same, starting in a small way in 1925, another name was moving rapidly to the forefront, the name of the nattily dressed, motorbike-riding, in those days clean-shaven figure of Johnstone (later to be known as Jomo) Kenyatta.

THE BIRTH OF LUO POLITICS

Political activity had not been confined to the Kikuyu. Administrators had cause to worry also about what was going on in Kavirondo (now Nyanza) Province on the shores of Lake Victoria. At the Church Missionary Society's station at Maseno, a telegraphy instructor from Buganda, Daudi Basudde, explained to a hundred Kavirondo students (divided between the Nilotic Luo tribe and the Bantu Luhya[79]) what damaging effect the supposedly harmless switch from East African Protectorate to Kenya Colony could have for Africans' holding of land. A strike at the mission school followed and the removal of Basudde did not end the matter because he was replaced by the Kikuyu James Beauttah, who was every bit as politically active and who inaugurated the alliance, which was so vital for the future development of Kenya politics, between Kikuyu and Luo.[80]

As the culminating point of a campaign of small meetings at first held at night under the slogan *Piny Owacho* ('The Country

Says'), just under 9,000 members of the Luo tribe on 23 December 1921 came out in the open at Lundha in North Gem to call for individual title deeds and to resolve 'that the meeting is strongly opposed against the word "Colony"'.[81] There were also demands to do away with the *kipande* and for a fairer tax system.

WINSTON CHURCHILL SPEAKS

At an East African dinner on 27 January 1922 attended by a delegation of settlers led by Lord Delamere, which went on from seven till midnight with too many speakers speaking for too long until it ended 'somewhat boisterously', the Colonial Secretary, Winston Churchill, started off by predicting that in fifty years' time Uganda would be a nice little earner for the Empire. Turning to Kenya, he confirmed that the White Highlands would remain exclusively white for ever and that all future immigration of Indians would be strictly regulated. He declared that nothing should prevent Kenya 'becoming a characteristically and distinctively British Colony, looking forward in full fruition of time to complete self-government'. Churchill had hit so many stops to the taste of the celebrating settlers that they seem to have paid little attention to his endorsement of Cecil Rhodes's principle of the equality of all civilized men, which implies votes for educated non-whites on a common electoral roll.[82]

The follow-up was all the more of a shock. First the settlers' beloved General Northey had overstepped the mark once too often by allowing the Legco, without prior reference to Whitehall, to vote for enormous protective duties on imports of wheat and wheat flour. Northey was abruptly recalled before the end of his normal term, in a Churchillian despatch that the *East African Standard* described as 'a frigid and calculated insult, cynical where its presentation of facts is accurate and carelessly or deliberately false where it finds facts inconvenient'.[83] He was replaced by Sir Robert Coryndon, the Governor of Uganda.

Worse, a new truce was negotiated between the Colonial Office and the India Office, which had been vigorously upholding the new doctrine of colour-blindness throughout the Empire, by the two Parliamentary Under-Secretaries of State.[84] This would introduce the settlers' pet abomination, a non-racial common electoral roll. It was intended, however, that this dose of imperial policy should be made more palatable to the whites by requiring property and educational qualifications for the vote. These, it was represented, had been specially crafted so as to keep the Indian element of the mixed electorate down to 10 per cent for the time being. Four seats in Legco would be reserved for Indians and their immigration would not be restricted. The question of access to the White Highlands, bitterly at odds between the two departments, was deferred for later resolution.

Coryndon advised Churchill against publication of the new plan as there was no hope at all of agreement by the settlers on these lines. No further steps were taken while there was a change of government and a General Election in Britain.

WHITES WILLING TO REBEL

On 10 January 1923 the Governor received a despatch from the new Colonial Secretary, the Duke of Devonshire, resubmitting the old proposals and instructing him to whip up support for them. Coryndon widened his consultations and in consequence substantial leaks occurred in the local press.

The white settlers went berserk. There were newspaper headlines like 'Be Prepared' and 'No Compromise'. A mass meeting at Naivasha threatened resistance and took particular exception to the appointment of William Ormsby-Gore (later Lord Harlech) as Colonial Under-Secretary, on account of a speech he had made as a backbencher predicting economic ruin for the white settlers and advocating the development of Kenya as a black African territory on the same lines as the Gold Coast and Nigeria. The snort of ducal indignation at this presumption to dictate to the Government its ministerial composition still rises from the page; the Governor was immediately instructed to pick out the two titled persons who had been present at Naivasha for a special dressing down. This Coryndon found himself unable to do.

The Duke addressed the Governor further on the great importance of the plan from the Imperial standpoint. But on 29 January Coryndon heard from Lord Delamere, on behalf of the unofficial members of Legco, that it would be useless to invite the white community's views on terms so incompatible with the principle of European supremacy. Wild talk was heard among the ex-Servicemen, including several ex-generals, of whom the Earl of Lytton's cousin Brigadier-General Philip Wheatley was said to be the chief, about preparations for a coup against the government, with a Vigilance Committee, 'connecting links' in each district, a plan to seize the railway and telephone systems and to kidnap the Governor.[85] 'I am sure complete machinery has been long prepared and recently stiffened to paralyze the functions of government,' Corydon warned Devonshire in a long cypher of 3 February. 'It is also possible that if things get so far steps will be taken to prevent me from issuing orders or those orders from being obeyed. I question if it is possible to call our British native troops against Europeans in their own Colony, but if I were compelled to do so it is most probable that they would refuse to come out. The reading of the Riot Act and the declaration of Martial Law will in such circumstances be meaningless.'[86]

This was a defining moment in Britain's tense relations with India. If the British Government gives way, the Viceroy, the Marquess of Reading, wrote, 'the Indian will then be convinced that the British Empire doesn't mean to treat Indians as she treats white members of her Empire and that India can never thus become in truth an equal partner of the Empire.'[87] With this in mind, the Duke of Devonshire replied to Coryndon on 9 February, 'Do you seriously anticipate such action before negotiations break down...? The Imperial and international embarrassments of HMG at the moment are in all conscience sufficiently grave without their being complicated by Englishmen in a British colony crying out before they are hurt.' Obviously riled by this reproach, Coryndon, who had just had the Indian editor M. A. Desai nearly thrown out of his office for impertinence, tried once more to spell out his condition of impotence:

> You will recognize that I must speak plainly... I thought I had made the position clear in previous telegrams all of which were carefully worded and containing no exaggeration. Read again my telegram of 1 February... The country is absolutely solid that the ultimate responsibility of government in this part of Africa with 5 million natives must remain in European hands... No persuasion or argument except that of superior force can now compel them to vary or abandon that standpoint... It will not be forgotten that the colony contains a very large proportion of trained soldiers, many of high military capacity. The supply, transport and intelligence divisions of their organization are almost exactly those which took part in the German East African campaign.[88]

On 26 February, 120 leading settlers, meeting at the Railway
Institute in the presence of the Governor, in an action that gave
African leaders whatever example they might need for future sub-
version, unanimously passed a resolution of loyalty to the King.
But that it was a special kind of loyalty was made clear by the
immense qualifying sentence which followed:

> But if, through the ill-considered advice of His Majesty's Minis-
> ters, his loyal subjects be forced into actions prejudicial to peace
> and abhorrent and ruinous to themselves, then full responsibility
> for such a calamity must rest on advisers who, in ignorance of or
> indifferent to the true issues involved, shall have advised His Maj-
> esty to sanction a policy disastrous to the future white colonization
> of Africa and the welfare of His Majesty's African subjects and,
> the Convention believes, calculated to endanger the integrity of
> the Empire.[89]

This was gesture politics deliberately fashioned after the style of
the Ulstermen of 1912 which was no accident in that it was being
forwarded to the Prime Minister of the day, Andrew Bonar Law.[90]

THE DUKE DECREES

How much substance there was in what became a major part of
the Kenya legend is difficult to determine. But right up until Mau
Mau the fear of a 'Boston tea party' if white settlers were pressed
too far was a very real factor in the relations between the home
country and the colonial territories of East and Central Africa. As
late as 1952 a ministerial aide was reporting to the Colonial Office
that if self-government by the Europeans in Kenya were not immediately granted it would be taken by force.[91] Over Nyasaland in
1960 Harold Macmillan was confiding to his diary that, 'The Boston tea party is a perpetual reminder to us of what English settlers
can do when angry.'[92]

In the end Coryndon persuaded the Conservative Government
to call a further conference in London. After two months' wran-
gling, the Government agreed to two of the settlers' essential points:
firm confirmation that the White Highlands would indeed stay white
and retention of the communal franchise. There should be no fear
that in twenty or thirty years, as Indians became more educated,

their superior numbers would prevail in a mixed electorate. The Legco was to consist of eleven elected settlers, five elected Indians, one elected Arab and one nominated Christian missionary 'to advise on the affairs of the African population'. Enough nominated members would be created to ensure an official majority. Nothing was said about the settlers' demand (and Churchill's promise) for tough restriction of Indian immigration.

For a whole tense weekend the parties to the London conference awaited the settler Vigilance Committee's reaction to the new White Paper. Thanks to a farcical error, a coded message from Nairobi that in fact related harmlessly to the budget was misinterpreted as signalling the onset of the crisis, after which all cable communications became temporarily cut off because of an exceptional flood. There was real fear that the Vigilance Committee had turned thumbs down and the coup had taken place.[93] In a panic Whitehall offered a further concession; a tough immigration bill would be drafted. But there had been no coup and by the time the text of the bill was actually ready there was a Labour Government and it was dropped 'on the grounds that the assurance was given on the false premise of a threat or fear of armed revolt by the Kenya settlers'.[94]

During the many weeks of the London conference the two great antagonists, the white settlers and the Indians, made lavish use of the opportunities for propaganda before the bar of British public opinion. The theme of each was their touching concern for the rights and interests of the black Africans, which each held themselves the more qualified to advance. The Duke of Devonshire was able to take both sides at their word. 'Primarily Kenya is an African territory,' his White Paper asserted, 'the interests of the African natives must be paramount and, where those interests and the interests of the immigrants should conflict, the former should prevail.'[95] Thus in the same year in which political power in Southern Rhodesia was being entrusted to its white minority it was officially decided that a similar fate should not befall Kenya.[96]

2 The Rise of African Nationalism

'Kenyatta was a braggart, a drunkard, a great womanizer but he knew his work well. He liked clean linen and was always well dressed. He was an expensive man but he also walked with courage.' (A Kikuyu contemporary reminiscing about the 1920s)[1]

Johnstone Kenyatta was in 1925 a Christian, mission-educated Kikuyu from Kiambu, not in very good odour with his Presbyterian mission (on account of beer-drinking and marital irregularities), round about 28 years of age, in good employment in Nairobi as a water-meter-reader and stores clerk. He was a dandy when dressed for best in sun helmet and plus-fours, sociable and in general cutting quite a dash. He was not politically engaged and had been no part of Harry Thuku's enterprise. James Beauttah,[2] one of the first Africans to be recruited in 1910 for training as a telephone operator, persuaded him during 1925 to take an interest in the Kikuyu Central Association (KCA), which, led from Fort Hall by Joseph Keng'ethe, Jesse Kariuki and other members of the new African trading class, claimed continuity with Thuku's East African Association.

Between 1925 and 1928, when he resigned his government job and took up full-time employment in Nairobi with the KCA, Kenyatta gradually increased his involvement, mainly translating and drafting letters. Although at that time not nearly as good an English-speaker as James Beauttah he was better than anybody else available. Kang'ethe and his much more energetic colleague Jesse Kariuki, neither of whom spoke English, knew that it was essential to have someone who did. Also, they wanted eventually to send a delegate to England to do for their crucial land question what the settlers and the Indians had done in their own interests, short-circuiting local authority by going to the fount of power; and Beauttah, the obvious choice, was not available.[3]

The Native Affairs Department's report for 1925 complained that, 'In the Kikuyu province an indeterminate collection of malcontents of no constitution, no representative authority and no constructive programme of reform calling itself the "Kikuyu Central Association" has achieved a notoriety and a prominence out of all proportion to its merits or its influence.' What worried the officials most was that money was being collected 'from the ignorant and foolish' which 'appears to be spent chiefly on the personal requirements and luxurious tastes of the collectors'. In 1927 the Department's report spoke of 'a continuous undercurrent of semi-articulate agitation' and of 'the growing antagonism among and a widening cleavage between the older and the younger generation'. Relationships were uneasy between the association and the new Local Native Councils (LNCs), with some elected members but also chiefs, and with the District Commissioner in the chair, on which the Government was relying to supply an outlet for African opinion.[4]

Kang'ethe, a mill owner who has been described as 'full-jawed and barrel-chested, who had the ability to lead men at the head of a machine-gun section during the war',[5] was himself elected to his LNC. But he was subsequently expelled for flouting his local chief over the holding of a meeting. Although some reports give an impression of continual antagonism between the administration and the KCA, there are others in the archives that show some practical co-operation of a workaday nature and some administrators ready to acknowledge the increasing support which the (partially) educated young men were gaining.[6]

An address from Kang'ethe and others in the KCA to the new Governor, Sir Edward Grigg, dated 31 December 1925, set out their views. It started off with warm greetings and promises of 'all possible co-operation and assistance' and then asked that the Land Ordinance 1915 be cancelled, that Harry Thuku be released, that the boundaries of the Kikuyu reserve not be drawn without consultation, that the Association be allowed to call meetings without the District Commissioner's interference, 'as is the case in the Kavirondo [Nyanza] district' and that the Kikuyu be allowed to grow coffee and cotton and be given the same degree of assistance as white farmers. The association also wanted government chiefs not to be able to try cases when they were themselves the prosecutors, the laws to be published in the Kikuyu language, and the Governor to 'appoint one Paramount learned Chief for our Kikuyu country with judicial powers for trying our cases, one who should be well educated and be elected by a majority of our own people'.[7]

This last was a very significant demand and at first sight a surprising one in the light of the tribe's chiefless tradition and the complaints about the artificial nature of the chiefs imposed by the

British. It almost certainly reflected the influence of James Beauttah who was now working in Uganda and who had repeatedly reported back that the Baganda were more united and respected because they had an African King.[8] In the course of a lengthy response mainly directed at rubbishing most of the KCA's points in detail, a British official had particular fun with the proposal for a Paramount Chief. 'Probably their idea, whatever it may be, has been so badly translated as to alter entirely the meaning,' he wrote. 'In point of fact I think it a form of authority most unsuited and foreign to the Akikuyu people.'[9]

In 1928 a vernacular Kikuyu newspaper appeared. It bore on its masthead the title *Muigwithania* ('The Unifier' or 'Reconciler'), the slogan 'Pray and Work' and the name of the editor, Johnstone Kenyatta, secretary of the Kikuyu Central Association.[10] It contained letters from readers, biblical citations, and pleas to remember the common origin of the Kikuyu tribe. The editor was evidently aiming at reconciling the traditions of the Kikuyu with the teachings of the Bible and also the particularities of different Kikuyu locations with the common origin of the tribe.[11] He also brought news from abroad. In the July 1928 issue Kenyatta tells his readers that 'the council of workers there in Europe who are called the BRITISH LABOUR PARTY understands the wants of black people'. It had agreed in a policy document that the *githaka* (land) should belong to black people, who should cease being pressed into forced labour and be allowed to grow valuable crops like coffee. Kenyatta ends, as his journalistic pieces almost invariably did, with an injunction to 'work hard to cultivate large fields and to build good houses on them', because it was not enough 'merely to say that it is our land' – and then do nothing about it.[12] It is not surprising that the Native Affairs Department found its contents 'for the most part unexceptionable and deserving of much commendation'.[13]

THE DRIVE TO FEDERATE

The imperial visionary Leo Amery, who was Conservative Colonial Secretary in the late 1920s, knew what should be done with East Africa. Since all three territories had since the defeat of Germany been under British rule, they should be set in train to become the single Dominion of the future. As a first stage, he breathed new life into the idea of a Federation or 'closer union' which as far as

Kenya and Uganda were concerned was as old as the century, and sent out to Nairobi as Governor a political appointee, Sir Edward Grigg, with the intention that he should become the first Governor-General of East Africa. Amery also wanted the two Rhodesias and Nyasaland to be formed into a Federation of Central Africa, with the ultimate intention that the two Federations should be linked.[14]

The first stage in Amery's plan would be to establish a central authority in Nairobi for East Africa to plan the economic development for the region; in Kenya the white community should be enlarged and brought into partnership with the colonial government in fulfilling the trusteeship role towards the Africans. Sir Edward Grigg was deliberately chosen because he believed in the Amery message and the Hilton Young Commission was set up to work out the details and give the concept additional weight. Unhappily for Amery the Commission came out with a majority report, signed by all members except the chairman, which instead put the emphasis on the Duke of Devonshire's notion of 'native paramountcy' and proposed a High Commissioner for East Africa whose main remit would be to unify policy towards Africans so that when they could pass a test of civilization they should qualify for a common electoral roll. The Central African Federation was turned down flat. In despair, Amery proposed to send his Permanent Under-Secretary, Sir Samuel Wilson, out to East Africa to rescue his ideas, but his departure was much delayed, Amery wrote bitterly, because of his colleagues' 'unconsciousness of the flight of time' and of Stanley Baldwin's 'conviction that the less a Government does the better'.[15]

When Wilson eventually got to Nairobi he received a petition from the KCA, presented by Kang'ethe, accompanied by Kenyatta as interpreter. It complimented the Commission on the majority report, accepted the formula of the equality of civilized men and went on to point out how 'paramountcy' could start to be interpreted here and now. 'Natives in Kenya wish to be represented on the Legco by two Europeans, one Indian and three Africans,' the petition said. 'The African prospective members will be Mr Johnstone Kenyatta, our representative whom we have deputed to visit England. . . . The other members will be forthcoming during the election.' One of the two Europeans should be Captain Dermot FitzGerald, 'in whom we have full confidence'. 'Ultimately the number of African representatives should predominate altogether'. The petition added that, 'The Association is absolutely afraid of settlers' government . . . Such settlers have presented an adverse barrier to native development socially, politically and economically.' The 1925 demands were repeated for a single, educated and elected Paramount Chief of the whole tribe and for an end to the Crown Land Ordinance of 1915.[16]

KENYATTA's IMAGE OF LONDON

Mr Johnstone Kenyatta, whom the members of the KCA wished to see in the Legco, arrived in London on 8 March 1929. Before leaving he had taken a special oath in a Church of Scotland church in which he swore to remain true to his tribe, never to forget the Kikuyu land or to marry a white woman, and to return to Kenya.[17] Official advice which had been pressed on him before he left was that his trip was a waste of time and money because, his Association being an unofficial one claiming to represent only one tribe and not doing even that, no one in authority would talk to him. In fact there was a Labour Government in office by the time he arrived, he was made a fuss of by left-wing activists and was received by the Parliamentary Under-Secretary. His correspondence with the Colonial Office was subsequently published.[18]

Kenyatta reported cheerfully to his readers in *Muigwithania* his witnessing of the return of King George V to Buckingham Palace after his grave illness:

On the evening of the preceding night the people spent the night as if it were a circumcision – as you may say, 'spending-the-night-outside'. . . . In the morning at dawn, the people opened their doors at the hour that the partridge calls for its young and went to seek for places to stand so that they might see the King. . . . And the soldiers formed files and lined the road like a line of sorghum. . . . My word, children of Kikuyu! The wonder I then saw I have never seen before and I do not suppose I shall see it again. . . . When I raised my eyes, behold there was the 'centre' [main body of a Kikuyu raiding party] that guards the peace of the King. I myself at first felt afraid, for this troop is a wondrous sight, for they wear metal garments of brass that flash like the sun and all of them are on horses and have drawn swords. . . . When they had passed by, as I wanted to see everything, I ran and went right to the King's house where they enter it. . . . I tell you, children of Kikuyu 'Going is seeing!' for I do not know to what I can compare the crowd that was in that place, unless I compare it to a great cloud of locusts, such as you see.

Kenyatta also saw the state opening of Parliament and a thanksgiving service in Westminster Abbey.[19]

In his articles he wrote of what the Kikuyu should learn from the British. In London he found a people who were industrious and united and it was that which made them strong. 'Exalt the Chiefs' he wrote, 'for the country that has no Chief is no country.' Wherever Kikuyus were to go in the employment of Europeans they are urged to remember that they are still Kikuyus and owe service to their own people. They should try to acquire a trade, so as to be self-sufficient. 'Here in Europe people respect each other very much ... Cease to disdain one another in argument for, if you disdain one another, the other races will also disdain you.'[20]

Above all, Kenyatta hammers home the theme of education:

> for you know that 'Wisdom is before force' and that is why we should find out where knowledge is and seize it with both hands ... But do not think that the education is that which we are given a lick of; no, it is a methodical education to open out a man's head.

Having got to know a Nigerian barrister in London, Kenyatta emphasises that there is no reason why there should not be Kikuyu lawyers and doctors.[21]

FEMALE CIRCUMCISION

According to a Political Situation Report dated 12 January 1930 from the District Commissioner, Kiambu (one of the three Kikuyu districts), 'The centre of gravity of political agitation shifted abruptly at the end of September from the land question to the question of female circumcision.'[22] This was an exceptionally difficult matter for all concerned. Modern opinion, especially female opinion, is extremely hostile on medical and psychological grounds to what is properly called clitoridectomy, which, especially when what is referred to as 'the major operation' is carried out, amounts to genital mutilation.[23] Even as sympathetic a friend of colonial peoples as Fenner Brockway, the left-wing politician who was chairman of the

Movement for Colonial Freedom, described it as 'barbaric'.[24] But, as Jomo Kenyatta was to explain in *Facing Mount Kenya*, circumcision, male and female, the turning of a child into an adult, was central to a Kikuyu's traditional sense of identity.[25]

What then was to be done? The administration, not wanting to stir up emotions, had been in favour of quietly persuading the tribe over a period of time to abandon the custom in the case of females or, as a compromise, limit it to the removal of the clitoris.[26] But this was an issue over which the Christian missions, which had been regarded as the main advocates of African rights and who had been used to acting as surrogates for the 'natives' in government councils, came into direct collision with African sentiment.[27] The Church of Scotland missions headed by Dr John Arthur, who now sat on the Governor's Executive Council as the representative of native interests, decided that on this most emotional issue conscience dictated that cherished Kikuyu custom be no longer tolerated among Christians. All native teachers must sign a paper renouncing the practice or be expelled. The rest of the non-Roman Catholic missions followed suit. A conference of Kikuyu church elders meeting at Tumutumu in March 1929 went further and resolved that 'all Christians submitting to it should be suspended by Churches everywhere'. *Muigwithania* denounced this in its May issue, Kang'ethe sent a letter to the *East Africa Standard* asking 'whether, because of circumcision being the custom of Kikuyu Christians, one is to become a heathen because he is a Kikuyu', and Jesse Kariuki travelled through the Rift Valley preaching that Europeans would soon take all their possessions, even their girls.[28]

When the storm burst, the Church of Scotland missionaries felt badly let down by the charge in official documents that they had suddenly and without warning precipitated the crisis in 1929 by their confrontational tactics. 'At the very moment when agitation was dying down for lack of a grievance,' the District Commissioner, Kiambu, had complained, 'Dr Arthur decided to take his leap in the dark. However much one may admire the courage and high purpose that prompted him, one cannot but regret that he acted with so little appreciation of the consequences.'[29] The missionaries pointed out that they had been preaching against the custom of clitoridectomy from the beginning but that in 1928 the KCA became more aggressive in insisting that members of the African church at Tumutumu revert to the old custom.[30] The Governor was sufficiently apprehensive of the consequences of Arthur's action to procure his resignation from the Executive Council because 'a clear differentiation between the policies of the Government and the actions of your church was imperative'.[31]

There was a dramatic fall in congregations and school attendance and parents turned to schools started by the Kikuyu Independent Schools Association and the Kikuyu Karing'a Educational Association in order to conduct education independently of the missions. These schools, whose educational standards were often considered questionable, were to prove in time to be prime generators of nationalism outside European influences. In parallel with them there sprang up many independent syncretic churches, preaching a colourful mixture of Christian and pagan beliefs, such as polygamy and speaking with tongues, though this phenomenon was by no means confined to Kikuyuland, being particularly strong also in Kavirondo/Nyanza, where it had been known since the end of the First World War.[32]

The highly emotional topic of circumcision radicalized the Kikuyu youth and provided the KCA, for the first time, with mass support. It polarized opinion within the tribe, the chiefs having to bear the odium of association with the government (which itself was bearing the odium of association with the missionaries). The object of hero-worship was normally Johnstone – or as they often said, 'John' – Kenyatta, sometimes linked with the name of the still detained Harry Thuku. Among young Kikuyu men and women there developed a passion for the Muthirigu dance-song, whose body movements were borrowed from the coastal Swahilis but whose words were freshly improvised.[33] They were directed against Senior Chief Josiah Koinange and other Christian government chiefs like Kungu Waruhiu and Philip Karanja, who had not subjected their daughters to the operation. Here are some examples:

Koinange, if you join issue with John Kenyatta on account of his journey to Europe, you will meet with the devil.

When Johnstone shall return with the King of the Kikuyu [Harry Thuku], *Philip and Koinange will don women's robes.*

The Government are fools. They have refused to hang Josiah Koinange and Waruhiu and Philip that John Kenyatta may be left to rule the land.

I have heard a great wonder – that Koinange's [uncircumcised] *daughter has given birth to a dog.*

Praise the elders of the KCA for sending John Kenyatta to Europe who is greater than the Governor of Kenya, for he defeats the Governor of Kenya.

Till John comes back, all the schools shall be closed and there shall be no teaching.

It is better to buy a donkey to carry your loads than a girl who has not been circumcised.

I shall proceed to commit adultery, then sign [the vow against female circumcision] *and be told 'You are forgiven.'*[34]

It was remarkable how rapidly Kenyatta had established himself as the putative redeemer of his people (one *muthirigu* verse actually went, 'We Kikuyu are delighted that John Kenyatta has been made Governor of all the Kikuyu by the Secretary of State'), especially as he was not present during the time that the circumcision controversy was at its height and his opinions about it were by no means clear. He stayed in Europe for some eighteen months, during the course of which he paid a visit to Russia. The emergence of the circumcision issue was evidently an embarrassment to him when in contact with church groups and progressive opinion generally; also the boycott of mission schools was a serious impediment to his emphasis on the supreme importance of education. Kenyatta was in all probability sincere when he muttered that, in the matter of changing the custom 'the way of gradual conviction is to be preferred to that of a direct attack by means of spear and shield'.[35] This put him, more or less, on the same side as the administration.

He landed back in Mombasa on 24 September 1930 and word went round the Reserve that he was 'our new king'.[36] He was politely received by administrators in the Reserve but his offer of services as a mediator were not accepted.[37] Dr Arthur, however, tried, against the administration's advice, to enlist his help and was left with the impression that, 'He is a man of guile, and thought he could gain credit with the Mission and at the same time keep up his end with his people. . . . Since Johnstone's return the opposition all over has stiffened and the numbers attending school have gone down.'[38]

This was the first manifestation of a recurrent problem for Kenyatta until, thirty-three years later, he was to achieve supreme power. As was said of Abraham Lincoln, he was probably one of those men who are equipped for no job except the top one and of this destiny he was increasingly prescient. There were at least three major occasions when his instinct as a modernizer came into conflict with his belief in strengthening Kikuyus' sense of self-worth by emphasis on tribal tradition. Female circumcision was the first of these; the issue of compulsory contour ploughing on the Kikuyu ridges after the Second World War was the second; the third, and much the most serious, was Mau Mau. In so far as Kenyatta claimed to be educated he was expected by whites to take the modern view; but in so far as he would be seen as collaborating with authority he knew that he would face the danger of being finished as the ultimate political victor.

CLOSER UNION FOUNDERS

In a limited sense the circumcision battle was the dog which did not bark in the night: there was no dramatic showdown between the colonial authorities and the Kikuyu tribe. For one thing, a Labour Government with Sidney Webb (Lord Passfield) as Colonial Secretary gave the impression of taking 'native paramountcy' seriously; Amery's drive for a white-led East African Federation had already been badly winded by the time that it came to be examined by a Joint Committee of the two Houses of Parliament. Even before the main hearings had started the Labour Government's Law Officers had found that in respect of Tanganyika the project was incompatible with Britain's obligations to the League of Nations as the mandatory for a former German colony. This the Germans had not hesitated to point out.[39] In any case the Joint Committee on Closer Union found against the scheme because of widespread local opposition to it, and Passfield, with pardonable exaggeration, claimed to his wife, Beatrice Webb, on 10 September 1931, 'We finished our African Report today . . . It has been really a triumphant success for the "pro-natives" as against the settlers.'[40]

The colonial government made an attempt through the Morris Carter Commission to resolve African land claims once and for all. This gave back to Kikuyu and others some lands or compensation for land to which they had laid claim, but did not satisfy many of the no doubt exaggerated family legends. In one particular case the settlement led to an important change of allegiance. Senior Chief Josiah Koinange, who had been the principal target of the young men's abuse in song, had been a prominent (and, according to George Bennett, an 'excessive and unrealistic'[41]) claimant. He was given one-tenth of what he had asked for. The land had been European and coffee-bearing; since Africans were not allowed to grow coffee because the settlers argued that Kenya's high production standards would be compromised by 'native' competition and the diseases that would spread from African to European crops, Koinange was ordered to grub up the bushes. Embittered, Koinange in his old age became the implacable enemy of the European settler.

KENYATTA, THUKU AND THE KCA

Three months after Johnstone Kenyatta had arrived back from Europe the British released the real 'King of the Kikuyus', Harry Thuku. Although three Africans, including one Kikuyu, Senior Chief Koinange, had been officially appointed as witnesses before the Joint Parliamentary Committee on Closer Union, the Kikuyu Central Association insisted on sending two additional representatives at its own expense. Thuku not being allowed to go, one of them was Kenyatta. He stayed fourteen years.

He was taken up by the network of black radicals that was already functioning in Europe, with the result that during 1932–3 he was in Hamburg and in Moscow. He and the Moscow communists do not seem to have impressed each other. John Lonsdale cites a Russian source for the contemporary Soviet assessment of Kenyatta's deficiencies in 'anti-religious questions' and in the theory of class stratification. He was found to hold to the heresy that 'the bourgeois school' encouraged more freedom of thought than its rivals and to treat as 'insolent' the Comintern's presumption in drafting a policy for him.[42] Back in London, he did occasional lecturing and journalism, wrote letters to the Colonial Office and the press on behalf of the KCA, earned a little money as a film extra and with London University as a Kikuyu linguist, and generally lived a fairly bohemian existence, being often in debt to his landlady. He was something of a celebrity in progressive circles and attended the classes in anthropology of Professor Bronislaw Malinowski at the London School of Economics. From this experience came his book *Facing Mount Kenya*, a fascinating picture from the inside of the customs and practices of the Kikuyu, though a static and idealised one.[43] Peter Mbiyu Koinange, the Senior Chief's son, who had been in London since 1927, lent Kenyatta his hyrax and blue monkey coat and they sharpened a wooden plank for a spear so that the front cover could give an 'authentic' impression of a tribal warrior. 'Let us,' said Mbiyu, 'put the author in a proper elderly background.' They then had to invent a first name for him that should retain the 'J' of Johnstone but sound authentic. They hit upon 'Jomo'.[44]

As it turned out, Kenyatta's instinct to stay away from Kenya during these years was sound. Indeed it was by not being there that his reputation remained unimpaired. Nationalist politics in Kenya followed a pattern that was to become only too familiar a feature of African politics in general. Harry Thuku was elected president of the KCA, defeating Joseph Kang'ethe, but soon he was found both too arrogant and too moderate. Kang'ethe and Jesse Kariuki formed their own breakaway party also calling itself the KCA. There were allegations of misapplying funds and Thuku brought a court action against his critics. Besides clashes of leadership style there were genuine differences of philosophy. Thuku now wanted gradual constitutional advance; Kang'ethe and Kariuki stood for making a fundamental challenge to colonial rule.[45]

When the Second World War had broken out, official patience with Jesse Kariuki and his friends ran out when they directly compared the compulsory relocation of some Kikuyu inconveniently placed in the middle of white-cultivated land around Limuru with Nazi policies on the compulsory transfer of people. It was decided to ban the KCA for the duration and to detain its leaders. When the war was over, though the leaders had by then been released, the ban on the party was never raised.

CHANGING COLONIALISM

Even before the war ended important changes had taken place in Kenya. There was a wartime boom which, in contrast to what had happened after the previous war, carried over into peacetime. In fact between 1947 and 1954 the Kenyan economy was growing at the astonishing rate of 13 per cent per year and over the whole period 1940–60 the average annual growth rate was 6 per cent. For the first time white income tax (which had been reintroduced in 1937) overhauled hut-tax as a source of revenue for the Colony.

The gain was mainly in the European sector and the distinction between this sector and the rest of the economy was accentuated by the increasing extent to which advances in technology enabled the European settler to lay off large numbers of his African labour force. As these were squatters in the Highlands they had no property rights to fall back on. Those who were allowed to stay had to sign regular contracts, which placed sharp limits on the number of cattle they were allowed to keep.[46] Young people from the reserves were flooding into Nairobi and Mombasa and living in the African townships in dismal squalor. When they had jobs they were lowly paid.

By contrast in the three years after the end of the war 8,000 white immigrants came out to strengthen the European population, much of it now in the commercial sector. But once again ex-Servicemen were encouraged to settle 'in an area permanently reserved for European farms and in which European influence was dominant'. Extremely generous and attractive terms were offered, but those who were accepted had first to liquidate all their capital assets. They originally had to have £800 but this was increased by three stages to £5,000 in 1949. Altogether two hundred ex-Servicemen took leases of Crown Land, with promise of security of tenure for 48 years and an option to purchase the farm after five years or at any time thereafter.[47] Again, the sponsors were going for the ex-officer type, well accustomed to command people and things and to respond to unfamiliar challenges by dint of improvisation. Other promotional schemes were continued right into the late 1950s.[48]

There flourished among some of the old settlers and the new a tradition, going back to the 1930s, of permissive social behaviour, a foretaste perhaps of the 1960s in Britain, that lent to white Kenya the name and reputation of 'Happy Valley'. Some of the leading settlers were planning to set up a small white self-governing Dominion, based on Nairobi and the Highlands, leaving the 'native reserves' to be looked after by the Colonial Office.[49] Sir Philip Mitchell, who was Governor when the war ended, tried to enlist the settler-politicians in something other than the politics of opposition by appointing one of them, Major Ferdinand Cavendish-Bentinck, the future 8th Duke of Portland, as Member for Agriculture, with responsibility for white settlement.

In 1940 there was a major change of principle in the policy of governing the colonial Empire. With the passage of the Colonial Development and Welfare Act, Britain moved from the rather passive concept of 'trusteeship' to a much more proactive one, in which British taxpayers' money was to be committed for the development of colonial peoples. This progressive concept was nevertheless liable to produce frustration and conflict; frustration because of the limited resources compared to perceived needs (for instance, in education) and conflict because development in, for example, African agriculture would involve the indigenous people in major departures from tradition, if only to fight the onset of soil erosion. When such changes were introduced in Kenya ahead of any fundamental reform in the political, social and economic relationship between Europeans and Africans this invited trouble.

The presence of a European population drew attention to such comparisons as, for instance, in the amounts spent annually on tuition in primary education: £49.6s.0d for a European child and £3.0s.0d for an African one. The European MLCs (Members of Legco) specifically rejected, in a debate in September 1947 on a Fiscal Commissioner's report, the concept that Kenya was a single political community, within which its resources should be allocated on uniform principles.[50]

THE BIRTH OF KAU

The first African member of Legco had been appointed rather than elected during the war. He was an educated Kikuyu, Eliud Mathu, with a South African university degree followed by post-graduate courses at Balliol College, Oxford, but it was noted that in appointing him the Governor had overlooked the claims of the first African university graduate, Peter Mbiyu Koinange, who was now back in Kenya and running the Kenya Teachers' College at Githunguri which supplied the staff for the independent schools. Koinange had been energetically canvassing support from notables across the tribal board and had sent a petition to the visiting Secretary of State 'by improper channels'.[51] This rejection further alienated his father, the Senior Chief, from the government.

Needing the advice of his fellow-Africans Mathu helped to found the Kenya African Study Union (KASU), with Harry Thuku as its first chairman. But the Thuku of 1944 was a very different man from the Thuku of 1921. Now a substantial progressive farmer, politics was not the first thing on his mind; and he felt uneasy with the more aggressive attitudes of the young men. Whereas the KCA had been deliberately a Kikuyu party, the leadership of KASU was deliberately multi-tribal, containing every ethnic group, except the Kalenjin. Its chief organizer was Francis Khamisi, a young journalist on one of the rapidly multiplying vernacular papers who came from the Coast. He was one of the only two founders who was outside the Government/teaching establishment.[52]

Significantly KASU was making little headway in the Central Province (which contained the Kikuyu reserve). Khamisi says this was because the Kikuyu now regarded Thuku as 'a government man'. He soon withdrew and was replaced as leader by a Kikuyu teacher James Gichuru, who was to be a major figure in the development of Kenya politics.[53] Gichuru, with the help of an energetic young Luo, Wycliffe Awori, compiled an impressive survey of what Africans in every part of the Colony required of their colonial ruler. The two top priorities were, unsurprisingly, education and land. According to them Africans would be prepared to pay higher taxes to finance compulsory education. A growing population required more and more land and, since the Europeans had taken what the Africans had lost, they alone could make good that loss. Gichuru and Awori concluded that 'the time is not ripe for self-government'. But, in case there was any misunderstanding, they added, 'The African people have a highly developed sense of nationalism. When the time will come it will be the Africans themselves who will petition HMG to grant self-government to Kenya.'[54]

But as Bildad Kaggia, one of the ex-Servicemen whose Forty Group[55] was to bring ginger to the opposition to colonialism, observed, KASU was necessarily confined to the educated Africans in Nairobi. 'The education the *mzungu* [white man] had given to Africans meant being divorced from ordinary African life,' Kaggia complained. 'Most educated Africans in those days despised everything African.'[56]

Although the Forty Group itself had a short life,[57] what it stood for had a major impact on the post-war scene. Seventy-five thousand Kenya Africans had served in the Forces during the war. According to James Beauttah,

> They had seen the white man do work that in Kenya only blacks did. They had seen white men killed and wounded, crying like babies with shell-shock; they had seen stupid white men get better jobs than Africans just because they were white; they had fought alongside white soldiers and learned that dirty white men stink just as badly as dirty black men. They returned with a confidence and fierce desire to change the system in Kenya.[58]

In 1946, KASU, now renamed KAU (Kenya African Union), decided to send a mission to London, and after several mishaps, Wycliffe Awori, a large young man with good English and a powerful voice, set off on the eight-day air trip to London (including a five-day stopover in Cairo, where he managed to lose almost all his money)[59] with the task both of publicizing the Kenya African's cause in the more hopeful atmosphere of a Labour Government and of convincing Jomo Kenyatta that his people wanted him back. Awori had been the first African to qualify as a health inspector with the Nairobi City Council. He also edited one of the new vernacular papers and had been treasurer of KASU. He was therefore representative of the new generation of non-Kikuyu politicians.[60] For Beauttah, who had the task of raising the cash for his trip, he was 'eager but was arrogant and lacked self-discipline'.[61]

Kenyatta said he was willing to return but he had no money. Awori also was broke, having lost his baggage for the second time. This caused some delay while more funds were raised – Khamisi says they managed to collect £30 or £40 every month. Finally Kenyatta travelled back to Mombasa on the SS *Alcantara*. There is in the Ambu Patel archive in Nairobi[62] an epic account of the voyage couched in biblical language complete with a miraculous occurrence when Kenyatta guessed correctly the length of one day's progress at sea. This seems in keeping with the style of the reception which Gichuru and Khamisi managed to organize for him at Mombasa.

Having got home in September 1946 he insisted (as he was to do fifteen years later) on taking time to reorient himself and on trying, unsuccessfully, to get his old party, the KCA, licensed again. He finally agreed to be elected President of KAU in July 1947; his task was to overcome the considerable reluctance of KCA members, particularly in Fort Hall district, where the banned party was still strong, to identify themselves with a new party that they considered too conciliatory.[63]

Kenyatta was faced with the same problem that he had formerly encountered over female circumcision: to what extent to lend his name to unpopular but economically progressive reforms over whose direction he had no control and thereby risk compromising his status as leader-in-waiting. He declined the Governor's suggestion that he enter local government. However, Walter Coutts, the long-time District Commissioner of the Fort Hall district in the Kikuyu reserve, whose excellent command of the Kikuyu language was acknowledged by members of the tribe, decided to invite his collaboration in the battle against soil erosion. This was part of Sir Philip Mitchell's plan to place the highest emphasis on the economic development of the African reserves.

The task Coutts was confronted with was what to do with the series of ridges at Fort Hall on which the Kikuyu were in the habit of growing wattle in a way that killed every form of life underneath, so that after heavy showers erosion set in. It was decided to dig trenches across the contour and allow the water to run off at special points. 'The terracing was extremely hard work,' Coutts admitted. Moreover it cut across traditional landholding, which typically ran in narrow vertical stripes down the ridges. The labour was supplied by government chiefs under the guise of traditional communal obligation. The men soon disappeared and left the arduous and not immediately rewarding work to be done by the women. Kenyatta was invited to come round with Coutts, both men explaining in Kikuyu the rationale of the operation. On the surface all seemed to be well but, says Coutts, 'there is no doubt in my mind that a lot of things were hatched up during that visit within the district'. Within two or three months of Kenyatta's visit 'the whole district fell to bits, both from the point of view of terracing and from the point of view of law and order'.[64] There was a women's riot, Forty Group activity and a general radicalization of the district.

While in later years Sir Walter Coutts was to say that he now doubted very much whether Kenyatta had any real control over the people he was dealing with, it seems clear that at the time and for many years afterwards he was intensely bitter about the man whom he blamed for this experiment in trust having ended so disastrously. Moreover, he suspected, with his knowledge of the parable-like uses to which the Kikuyu language is particularly prone, that Kenyatta had been deliberately speaking with forked tongue. Given his reputation for expertise about the Kikuyu tribe and language, Coutts was to become for Kenyatta a dangerous enemy.

In the autumn of 1948 Coutts reported to Nairobi that there was a new secret society abroad, its name at that time unknown, whose object was to get rid of the European. 'If it was necessary to kill, they would kill.' It was not quite the first intimation of Mau Mau – the use of that name itself had already been reported from the Rift Valley during an enquiry into intimidation among Kikuyu squatter labourers in May of that year.[65] But neither the one episode nor the other produced a reaction out of Nairobi.

The ambiguity of the role of Kenyatta and the party over which he presided – as to whether they genuinely spoke for Kenya Africans as a whole or whether they were a cover for the old tribalist Kikuyu Central Association – remained for a number of years. Kenyatta himself took over from Peter Mbiyu Koinange the control of the Kenya Teachers' Training College at Githunguri, where he was surrounded by former KCA personalities. Wycliffe Awori, whose Swahili paper *Radio Posta* had been a great booster of Kenyatta and KAU in the early days, resigned his vice-presidency of KAU and went off to Uganda to hunt crocodile, because he objected to the way important decisions got reversed at secret meetings at which non-Kikuyu were not present.[66]

On great occasions Kenyatta could be absolutely relied upon to produce an inspiring speech which would lift the spirits and the aspirations of his audience.[67] But the day-to-day running of the party in its Nairobi headquarters was left to its Swahili vice-president, Tom Mbotela, the son of a freed slave, whose father had long lived among the Kamba but was probably of Malawi origin. Mbotela was far too moderate for the young radicals' tastes. He and Kenyatta were continually postponing holding a party conference because, it was suspected, they feared the young men would take over. The really radical work was being done by the trade unions led by the Asian communist Makhan Singh and Fred Kubai, culminating in 1950 in a violent campaign against the granting of a Royal Charter by the Duke of Gloucester to Nairobi. The arrest of Makhan Singh and Kubai was followed by a general strike, which was supported by the radical KAU leaders Bildad Kaggia and James Beauttah, whereas Kenyatta and Mbotela held aloof. Beauttah, who had been busy mobilizing young men into various overlapping organizations of motorists, traders, and so forth, told his later biographer John Spencer that in 1950 he had recruited ten youths into an 'Action Group' that would practise marksmanship so they could kill the Governor. He inspired them with a simplified version of how the Sudanese people freed themselves by killing Gordon at Khartoum. But one of Senior Chief Koinange's sons who belonged to the group got himself killed by one of the guns and Beauttah gave up on the idea. 'I learned that a good many of the Action Group were drunks. I couldn't trust them,' he said.[68]

It was not until 1950 that a serious attempt was made to organize KAU in Nyanza province, the second area of political awareness, and it was not until 1952 that Kenyatta himself came to Kisumu, the capital of Nyanza province, to expose the Luo and Luhya to the magic of his personality.[69] Then his impact was electrifying. Among other things it led the *ker* (chief) of the Luo Union – a non-political association which linked together members of the tribe wherever they might be in East Africa – Oginga Odinga, to take the plunge into politics. Hitherto his pioneering business career had been his first priority.[70]

THE GATHERING STORM

On the whole the post-war Attlee Government was a great disappointment to Kenya Africans, who had looked to Labour Party personalities as their friends. There should have been none more so than Arthur Creech-Jones, a great pillar of the Fabian Colonial Bureau before the war, who became first Colonial Under-Secretary and then Colonial Secretary. In Kenya he agreed in 1947 to increase the African representation in the Legco to four, but they were still not elected, and at the same time the unofficial members of all races taken together were, for the first time, placed in a majority. Among unofficials the European element was equal to a combination of the other races. But Creech-Jones's main interest everywhere was to develop local government, which for ambitious Kenya Africans, particularly if they were Kikuyu, was simply not the heart of the matter, though to be sure many Africans did get their first taste of responsibity in this way.

Kenyatta wrote in 1950 to John Dugdale, the Minister of State for the Colonies and supporter of African nationalism, 'We have been claiming for better representation all these years and we have been loyal to the Government throughout the great two wars [*sic*]. We urge with earnestness that it is time now to give to Africans at least half the seats in the Kenya Legco by election.' He called attention to the contrast of immigrant settlers being heavily subsidized while 'we Africans who are also British' were squeezed into small, overcrowded reserves; and he ended with a warning, delivered with feeling, that 'because action is delayed . . . young elements in our community have on some occasions got out of our control and have stopped listening to our advice'.[71]

When James Griffiths, who succeeded Creech-Jones as Labour Colonial Secretary, came to Kenya in May 1951 he received memorials from Kenyatta on behalf of KAU and separately from Beauttah on behalf of the party's Central Province branch.[72] They both set out a powerful African case against the legal structure under which European possession of land was underpinned while Africans did not possess any security of tenure whatever. 'The African people in Kenya,' KAU said, 'do not recognise the moral authority' of the laws concerned. They should be withdrawn and Africans should be given rights to the occupation of land and individual land ownership in any part of Kenya. All immigration should be stopped.

Beauttah, who was believed by the authorities to be behind much of the trouble over soil conservation, was anxious to insist that the Fort Hall branch of KAU was not against fighting soil erosion as such, merely against the methods used to implement it. 'Contour terracing is such that there is no foreseeable end of the work.' There should be better ways of conserving the soil – Beauttah suggested a couple, on which his Provincial Commissioner heaped derision and contumely[73] – and African students should be sent abroad to find out about them.

The expenditure on African education was pitiful when compared with what was spent on European and even on Asian children. African farmers, although in principle now allowed to grow cash crops, had no loans or research stations as European farmers did. As in Kenyatta's letter to Dugdale, the claim for representation was that the position of white and black MLCs should be reversed, so that it should be Africans who had the same numbers as the other races combined.

Griffiths promised a constitutional conference within a year and in the meantime adjusted the Legco membership at the edges: six African nominated seats instead of four; Asian also six but elected, and two Arabs, one of them elected; Europeans kept their parity by moving up from eleven to fourteen. There were 26 nominated official members, placing them in a minority of two on such occasions as the unofficials could vote the same way.

Michael Blundell, who was elected leader of the European unofficial group in Legco in 1952, wrote in retrospect, 'I now believe that we were wrong in our attitude and that we would have been wiser to have accepted a far greater advance for the Africans in the responsibilities and intricacies of government. All of us were unaware of the intensity of political feeling among many Africans and had little conception of the stirrings of nationalism which were all around us.'[74] But by 1952 the settlers were aware enough of mounting subversion and by mid-year were agitating for the arrest of the Kikuyu leaders. The terrible Mau Mau struggle was about to begin.

3 The Politics of Mau Mau

'I speak the truth and swear before Ngai [God] *and before every-one present here that if I am called upon to fight or to kill the enemy, I shall go, even if that enemy be my father or mother, my brother or sister. And if I fail to do this, may this oath kill me, may this thenge* [he-goat] *kill me, may this seven kill me, may this meat kill me.'* (One of the seven parts of the *batuni* (platoon, or warrior) oath)

'Poor Mitchell, though a first-class Governor in many ways, had been entirely caught out by the Mau Mau movement and had told the Colonial Office there was no serious danger,' Sir Evelyn Baring, who replaced Sir Philip as Governor in 1952, told Margery Perham after independence.[1] Although cheerfully paternalistic in manner, Sir Philip Mitchell did not socialize with Africans and had sounded preoccupied by the thought that they had not invented the wheel.[2] Because Baring had nearly chopped off his arm with an axe, there was a three-month gap while he recuperated between Mitchell's departure and his own arrival. In the course of it only one high-profile arrest was made, that of Jesse Kariuki, who had made a speech inciting the police to disobey orders.[3] But the police, increasingly frustrated at the lack of response to their warnings of really serious subversion, claimed that events were taking a set pattern. First, there would be a political meeting in some area at which Kenyatta was the main speaker and for which crowds were shuttled in from Nairobi; next Mau Mau meetings would occur in that same area, at which oaths were taken and dead dogs hung up in front of the houses of non-supporters; then would follow the murders. During the three months before Baring arrived thirty-six witnesses who had been subpoenaed had been assassinated as well as twenty-four headmen.

It was true that Kenyatta had on request made speeches denouncing Mau Mau but these appeared to have had no effect whereas his pronouncements on other subjects had been instantly obeyed. The new Governor was told that these obliging speeches must have been accompanied by sayings and gestures that made it clear to the audience that he did not mean what he said. Kenyatta's name

45

was constantly appearing in hymns and prayers designed to empty the mission schools and fill the independent schools and churches. The situation was clearly slipping out of control.[4]

The question has been much debated as to Kenyatta's share of responsibility for the traumatic experience which was Mau Mau. Most British opinion during the Mau Mau Emergency and for some time thereafter held that he was the fount and origin of it all, an African who had been well received in Britain and partly educated there, yet who, with all these advantages, had with satanic perversity chosen to cast his tribe back into the most degrading barbarism. The oath was the essential bond; it carried men out of their previously normal selves and across a behaviour barrier which was meant to debar return. Thus, for instance, loyal and trusted Kikuyu house servants could be turned into murderers of their employers. And as, later, the screws were being turned on the fighters who had retreated into the forests, pursued not only by the British but also by loyalist home guards and pseudo-gangs from their own tribe, more and more horrific and disgusting oaths were introduced to keep the survivors up to the mark. In the mind of the European, oaths of every degree were attributed personally to Kenyatta, albeit he had been out of circulation from the beginning of the Emergency.

Without an understanding of the intensity of this feeling about Jomo Kenyatta and Mau Mau, much of the story in the second part of this book will not make any sense. Dr J. C. Carothers, a psychologist employed by the Government of Kenya to guide them through the baffling phenomena with which they were confronted, identified resemblances between the Mau Mau oaths and freemasons' initiation oaths and rituals in mediaeval Europe. He inferred from the fact of Kenyatta's anthropological studies in Britain that he was the most likely agent of transmission.[5] 'He had the opportunity and it is easy to imagine more than one incentive,' Carothers wrote, though adding wisely, 'No dogmatic answer can be given.' Walter Coutts was still saying in 1960 when he was Chief Secretary that those who had not known Kenyatta 'seem to have forgotten the man's foul wickedness. He was hardly human in his evilness.'[6] For most white settlers he was indeed Satan Incarnate.

And yet there is the positive record of his later achievements and the changed opinions of those who lived to see him functioning benignly as Prime Minister and then President of Kenya. One after another in a long line they testify that without him Kenya could have been another disaster like the former Belgian Congo. 'I have no doubt that Kenyatta has been an absolutely first-class Prime Minister by African standards or even by any standards,' said Sir Evelyn Baring (then Lord Howick) in 1969. How are such views to be reconciled?

There is in the library of Rhodes House, Oxford, a fascinating exchange between Sir Evelyn Baring and Dame Margery Perham on this topic. Baring says that there are three theories about Kenyatta: that he was a great villain and remained so despite all appearances; that he was always an able and perfectly reasonable man and not really the leader of Mau Mau; and finally – and this he described as being his own theory – 'that Kenyatta was a double man'. Baring continued to believe that in the 1950s Kenyatta was the master, able to switch murders on and off at will, but that later his character changed.

Dame Margery found it difficult to believe that Kenyatta was the instigator of Mau Mau or that a man could change character so radically late in life. 'Obviously he was a great leader but is it not possible that some rather less enlightened men thought he wasn't going fast enough and developed this Mau Mau technique? And that Kenyatta was afraid of it as it developed and didn't dare come down against it or commit himself wholly to it and he followed a kind of ambivalent double position . . .?'[7]

Much support is given to this latter view by the account provided by Bildad Kaggia, one of the younger leaders who was to be tried and convicted with Kenyatta. Kaggia together with Fred Kubai, another co-defendant, had in June 1951 taken over the Nairobi branch of KAU as secretary-general and chairman respectively and established a headquarters in Kiburi House, which at this time was the only building owned by an African in the Nairobi business centre.[8] Kubai was a rough-hewn, rough-spoken trade union leader who had emerged as General Secretary of the Transport and Allied Workers in the abrasive atmosphere of the late 1940s, the cowboy era in Kenya's industrial relations. In 1949 he had become President of the East Africa Trade Union Congress which had largely been the handiwork of an Indian communist, Makhan Singh, who was its General Secretary.

Bildad Kaggia was in appearance very different from Kubai. Neatly turned out with a watch-chain across his chest he spoke very correct English and, unusually in Africa, was known everywhere as a fanatic for punctuality. Both he and Kubai were ex-Servicemen and had been leading figures in the Forty Group. It was former members of this group, including Eliud Mutonyi and Isaac Gathanju, who planned to give leadership to what for reasons that are more than a little obscure became known as 'Mau Mau'.[9] This name, which first came to the surface in 1948 and was formally outlawed in 1950, was never used by the movement itself. It has been speculated (and most clearly asserted by Josiah Mwangi Kariuki, author of *'Mau Mau' Detainee*) that 'Mau Mau' was a childhood anagram for 'Uma Uma' meaning 'Get out! Get out!' which police once heard shouted by a look-out when they had been raiding an oath-taking ceremony. It is not an expression in either Swahili or Kikuyu.[10]

Bildad Kaggia, who reached the rank of staff sergeant during the war, was a very religious man as a result of his education by the Church Missionary Society and quick with the biblical reference which he was given to throwing out in the course of conversation.[11] When serving in the Middle East it seemed natural to him to spend his leave in Jerusalem. The experience, however, was a very disillusioning one. He was offended by the duplication of holy sites and the venom of holy feuds. When he came to England he sensed racial discrimination within the church, except among the nonconformists. When he was discharged from the Army he went round the churches in Kenya preaching against the foreign religious yoke. When this was stopped he began speaking in the markets and streets, arguing that it was not right to interfere with people following their own way of marriage and questioning the taking of collections. There was no need to build churches, he said, you can pray under the trees.[12]

Although he was sent to prison several times for illegal assembly Kaggia refused to form his own independent church (which probably would have been allowed) because he was opposed to denominationalism. He disbelieved in KASU and the original KAU because of their moderation and their isolation from the ordinary African. But when Kenyatta reappeared and took the KAU presidency, he was at first impressed, agreeing to join KAU and disband his own movement. He was once more disappointed. He found Kenyatta incomparable on the great occasions, but in between these rather infrequent meetings nothing appeared to be happening.

After a while Kaggia took a job as a bank clerk in Nairobi and then created the Clerks and Commercial Workers Union, which he fashioned into an instrument of increasing militancy. 'Because of the new revolutionary atmosphere in the early fifties, "Mau Mau" was able to succeed,' he has written.[13] In the Kikuyu reserve the old Kikuyu Central Association continued to operate underground. Its leadership overlapped with membership of the so-called 'Kiambaa Parliament' which met at the home of the now seriously disaffected ex-Senior Chief Koinange at Banana Hill. Both of these organizations concentrated on the land issue and employed oathing as a means of binding together the various elements of the Kikuyu people in preparation for the mass action which the leaders anticipated would be needed.

Kenyatta's relationship with these elements was ambivalent. Living at Githunguri, which was a hotbed of plotting and radical politics, he could not possibly have been wholly unaware of what was going on. He had certainly been involved in promoting the use of loyalty oath ceremonies, using goat's blood and meat, for political purposes in the period after he had returned from England at a time when oathing was not yet illegal. But he did not originate this. It had begun in 1925 and was resumed in 1944 after the banned KCA leaders were released from detention.

Kenyatta himself was oathed after his return in 1946; he sanctioned the spreading of the oath in the late 1940s both in the Central Province and in the Rift Valley as a way of giving KAU a wider appeal among Kikuyu as the genuine heir to the KCA. In the early days Kenyatta sometimes supervised the oaths but never administered them. Later, during the large-scale oathings and particularly after they were made illegal, he was rarely seen when they took place.[14] (Whether he was then seen at all at such a ceremony is one of the disputed matters about his subsequent trial.)

What does seem clear from Kaggia's account of his dealings with him is that Kenyatta was worried about premature resort to direct action and to all appearances much preferred the constitutional path, either on principle or because, as he repeatedly told the young militants, he believed that they gravely underestimated the probable strength of the British response.[15] He may well have hoped that the contingency plans for direct action would prove unnecessary because the Labour Government would respond to the various representations that were being made including a petition organized by the left-wing Labour MP, Fenner Brockway, which received 67,000 African signatures or marks. But before all else he intended to remain the leader; he would not allow himself to be put on one side like Harry Thuku.

In 1951 he acquiesced in the militant trade unionists taking over the Nairobi branch of KAU, and accepted their demand to hold an overdue national party conference, the first since 1949. At it the moderate office-holders like Mbotela were all overthrown (and he was later to be murdered). Only Kenyatta was re-elected as President unopposed.[16] Still, there was a sharp passage between Kenyatta and the Nairobi branch, which wished to elect Kaggia to the key job of Secretary-General. Kenyatta, who had never felt comfortable with him, insisted on the impropriety of having Kikuyus in both the two top posts. At one stage the Nairobi branch walked out and threatened to form a new party. In the end they accepted a Luhya Secretary-General. The policy resolutions, after all, met their requirements: for the first time these called for an independent Kenya under African rule. A mere dozen years later they were to get it.[17]

Kaggia and his Forty Group comrades had begun seriously to question Kenyatta's leadership. It seemed to be leading nowhere. Even after their long period in detention together, even after independence, Kaggia said he was not sure where Kenyatta had really stood and what he had really wanted.[18] 'Our protest at the [party] election,' he wrote later, 'was the first organized opposition Kenyatta had faced at home. Almost inevitably there was tension between us. I was naively outspoken at [KAU] Committee meetings and as a result I could neither expect, nor did I get, much help from him.'[19] At one time Kubai, Kaggia and some others talked of kicking the *Mzee* ('the old man') upstairs to some honorary post and appointing a leader who would prepare for revolution.[20]

Kenyatta got the various sections of his movement to agree that a Luo, Achieng Oneko, who had been both a business colleague of Odinga's and a political favourite of *Mzee*, should join Peter Mbiyu Koinange in London in a final effort to achieve a breakthrough over the land question.[21] It was the understanding of the radicals that no further opposition would be offered to physical force if this last chance for peaceful methods failed. Kenyatta's options seemed to be closing. The radicals were preparing for action.[22]

As Oginga Odinga describes it, guns were acquired by illegal purchase or stealing; ex-servicemen gave small arms instruction under cover of dynamiting in quarries; the taxi-drivers in Fred Kubai's union were mobilized, black marketeers and prostitutes were enlisted and lines of communication established with the thick forests of Mount Kenya and the Aberdares where the war between Mau Mau and its opponents was to be fought. These plans and preparations, says Odinga, were not revealed to the official committees of KAU, of which he had recently become a member.

A Central Committee was formed to co-ordinate the preparations for violent rebellion, but although its meetings were held at Kiburi House, they happened, according to Kaggia, late at night after the others had left. There were only two members in common between the KAU Committee (which represented a variety of tribes) and the Central Committee (which consisted only of Kikuyus) – Kubai and Kaggia. Even these two held no office in the Central Committee, whose chairman was Eliud Mutonyi and the secretary Isaac Gathanju, both ex-Forty Group members.

The Committee was able to keep in touch with the locations and districts by means of the 'group of 30', runners who had the vital task of delivering Central Committee orders and bringing back intelligence. The centre of oath administration was at Kiambaa in Kiambu District and hundreds of people were transported there from Nairobi throughout the night. Kaggia makes plain that the Central Committee imposed the death sentence on anyone who informed to the authorities, and has described in his book and in an article in *Drum* how he, Mutonyi and two others held a drumhead court-martial in a taxi in which a fellow-Committee member who confessed to having informed about a proposed leadership oath ceremony at which the entire Central Committee would have been present was condemned to die. They immediately executed the sentence.[23]

Kenyatta, says Kaggia, deliberately knew little of what was going on, being in any case under constant supervision from the Special Branch. Although the Government's view of his speeches in 1952 denouncing Mau Mau was that, through subtle use of Kikuyu metaphors, he was managing to convey the precisely opposite message, that was not the view of the Central Committee which decided that 'such meetings could not be tolerated'. Kenyatta was summoned before them for the first time. He apparently did not know Mutonyi and Gathanju and was surprised to find Kubai and Kaggia there. The committee asked him to stop these speeches forthwith because although, they said, they did not question his motives the terms in which he had denounced Mau Mau were too strong and would hamper the work of the organizers among those weaker brethren who might take him seriously. After some discussion he agreed to desist.[24] It was clear that his leadership (and perhaps his life) was at stake. It was a bad time for Kenyatta personally. The strains showed in bouts of heavy drinking; he kept away from people and Asian shopkeepers were complaining that he was taking out his frustrations on them.[25]

Achieng Oneko had by now returned from London, not having been received by Oliver Lyttelton, the Colonial Secretary, and not having much to show for his visit other than the repetition of a promise of a Royal Commission on the land problem. Preparations for rebellion were pressed ahead more urgently.[26]

On 7 October 1952 Senior Chief Waruhiu, a pillar of the establishment in the Kikuyu Reserve, was assassinated. Special Branch told the new Governor, Sir Evelyn Baring, that Kenyatta had known that it was going to happen though he had argued against it with ex-Senior Chief Koinange and one of his sons on the familiar grounds that it was too provocative an act and that they were underestimating the likely reaction.[27]

Baring had decided by 10 October that it was necessary to act. The Colonial Office had not until then considered the situation in Kenya at all urgent. 'Mau Mau I believe to be more hooliganism than a deep political convulsion,' Oliver Lyttelton had noted.[28] But when the new Governor did make known his decisive assessment he received four days later the Churchill Cabinet's authority to proceed. Baring wanted to arrest and intern Jomo Kenyatta and 186 KAU activists, nearly all Kikuyus, though including Achieng Oneko, a Luo, and Paul Ngei, a Kamba. Because he anticipated large-scale violence in response the Governor preferred not to act, as he could have done, under his existing powers, but to declare an Emergency. He asked for an additional battalion of troops from the Middle East to reinforce the existing three KAR battalions on the spot as well as troops he would arrange to bring in from Uganda and Tanganyika. Word of these plans was leaked to Kenyatta and to the Central Committee, probably by way of Kikuyu clerks or policemen, but he made no attempt to evade arrest.[29]

On 19 October the order went out from Eliud Mutonji, who was not on the arrest list, to the guerrilla forces stationed in the forests to take independent action. The British struck forty-eight hours earlier than originally planned. Kenyatta and the others including Kaggia, Kubai and Oneko were arrested in the small hours of 21 October. There was no immediate outbreak of general disorder. What did follow was a succession of individual assassinations, most prominently of Tom Mbotela, the former KAU vice-president, and attacks on isolated Europeans, made the more horrific by the mutilation of the bodies.

Altogether only thirty-two European civilians were murdered in the whole course of the Mau Mau rising as against eighteen hundred African civilians. But each individual European murder was well publicized, with all the exceptionally distressing circumstances and with frequently the elements of betrayal and of barbaric treatment of the victim.[30] An elderly resident in the Nyeri district, known for his friendship for Africans, was buried alive.[31]

BRITISH COLONIAL ATTITUDES

The House of Commons was informed about the Mau Mau Emergency by Lyttelton on the afternoon of 21 October and there was a wider debate on the Address on 7 November.[32] In his speeches Lyttelton set what was to be the predominant tone of British attitudes to Mau Mau throughout. 'Across the page of Kenya's history has fallen the shadow of witchcraft, savagery and crime,' he said. 'Mau Mau is the unholy union of dark and ancient superstition with the apparatus of modern gangsterism'. Asked for an example of oaths taken, he cited, 'When the reed-brick horn is blown, if I leave the European farm before killing the European owner, may this oath kill me.'

Although Britain's international standing had rested so much on her being at the head of a large Empire, colonial policy had always been a distinctly minority interest in the home country. Specialist magazines like *East Africa and Rhodesia* were given to raging at the poor attendance at colonial debates. But there were MPs on either side who specialized in and were quite knowledgeable about either colonial matters in general or particular regions. Sir Roland Robinson, Patrick Wall, Frederic Bennett and Philip Goodhart were prominent among Conservatives interested in East Africa. On the Labour side members like John Dugdale, John Stonehouse, Barbara Castle, Leslie Hale and Fenner Brockway regularly raised the problems of colonial peoples. George Wigg challenged the wisdom of arresting Kenyatta just when, so he said, he was on the way out, thus making a martyr of him. 'It is said that Kenyatta is a wild, untidy and arrogant fellow and that he is a political vagabond. But that is no reason for arresting him.'[33] When the Emergency was proclaimed Brockway went immediately to Kenya accompanied by Leslie Hale.[34] They found KAU still functioning. The presidency had been taken over by Walter Fanuel Odede, a Luo Member of the Legislative Council, assisted by another MLC, Wycliffe Awori, together with the bright part-Goan, part-Masai, Joseph Murumbi, and a 22-year-old director of information, Tom Mboya. But their relationship with the colonial administration was uneasy. They told Brockway and Hale that they were prepared, if given permission, to address meetings repudiating Mau Mau and the use of violence; they were not given permission because they would not repudiate Kenyatta.[35]

On the political right in Britain the opportunity was seized to strike back at Fenner Brockway, the Fabian Colonial Bureau and other champions of colonial peoples, rubbing the noses of liberal opinion generally in the disgrace of what was supposed to be an advanced tribe. 'This outbreak of violence,' said F. S. Joelson's *East Africa and Rhodesia*, 'proves that the Kikuyu are completely unfit for the political medium presented for them by Fabian and other theorists. Perhaps even these fanatics may now realise that the Africans whom they had insisted on regarding as cadets in democracy are but little removed from barbarism.'[36]

Yet in the African continent the train of decolonization had already left the station, and the pace was quickening, though how much so could not yet be assessed. When the Conservatives came back to office in October 1951 they were surprised to be told by their civil servants that the Gold Coast (Ghana) was irreversibly headed for independence. The question then arose of which colonies could be expected in the next ten to twenty years to arrive at that goal. A Cabinet committee under Lord Swinton answered that in Africa it was three territories only: Gold Coast, Nigeria, and the (white-ruled) Central African Federation. Accompanying the Swinton memorandum was a powerful and persuasive appendix by Sir Norman Brook, the Cabinet Secretary, in which he argued that the process of decolonization

> cannot now be halted or reversed and it is only to a limited extent that its pace can be controlled by the UK Government.... But in the main the pace of constitutional change will be determined by the strength of nationalist feeling and the development of political consciousness... Political leaders... normally expect that the promise of independence will be attained within their own political lifetime and, if they cannot satisfy their followers... their influence may be usurped by less responsible elements.[37]

It is evident from the subsequent Cabinet Minutes, which Brook had to compile, that for several Ministers this was very bitter medicine indeed. They recorded their view that 'it was unfortunate that the policy of assisting dependent peoples to attain self-government had been carried forward so fast and so far'.[38]

Where did the East African territories fit in with this? In his 1954 appendix Brook put Kenya, Tanganyika and Uganda into an indeterminate category. If they could manage to club together to create an East African Federation this would be robust enough to qualify for the list of new members of the Commonwealth by 1974; if not, not. There had been renewed discussion of Federation since the war; the only trouble was that whereas the three territories were always said to be progressively converging over time, the actual decisions made in each of them were driving them further apart.

There had been in existence since 1948 what had been planned as the first instalment of closer union: an East African High Commission and Central Legislative Assembly, with responsibility for common services including railways and harbours, civil aviation, posts and telegraphs, customs and excise (but not their rates) and defence. That sounded impressive but the High Commission had no enforcement powers or revenue of its own and its decisions were subject to the veto of each of the Governors.[39]

It was the political and economic prominence of the white settler in Kenya and the prospect that this would be extended within a Federation economically dominated by Kenya that generated opposition to the project in Uganda and Tanganyika. In Tanganyika the obstacle was the one raised in 1930; the territory was not a colony but a UN trusteeship.

The Colonial Office was forever fighting an unequal battle to bring about consistency between political developments in the East African territories and indeed between them and the territories of Central Africa. The presiding theme was to be the principle of multiracialism, which was favoured by Oliver Lyttelton and even more enthusiastically by his successor Alan Lennox-Boyd, who took over as Colonial Secretary on 28 July 1954, after having been for a while Lyttelton's Minister of State. He was a large man with a very pronounced personality. The principle was variously expressed, sometimes in terms of actual parity between European, Asian and African representation, sometimes as incentives or even requirements for political parties to be rainbow-coloured. But what these ideas had in common was that they involved a major exercise in social engineering whereby people of all races would be conditioned into believing and acting as if race did not count. When, and not before, that had been achieved the territory, or territories put together, could be considered ready for independence. This idea began to fall apart in East Africa in the 1950s, in the first instance in Uganda and not long afterwards in Tanganyika.

To make clear what happened in Uganda, it should first be mentioned that, beginning under the Labour Government and continuing under the Conservatives, the very idea of Federation had been poisoned as far as Africans were concerned by the long conception and final inauguration on 3 September 1953 of the Central African Federation covering the Rhodesias and Nyasaland. This construct, which was white-run and in which the multiracial principle, though proclaimed, was a farce, was bound to give the idea of Federation a bad name in East Africa – it was no accident that among Bildad Kaggia's many organizations was an Anti-Federation League.[40]

The one thing that was certain to sink the frail barque of an East African Federation was anything that linked the one venture with the other. This is precisely what, through loose thought or clumsy wording, Oliver Lyttelton proceeded to do in the course of an after-dinner speech to the East Africa Dinner Club on 30 June 1953. This was enough for the *East African Standard* to launch a headline 'Great New Dominion Foreseen: Union of Central and East Africa', and thus to precipitate a major crisis in Uganda.

The young Kabaka Mutesa II ('King Freddy'), whom the powerful Governor, Sir Andrew Cohen, dismissed as 'a weakling', took the occasion to assert his leadership. Relying on the special nature of Britain's historic relationship with his kingdom, he required that Britain should recognize Buganda's independence (and thus separation from the rest of Uganda) and that his relations with Britain should in consequence be transferred from the Colonial to the Foreign Office. Failing to move him from this position and regarding the Kabaka as an anachronistic impediment to political advance, Cohen recommended that Britain get rid of him. Lyttelton hesitated – 'His Highness speaks perfect English, has agreeable manners, was an honorary officer in the Grenadier Guards, my old regiment'[41] – but in the end backed the man on the spot.

The Kabaka was deposed and deported to Britain. Fenner Brockway and Leslie Hale put down a motion of censure. In his reply Lyttelton felt himself obliged to declare that Uganda was to be an essentially African state and that unless public opinion changed there would be no more federations. It was a decisive moment. As soon as Lennox-Boyd took over in 1954 he was advised by the Governor to return the Kabaka; he was inclined to agree but it was a year before he could overcome the combined opposition of the civil service at home and on the spot and send him back.[42]

A year after that in Tanganyika, the Governor, Sir Edward Twining, who had been talking about carrying on without much change until 1967 or 1970, suddenly altered his tune and began in November 1956, the month of Suez, talking to the Colonial Office about the need for major changes which would clearly point the way to African leadership. The immediate reason given for this switch was that 'the unofficial European element . . . has had an opportunity to display capacity for political leadership and has taken this opportunity to demonstrate that it has none'.[43] But major contributory causes were circumspection about the UN (especially in the weeks after Suez) and the personality of the principal African leader, Julius Nyerere. Nyerere was able and intelligent, scholarly in his approach, moderate in manner and not given to demagogy; he was to make an excellent impression before the UN Trusteeship Council. If Britain could not get along with him, whom could she get along with? 'Nyerere's personal position is more important than we perhaps like to admit and therefore it is very strongly in our interests that we should try to gather him into the fold, although this might mean making some concessions,' the Governor declared.[44]

From then on, the need to keep Nyerere on side, and thus to allow him to become a pacemaker, was an important factor in any calculation that tried to preserve some harmony between the progress of the three East African territories.

THE CHALLENGE FROM THE FORESTS

Nothing could be finally resolved about the future of East Africa until the Emergency was over in Kenya. There is no space here for describing in any detail the nature of Mau Mau or the successful campaign fought against it. There is by now a sizeable literature about the uprising and its suppression, to which this book makes no attempt to add.[45] But its special horror – the feeling that the most advanced tribe in Kenya had turned its back on modern culture – invested the drive first for military victory and then for a political settlement with menace and urgency.

Odinga records that, as the Government had struck before the rebellion was ready to begin, almost the entire educated leadership had been removed ahead of the battle and that the initial effect was to paralyze the secret organization at the centre. In the first days there was not the carefully planned campaign of slaughter and sabotage, disrupting communications and damaging buildings and installations which, in the opinion of many, could have brought the colony to its knees.[46]

Nevertheless on 15 January 1953 Lawrence Karugo Kiburia, who had replaced the arrested Fred Kubai at the head of the still legal Nairobi branch of KAU, summoned a meeting of those few who were left of the secret organization. They decided on a fresh oath and 'war against the imperialists'. They seem to have been able to preserve a secret War Council among the mud huts of Mathari in Nairobi until April 1953, and Eliud Mutonji, the chairman, avoided arrest until November of that year. Each KAU branch in the Kikuyu Reserve was required to raise a thousand fighters who were to be deployed in the forests, and firearms were passed to them, many by way of the Indian radical Pio Pinto. Odinga calculates that about 15,000 Kikuyus entered the Aberdare Forests after the Emergency was declared and others went into the forests of Mount Kenya. Round such military leaders as Dedan Kimathi and Stanley Mathenge in the Aberdares and 'General China' on Mount Kenya, says Odinga, 'rallied the men who had taken not only the unity oath of the KCA but also the later fighting oath'.[47]

The unity oath was relatively simple. Performed under an arch made of two banana stems joined at the top, through which the initiates passed seven times, the ceremony consisted of an oath administrator circling each initiate's bowed head, also seven times, with the lungs of a goat which he was then required to bite. The pledge taken was to fight for the lands that had been seized by the Europeans – 'And if I fail to do this may this oath kill me, may this seven kill me, may this meat kill me.' The initiates were afterwards anointed on the forehead with the blood of the goat mixed with grain, as a warning that they should never sell their country. Three cuts were made on the left wrist and the blood of all of them was mixed with goat's meat and other Kikuyu foods which they would then eat as a symbol of unity.

This was the ceremony as described by one who took the oath, Josiah Mwangi Kariuki, in his book *'Mau Mau' Detainee*. The account of Harrison Njoroge Kimani, the Fort Hall oath administrator who spoke to Dr John Spencer in 1972, contains a number of additional ceremonial flourishes, including seven cuts instead of three and the pricking of the eyes of the dead goat (or, in some cases, ram), and a number of more specific pledges, such as 'If you ever disagree with your nation or sell it, may you die of this oath . . . If you ever sell a Kikuyu woman to a foreigner, may you die of this oath . . . If you ever report a member of this Society to the Government, may you die of this oath.'[48]

Kariuki, who unlike most of the forest fighters had had some education, wrote that after taking the oath, 'I felt exalted with a new spirit of power and strength. . . . Even my education, of which I was so proud, appeared trivial beside this splendid and terrible force that had been given me. I had been born again.' An informant of Donald Barnett, whose book co-authored with Karari Njama, *Mau Mau from Within*, was endorsed by four of independent Kenya's nationalist leaders, concedes that the taking of this oath was not always voluntary. In Njama's particular case a group of young men had been gathered together after dark on a social pretext and had then been threatened with death if they did not take the oath. One man objected. 'Before he had completed his statement, however, he was hit very hard in the face. This convinced him . . . The man pleaded to be allowed to take the oath and have his life spared.'[49]

Both Kariuki and Njama give details of the warrior's or *Batuni* oath which the forest fighters subsequently took. In Kariuki's version it had seven parts, undertaking to shed the blood of Europeans when so ordered, never to betray, to hide a comrade on the run, never to disclose secrets and to 'abide until my death by all the promises that I have made this day'. Njama swore to a rather longer version, ending up as a twenty-first point with, 'I shall always follow the leadership of Jomo Kenyatta and Mbiyu Koinange.'[50]

The taking to the forests had important symbolic effect. Traditionally, the Kikuyu were people of the forest and, traditionally too, they were not thought by other tribes to be much good as warriors. They now sought to refute that aspersion by reverting to their former habitat. Odinga says that as the struggle grew more desperate there were perversions and abuses of the basic oaths.[51] The Corfield Report on the history of Mau Mau alleges that 'the use of menstrual blood and public intercourse with sheep and adolescent girls were a common feature of most of these ceremonies... Concoctions of the foulest and almost unimaginable ingredients were eaten and drunk.' According to some Mau Mau confessions after capture, parts of human bodies and body fluids sometimes were incorporated in the magic cocktail. Kariuki comments that if these things happened they must have been the work of perverted individuals driven crazy by their isolation in the forests. In their psychological war against Mau Mau the authorities made maximum use of the extent to which these extreme extensions of the oath carried initiates beyond the pale of acceptable tribal behaviour.[52]

As Kaggia, Kubai, Murumbi and Oneko, the authors of the preface to *Mau Mau from Within*, said, those who went into the forests when most of their educated leadership had been arrested were almost all humble men and women. They attempted, nevertheless, with all their handicaps to adopt a stance of some dignity in their forest camps. They created a 'Parliament', chose a 'Prime Minister' ('Field-Marshal Sir Dedan Kimathi, Knight Commander of the East African Empire'), honoured his new wife ('Knight Commander of Gikuyu and Mumbi'), distributed high military ranks and even once or twice corresponded with the Governor and the British general ('... We demand a written proof that this is a true negotiation and signed by you both.... Yours faithfully, Brig. Gen. Sir Karari Njama, Chief Secretary, Kenya Parliament.') Nevertheless they were unable to avoid damaging splits, particularly with Kimathi's chief rival for leadership, Stanley Mathenge.[53]

THE GOVERNMENT'S RESPONSE

The Government rather belatedly realized the scale of the challenge they would have to face when a co-ordinated operation requiring some military professionalism to mount was carried out on the night of 26 March 1953 both on the Naivasha Police Station and on the village of Lari nearby. At Naivasha the rebels captured a large haul of weapons and ammunition and at Lari there was a horrible massacre of ninety-seven loyalist Kikuyu, including an ex-Chief and 26 members of his family. The scale and shock of this event had two all-important consequences. It convinced the authorities of the need for a major military operation and it ensured that the subsequent struggle would take on the character of a Kikuyu civil war.[54]

A senior military commander, General Sir George Erskine, arrived in June 1953, and with eleven infantry battalions, assisted by 20,000 police and 25,000 Kikuyu loyalists who were enlisted in the Home Guard, and at a cost to Britain of £60 million, which was a big sum in those days, an elaborate and systematic plan to suppress the rising slowly but relentlessly, area by area, was put into action over the next two years. The whole Kikuyu tribe except those who, through attachment to a Christian mission or manifest adherence to a government chief and service in the Home Guard were dubbed 'loyalist', were treated as suspects. Kikuyu 'pseudo-gangs' were used against the fighters in the forests. With the exception of some elements within the related Embu and Meru people, the uprising was confined to the one tribe, and the traditional prejudices against that tribe as being sour, secretive, subversive folk were exploited for its discomfort.[55] Of the security forces about six to seven hundred lost their lives (of whom 63 were Europeans); estimates of Mau Mau deaths have been put as high as over 11,000. In addition there were more than a thousand executions, less than a third of which were for homicide, the rest being for such offences as 'consorting with terrorists' and 'illegal possession of firearms'.[56]

Kikuyu families did not live traditionally in villages; they were now compelled to do so. 'Operation Anvil' on 24 April 1954 cleared 30,000 Kikuyu from Nairobi and placed them in reception camps, where they were screened (with the help of loyalist informers) and those held to be infected with the Mau Mau disease were forwarded to detention camps. Altogether nearly 80,000 tribesmen were subjected to rehabilitation on the principle that men so psychologically disoriented could not otherwise resume a rational existence.

These operations, often involving techniques that were rough-and-ready at best and at times abusive, broke the effort that was made to give any co-ordination to the rebellion from the city. When Colonel Arthur Young, who had been picked by Oliver Lyttelton as Kenya Police Commissioner in early 1954 because of his recent Malayan experience, arrived in Nairobi, he was told by the head of the crime department that 'many serious and revolting crimes were being perpetuated both by "loyal" Africans and Europeans, not infrequently with the tacit approval of the administration, concerning which no reports were being received at police headquarters.' No action was subsequently taken over well-substantiated cases of extortion, torture and murder in order not to endanger the morale of the civilian security forces.[57] When Lennox-Boyd retired in 1959 he briefed his successor about 'all the skeletons . . . of people whose breaches of discipline I had tolerated on the Governor's advice.'[58]

Intense propaganda stiffened the other tribes of Kenya against the Kikuyu and the loyalist Kikuyu against the rebels. Emphasis was placed on evidence pointing to the mental debasement of Mau Mau involved in some of the oathing routines, and the zombie-like appearance of 'hard-core' detainees; internationally, every effort was made to prevent the rising from acquiring the status of a 'war of national liberation', which Cairo radio and Communist bloc countries were only too ready to give it.[59]

THE AIR-BRUSHING OF KENYATTA

The involvement of the KAU structure – or rather of the Kikuyu parts of that structure – with the uprising was too apparent[60] and on 8 June 1953 the party as a whole was banned. Jomo Kenyatta was placed on trial, together with Fred Kubai, Bildad Kaggia, Kungu Karumba, a Kikuyu who was a branch chairman of KAU, Paul Ngei, a Kamba, an ex-NCO and member of the Forty Group with a short fuse and very rough tongue, and the Luo Achieng Oneko on charges of managing Mau Mau. The trial took place in the schoolroom of an agricultural training college in Kapenguria, a remote region 280 miles from Nairobi near Kenya's northern boundary before a retired judge who sat as a resident magistrate.

The accused were defended by the extreme left-wing lawyer and politician D. N. Pritt. All of them were convicted of 'managing Mau Mau', though one, Achieng Oneko, was acquitted on appeal but nevertheless detained. The evidence against Kenyatta, which placed him at three Mau Mau initiation ceremonies in March 1950, five months before Mau Mau was made an illegal organization, sounded none too convincing at the time and in one instance was disbelieved. It became even less convincing subsequently when the main witness of what had appeared to be one clearcut instance, Rawson Macharia, withdrew his evidence by an affidavit that alleged government bribery.[61] The rest was mainly circumstantial, such as the use of Kenyatta's name in Mau Mau songs and hymns.

At the end of the trial Kenyatta and the five other prisoners were sentenced to seven years' hard labour and indefinite restriction thereafter.[62] They served their sentences at Lokitaung, in the intensely hot and arid country near to the northern end of Lake

Rudolph and the Ethiopian border, before being moved under restriction ninety miles south to Lodwar. Relations between Kenyatta and the young revolutionaries were not good. The latter formed their own 'political party' with Kaggia as the president and Kubai the general secretary. On one occasion a knife attack was even made on the old man.[63]

The Government had resolved that it should be as if Kenyatta had never been. His very substantial house at Githunguri was demolished; it was decreed that he would never be allowed to return to Kikuyuland. Like Trotsky and the Russian revolution the name and fame of Jomo Kenyatta were to be air-brushed out of Kikuyu history.

THE LYTTELTON CONSTITUTION

Sir Evelyn Baring, having originally been of the view that talk of changing Kenya's constitution should wait until after the Mau Mau uprising was over, had changed his mind when he observed what strains the emergency had involved. During 1953 there was repeated friction between the authorities and the settlers, now led by Michael Blundell, a man of forceful personality, considerable intelligence but volatile temperament who was just beginning to feel his feet politically. The settlers wanted to take over the Government and regarded the rather aloof and aristocratic Baring and his advisers as much too slow and hidebound in their reaction to the crisis. On 26 January 1953, following a particularly terrible murder of a young woman doctor, her farmer husband and their son, there was an ugly demonstration by Europeans outside Government House, which was only containable because Blundell kept his head.[64]

But the cost to the British taxpayer put the whole position of the settlers in perspective. In 1954 Lyttelton came to Nairobi and with Baring confronted Blundell and the settlers with the proposition that after this convulsion Kenya would never be the same again. Lyttelton spent three weeks in Kenya and gave them a choice, 'Either you agree [with reforms] or if you don't we have a military Governor with complete powers.'[65] General Erskine had made no effort to conceal his belief that military methods alone were not enough. 'If anyone thinks,' he said, 'that the re-establishment of law and order is a signal to return to old ways they will be sadly disillusioned.'[66]

Under the Lyttelton Constitution of 1954, which was essentially devised by Baring, a Council of Ministers was for the first time formally established with, in addition to the Governor and the Chief Secretary, a multiracial element of three elected European ministers, two Asian ministers and one African minister, together with two (European) nominated ministers (Vasey who was very liberal and Cavendish-Bentinck who was very conservative) and five portfolios, including Internal Security and Defence, Legal Affairs and African Affairs which were still entrusted to civil servants. By having the elected Ministers keep their seats in Legco the Government regained its majority, whose absence under Mitchell's arrangements had been considered by Baring as a serious anomaly. For the first time an Asian, Ibrahim Nathoo, an Ismaili Muslim, acquired the portfolio of Works, to the dismay of many Europeans, in addition to the appointment of a prominent Hindu as Minister without Portfolio. The Africans regarded their single portfolio – that of Community Development – as seriously deficient as an indication of what Britain had in mind by multiracialism. At first there were no takers. Eventually a willing candidate was found, though it inevitably followed that he could have little political future.[67] But Cavendish-Bentinck understood what had happened. He told Blundell, 'You have destroyed everything for which I have worked all my life.' When asked what that could be, he replied, 'A white dominion in East Africa.'[68]

By the end of 1955 there was no military problem but there were many other problems created by the Emergency. The scale of the effort required convinced men like Blundell, who had grown in authority and understanding during his service from March 1954 onwards as the one settler in the four-man War Cabinet, that the white settlers could never rule the country alone. In 1955 Cavendish-Bentinck was persuaded to take the Speakership of Legco, and Blundell, now a convinced advocate of multiracialism, took over as Minister of Agriculture while remaining an elected member. 'The greatest need from our community is responsibility and a realisation that the country is not just two old gentlemen with pink gins sitting in the Muthaiga club,'[69] he said.

In addition to the multiracial executive the Lyttelton Constitution provided that for the first time the African MLCs should be elected. How was this to be done? Lennox-Boyd, now Colonial Secretary, was clear that 'it will not be possible for many years to come to allow African members to be elected by universal adult suffrage'. What was needed was a new principle of 'qualified democracy' to prevent 'backward tribes from being exploited by the more advanced, the illiterate peasant by the townsman, the real intelligentsia from being swamped by the half-educated demagogue'. Walter Coutts had conducted an enquiry to devise such a franchise and had come out with a list of ten qualifications – such as education, property and practical public service (for instance, as tribal leaders) – any three of which would convey a vote and more would convey a bonus up to a total of three votes.[70]

The Coutts plan was adopted, though modified in detail and somewhat simplified so as to admit 50 per cent more voters.[71] While the European elections took place on time in September 1956, the voting for the first eight African members had to wait until March 1957. When it occurred an altogether new phase in Kenya politics was to begin.

Part II

The Independence of Kenya 1957–63

4 Tearing Down Lyttelt

*'What we really want to do is to ensure that the minorities obtain
not proportionate but disproportionate representation both in
executive and in legislature.'* (Ian Buist, Colonial Office official
commenting on Ministerial arguments for PR in Kenya, 20 May
1959)

On 28 January 1957, within less than a month of his installation in
No. 10 in the wake of the Suez fiasco, Harold Macmillan called on
Lord Salisbury, as chairman of the Cabinet's Colonial Policy Committee (CPC),[1] to supply him with 'a profit and loss account for
each of our colonial possessions'. The stated object was 'to gauge
whether, from the financial and economic point of view, we are
likely to gain or lose by its departure'. The whole Cabinet ought to
be told 'which territories are likely to become ripe for independence over the next few years – or even, if they are not yet ready
for it, will demand it so insistently that their claims cannot be denied – and at what date that stage is likely to be reached in each
case'.[2] The Colonial Secretary, Alan Lennox-Boyd, objected to the
unsentimental realism of this approach, which seemed to him to
leave out of account 'the moral obligations which we have inherited – the long and historical association which no amount of
economic argument could blot out of my memory or my feeling of
duty'.[3] His response to Salisbury warned him that the exercise would
take a long time and added 'one or two glosses' to the Prime Minister's choice of words.[4]

The first civil service reaction to the Prime Minister's directive
was to take his words about 'profit and loss' literally; happily the
experienced Cabinet Secretary, Sir Norman Brook, was there to
reinterpret Macmillan's wishes.[5] What the new Prime Minister really
had in mind, Brook said, was a detached account of all the factors
Ministers would need to weigh up when deciding about the future
of each colony. It took the departments a long summer to compile
this Imperial Domesday Book. It was September before a final report
was ready for the Prime Minister.[6]

This reply was not couched in a profit-and-loss mode, though
there was a Treasury paper, which unhelpfully concluded that,

'Economic considerations tend to be evenly matched and the economic interests of Great Britain are unlikely in themselves to be decisive in determining whether or not a territory should become independent.'[7] In line with his report already noted to Winston Churchill, Brook said that in Africa the only territories to whose independence Britain was committed during the next decade (apart from the Gold Coast which was to become independent as Ghana in a little over a month) were Nigeria and the Central African Federation. As for East Africa Uganda was pressing for internal self-government in 1961 and independence in 1967 but 'it cannot be expected by then to have acquired the skill in government or to have developed the racial harmony which would justify the UK Government to relinquish their authority'. Brook had warned the CPC that, 'HMG may therefore be obliged to maintain its authority in the face of opposition and criticism.' When it came to Kenya Brook's advice was that 'the devolution of responsibility will largely depend on the growth of inter-racial confidence, which cannot be predicted in terms of time'.[8]

FIRST AFRICAN ELECTION, 1957

But 1957, in addition to seeing Ghana's independence under the Premiership of Kwame Nkrumah, saw the first African election in Kenya. The previous year, in voting for the European seats in the Legco, right-wing opponents of the Lyttelton multiracial constitution, under 'Puck' Briggs, had outnumbered Michael Blundell's supporters by eight to six; now, the Africans' eight seats all went to vociferous critics of Lyttelton from the opposing camp. Both kinds of Europeans in the end accepted office, Blundell staying on as Minister of Agriculture and Briggs becoming a Minister Without Portfolio. The Africans refused to serve and the one existing African minister, who had been rejected at the election, resigned. Multiracialism was not off to a very good start.

All colonywide African parties had been banned when KAU was banned. They were still banned in 1957 when African MLCs were elected. On the other hand, district parties had been allowed, though this had not been implemented until June 1955 and even then not in Central Province which included the Kikuyu reserves. This conveyed a sinister message to those educated Africans who treated tribalism as the great enemy of nationalism and suspected Europeans of using the Emergency as an excuse to divide up the huge African majority that they faced. J. P. Mathenge, a Kikuyu student at the University of East Africa at Makerere in Uganda and a future political leader, wrote in *Politica*, the monthly journal of the College Political Society, for 2 June 1953,

> It must be kept in mind that the present government is deeply penetrated by settler influence and leaders. It aims at breaking up the political growth of the national unity of the African people, splitting them into tribes which will come under rigid state control under the offices of the chiefs. The objective is 'Back to the Days of the Dark Ages', . . . a policy of European perpetual superiority and domination in the social, political and economic fields over the non-European population . . . [and of linking] Kenya in a Federation to the other East and Central African territories.[9]

'A-K' VERSUS TOM MBOYA

Nevertheless, educated Africans, including the by now eight nominated MLCs, set to work in advance of the election to found such political organizations as were permitted. In the absence of national parties, a Nairobi party would have the highest profile and, since Kikuyus except those with special certificates of loyalty had been massively expelled from the capital in 'Operation Anvil', it was the Luos and Luhya who filled the vacuum. At first the dominant personality would appear without question to be Clement Argwings-Khodek. Thirty-two years of age in 1955 he was the son of a wealthy Luo landowner from the Uganda border, whose parents were among the earliest Christians in Nyanza. After attending Catholic schools and Makerere College he took a degree at Cardiff and was called to the English Bar, having pursued legal studies against the express wishes of the Kenya Government. In December 1951 he arrived back in Nairobi, a flamboyant barrister with an Irish wife, a nurse from Armagh.

Only after a year's delay was he allowed to practise. Argwings-Kodhek joined KAU in May 1952. According to a profile in the *Sunday Post* Kenyatta gave him 'a right royal reception', pressing a bottle of brandy on him and rushing him to a photo studio to be pictured with KAU committeemen.[10] Under the Emergency, as the only African member of the Nairobi bar, he appeared frequently as defending counsel in Mau Mau cases. His 'commanding resonant voice will be his most powerful political attribute,' said the *Sunday Post*. 'He has as much presence and personality as all the African unofficial MLCs put together.'[11] Unhappily, in the long run his liking for alcohol was to damage his political career.[12]

What political discussion there was at that time in Nairobi centred on the Kaloleni Club. Members were principally Luo but an influential role was played nevertheless by the future Ugandan Prime Minister Milton Obote whose residence, L 10, was crammed with books and became known as No. 10 Downing Street. Frail in appearance and reserved in manner, he took others by surprise when he did speak by the force and ardour of his oratory. He was prominent among those Kaloleni Club members who in 1955 met in Wycliffe Awori's office to start what they wanted to call the 'Kenya African National Congress'. They nominated Argwings-Kodhek as president and created a committee of eight, including 'A-K' and Obote, to draft a party constitution. A well-attended public meeting at Pumwani Hall on 18 December, at which Kikuyus were present, changed the name by majority vote to 'The African Congress' and the plans were then unanimously endorsed.[13]

The Government at this stage took fright at the prospect of political developments running away from their control. 'A-K' was a man given to throwing out bold, controversial statements, often a little off-beam in their wording, and then, under challenge, retreating with a smokescreen of professional circumspection. He was willing when it came to it to settle for Nairobi District African Congress (NDAC). The party secretary wrote that, 'We will not rôle [*sic*] any Kikuyu before the necessary loyalty certificates can be obtained and our [only] Kikuyu office-bearer must of necessity stand down until then.'[14] The registrar granted a licence in March 1956 providing that the congress should not 'affiliate, merge or otherwise combine with or participate in any other association, organization or society or any combination of such bodies'.[15]

Nevertheless the new party pledged itself to national aims, to 'smash the Lyttelton constitution', open the White Highlands to African occupation, abolish the colour bar, establish universal adult suffrage and fill half the unofficial seats in Legco with Africans.[16] Even more radically, its leader, Argwings-Kodhek, launched the slogan 'Africa for the Africans' and called on Eliud Mathu, the nominated Kikuyu MLC, to resign. 'The Congress will in future,' Argwings-Kodhek declared, 'oppose the quasi-Kenyan-traditional practice of making [as] councillors and legislators certain classes of Africans who are so ill-equipped that they are merely used as enlarged pictures on the wall'. Mathu replied on the radio that he refused to listen to this 'Mussolini of Kenya'.[17] Africans found 'A-K' an exciting speaker but those who tried working for him in the party office found him a hopeless organizer. He was considered to be easily the front-runner for the high-profile Nairobi seat and was nominated at a meeting at Kaloleni Hall that was so packed that his nominator had to be put on somebody's shoulders before he could be heard.[18]

There was, however, to be an even younger contender. Tom Mboya, the General Secretary of the Kenya Federation of Labour, now twenty-six, arrived back on 31 October 1956 from thirteen months in Britain and the United States. Of medium height and stocky, jet black and round-faced, he was of high intelligence and fleet of speech. Some held him vain and he was certainly attractive to many women, both white and black. While he had been away he had attended classes at Ruskin College, Oxford, published a Fabian pamphlet called *The Kenya Question: An African Answer*, and in America laid the foundation of his enviable international reputation as a public speaker. He was shortly to become, to borrow an expression from American politics, Kenya's boy wonder.

Coming from Rusinga island in the Kavirondo Gulf of Lake Victoria, though not actually born there, Tom Mboya was a Luo but not of that Nilotic tribe's mainstream. He belonged to the Suba clan, which is of Bantu extraction, a remnant of previous inhabitants whom the Luos assimilated when they moved south.[19] Some use of this was to be made against him politically by opponents within the tribe. At an early stage in life Mboya acquired a remarkable facility in English and a much more disciplined approach to work than most of his fellows. Starting as a sanitary inspector in the Nairobi Health Department, he soon became involved in the trade union movement. After a brief experience of politics in 1952–3 as Awori's protégé in KAU, he joined the Kenya Federation of Registered Trade Unions (KFRTU), and when in October 1953 its General Secretary was dismissed following a major internal row, Mboya, who had already displayed his cool practical competence, was elected in his place.[20] In the absence of KAU, he turned the KFRTU into the principal voice of Nairobi's Africans. At the same time he began to build up white patrons such as Ernest Vasey, the liberal-minded and highly talented Minister of Finance who later

loaned him the money to buy his first car, and British trade unionists working within the Labour Department.[21]

Because the KFRTU was affiliated to the International Confederation of Free Trade Unions (ICFTU) Tom Mboya was able to
make his mark early at the international and, above all, American
trade union level. The ICFTU was founded as a breakaway from
the World Federation of Trade Unions (WFTU) which was more
and more slipping under communist leadership. The breakaway had
been masterminded by an American Jay Lovestone, who had been
General Secretary of the American Communist Party in the 1920s
until he was personally expelled by Stalin[22] and had since been
engaged, at the right hand of the president of the American Federation of Labour, in a relentless anti-communist crusade. One of
ICFTU's main tactics was to get in first with emerging nations while
they were still at the colonial stage and sign up their future labour
stars. From that perspective Mboya was an obvious target.

For Mboya the great advantage of this connection was the links
with the American unions, who financed the building of Solidarity
House, the first African-owned purpose-built office block in Nairobi which was the headquarters of the Kenya Federation of Labour
(KFL) (the former KFRTU); they also made other funds available
for what were in effect political activities. His immense popularity
as a speaker in the United States gave him a certain protection. It
made him a very awkward person to detain. The disadvantage, which
only gradually became apparent, was that while Mboya saw in the
United States an anti-colonial superpower which could be used, if
necessary, to checkmate Britain, there were other Africans who
came to see America as the great Satan of imperialism whose influence should be repelled.

As a union leader in Kenya before going overseas Mboya had
earned near-universal applause for his success in presenting the
workers' case in a major strike at the Mombasa docks before a
judicial tribunal and securing a satisfactory outcome. He received
public congratulations from Mr Justice Windham, who later, in
a union recognition case concerning the Nairobi City Council in
which Mboya appeared for the employees, once more rewarded the
thorough preparation and forensic skills that had seen the city
fathers simply outclassed by the youthful African.[23] Sir Walter Coutts,
who was Minister of Education and Labour at the time, later remarked rather sadly, 'In trade unionism he was always correct, he
always knew his law, he knew his employers, he knew exactly how

far he could go . . . But he didn't push the employer over the edge.'
But he went on, in a bewildered manner, 'Given all these qualities
in trade unionism he never applied them to politics . . . This to me
is a complete enigma. I never really understood it.'[24]
Unfortunately Mboya acquired enemies for other reasons. Although
he had great charm for people he liked, he could be very arrogant
towards his fellow-Africans, as well as displaying vanity. Malcolm
MacDonald, the last Governor, who had the highest regard for him
and who described him as a man of the first rank by any standards,
added, 'he has one awful defect: he has an insufferable arrogance.
He offends all sorts of people whom he could otherwise easily command as supporters.'[25] In Nairobi he could command the streets
and the assembly halls, but the number of personal aides who ended
up in the ranks of his enemies was nevertheless rather daunting.

Now Mboya was back and feeling that it was time openly to enter
politics. He tried to borrow Argwings-Kodhek's car to examine
prospects in South Nyanza but the car was broken and the prospects did not look much better. So he decided to contest the Nairobi
seat, which meant taking on 'A-K'. Argwings-Kodhek launched his
campaign by producing the 'A-K Plan', to which three other candidates, including Oginga Odinga, standing for Nyanza Central,
promptly subscribed. It included a highly desirable but economically implausible pledge of compulsory education for all African
children, no Federation for East Africa until all three governments
were African-led, African access to land in the White Highlands
and universal adult suffrage. Most other candidates subsequently
incorporated these pledges into their campaigns. The election was
in essence politics without the Kikuyu, since only loyalty certificate-
holders were allowed to vote. Although Nairobi had a Kikuyu
candidate in the incumbent, Muchohi Gikonyo, he was never considered a serious contender and with only 238 votes lost his £25
deposit.

THE ELECTION CAMPAIGN

Hardly had the campaign begun than Argwings-Kodhek's principal
asset, the Nairobi District African Congress, imploded. The candidate himself was suspended as the Congress's president, as also
was the party secretary, for mismanagement by the Executive Council.
New office-bearers were appointed, headed by Obote as Acting

President. This was not a good beginning. Argwings-Kodhek at a public meeting bitingly denounced 'the K[enya] F[ederation of] L[abour] group' whom he accused of masterminding dirty-work on Mboya's behalf. The tone of his speech can be gauged by this passage devoted to the man purporting to replace him, Milton Obote:

> We are trying to get rid of imperialism. We are not used to imperialism across the border. People of Obote's clan in Northern Uganda are very primitive, so that you can see a lot of flies around their eyes. Obote should get the flies from his mother's eyes instead of teaching people about politics.[26]

Mboya promptly denied his involvement in A-K's embarrassments. That may be so, but accidents of this sort were rather liable to happen to his political opponents and it was noted that three of A-K's internal opponents were in the KFL.

The polling which took place over two days (9–10 March 1957) was an orderly affair. The electorate was tiny. In Nairobi there were only 2,078 voters casting (under Walter Coutts's multiple voting scheme) 4,255 votes. G. F. Engholm of the University College of East Africa, who was observing the process, noted that crowds were passive except that with ten minutes to go on the second day cheering and catcalls broke out outside one of the polling stations until 'eventually there emerged a woman voter who can only be described as an African Marilyn Monroe, dressed in black jeans and a yellow and black checked shirt'.[27] The result of the poll was that Tom Mboya had beaten Clement Argwings-Kodhek by 2,138 votes to 1,746.

In the election generally every one of the original six nominated members was defeated with the sole exception of Daniel arap Moi, the great survivor of Kenya politics. (One of the two recently added MLCs also survived.) Thus, except for Moi, all who had had a first taste of Western-type political responsibility had been rejected, which must say something about the usefulness of nomination as a first stage in political education. On the other hand, the fact of election rather than the particular franchise was what counted: almost all the men elected under the restrictive Coutts formula were also to flourish in the world of universal suffrage. Eighteen months later Sir John Macpherson, a senior Colonial Office official who had had West African experience, was to conclude that fancy franchises were no good and that 'whatever the qualifications Africans will vote for nationalist Africans. . . . The only effective way of dealing with African nationalism that I know of is to roll with the punches.'[28]

Of the four upholders of the 'A-K Plan', only one triumphed but he was a major figure, Oginga Odinga. It was an augury of future politics that his ally, Argwings-Kodhek, had been worsted by Tom Mboya. The registration of the Kikuyu was so restricted that this tribe which, ahead of all others, had pressed for political advance was unrepresented in the first Legco with African elected members. The Legco pioneer Eliud Mathu was unseated in the Central Province by a Meru candidate because, while the Kikuyu made up 1,150,000 of the Province's 1,750,000 inhabitants, only 10,500 Kikuyu were registered, but 21,150 Meru had been signed up to vote by a keen District Commissioner. All otherwise qualified voters required loyalty certificates in this Province and it had been ruled that the DC was 'the sole judge of such loyalty'.[29]

Daniel arap Moi, the one nominated member who saved his seat, came from a small pastoral tribe, the Tugen, which like the Nandi belongs to the Kalenjin-speaking peoples, who were not at that time very interested in elective politics. He was a schoolmaster and did not have much in the way of opposition.[30] Within just over a year of his election he had created out of his backward pastoral tribe a Baringo District Independent Party, because, he said in defiance of the received wisdom of the intellectuals, 'tribalism will live for at least another fifty years'.[31]

THE AFRICAN ELECTED MEMBERS

Oginga Odinga was chosen because of his seniority in age as the first chairman of the African elected members and Mboya was elected secretary. The latter from the first showed in debate his easy, unforced superiority, not only over the black members but over the white members too. He also adopted towards the Lyttelton Constitution a stance of total hostility. It could not be worked; it must be brought down. These two men, both Luos, were to be the stars of Kenya politics until the 'old man' (*Mzee*) was to be released. They seldom got on and could hardly be more different, yet when divisions occurred over issues they were more often than not on the same side.

Odinga was an important transitional figure, part tribal, part national, a pioneer capitalist and a pioneer pro-communist. Generationally he came mid-way between Kenyatta and the younger leaders like Mboya. But at the age of fifteen when Kenyatta was at mission school and working for a European, Odinga was minding goats and cows for his father. When the first school opened in his region, his elder brother trekked miles on foot to attend and then taught him at night, by improvised candlelight, to read the Bible. A strong-willed missionary got him away to boarding-school against his father's wishes, whereupon he ran away and lived wild for a year. Finally, he was picked up in a barley-field and returned to school, from where after passing exams and doing duty as a pupil teacher he entered Alliance High School. This famous academy which turned out a high proportion of Kenya's African élite accepted Odinga at the age of twenty-five; his favourite master was his future colleague, James Gichuru. He went on to qualify as a schoolmaster himself at Makerere College, in Uganda.

Having taught at a mission school and as the first headmaster of a new veterinary school, Odinga got fed up with the profession. While as a teacher he enjoyed 'a fictitious sort of respect' in some circles, he noticed that those Africans who were getting on and making money, like the owners of rural buses, despised education and regarded the educated as 'accomplices of Europeans'. He persuaded some of his colleagues to join with him in proving that education was helpful to business. They founded the Luo Thrift and Trading Corporation, whose offices were the first African-owned building in Kisumu, the Luo capital; they opened shops, a hotel and three flour mills and launched a printing press, on which was printed Achieng Oneko's vernacular newspaper *Ramogi* (the legendary ancestor of all Luos) and many others such as Awori's Swahili *Radio Posta* and Paul Ngei's very radical organ *Uhuru Wa'Afrika*.

They had their setbacks – Odinga admits that the attempt to market fish from Lake Victoria was 'a financial disaster' and that one of his trusted employees misappropriated funds. At one point he was in trouble with his tribe because of wife-beating; he was also successfully treated for epilepsy. (Hence his later remark in the Council of Ministers that he was the only one present who had been officially certified as sane.) Unlike Kenyatta, who disdained local government, Odinga was elected to the Central Nyanza African District Council, where his conduct towards the District Commissioner who was chairman was less than decorous. Among the Luos of Central Nyanza he succeeded in gaining a unique stature reflected by his nickname of 'Ja-Ramogi'.[32]

As we have already seen, Oginga Odinga made his entry into

national politics in 1952 by joining KAU shortly before its president, Kenyatta, was to be arrested. Since then he had concentrated on his business activities. In 1957 he was about 45 years of age. He had an original appearance as he had designed his own tribal uniform which he wore as if it belonged to him, whereas Tom Mboya's ethnic accoutrements, when he bothered with them, looked as if they were fresh from a theatrical costumier. Odinga had a hoarse, high-pitched voice with which he used to express himself in great rushes of language that often culminated in a near-hysterical shriek. Anyone reading his handwritten notes would realize that his command of English was much more exact than his style of oratory would suggest. His traditionalist manner consisted of a partly natural, partly cultivated combination of old-world courtesy, an elder's cussedness and an acute awareness of what was due to him. His total absence of intellectual snobbery made it absolutely impossible to say of him as some Africans said of Tom Mboya that he was 'a black European'. He was also capable, if he felt the occasion warranted, of some extremely plain speech.[33]

From the start the African Elected Members took the view that Lyttelton's constitution under which they had been elected was designed to head Kenya off from following the road of Ghana and was therefore unacceptable. It was formulated, the Africans argued, on the assumption that all the races could be persuaded to support its proposals for a multiracial ministerial system. 'But the Europeans are divided in their support of it and the Africans are totally opposed to it,' as Mboya wrote.[34] To them multiracialism stood for the same exceedingly unappetising solution as the Central African Federation, to be arrived at by a gradual replacement of official Europeans at the head of departments by local ones. They demanded immediately fifteen more African seats, since it was more onerous to represent illiterate constituents than educated ones, and they despatched Mboya and Ronald Ngala, a Giriama from the Coast, to press their case in London.

Baring reported in advance to the Colonial Secretary, 'Mboya holds his group together. I do not think they all like him; about half would prefer a more moderate course. . . . Mboya is by far the most intelligent. He expresses himself admirably and his English is perfect. Secondly he has a plan . . . Thirdly, I think there is a veiled threat of violence to "dissident" Africans.'[35]

What the Governor was aiming for was a small increase in African seats and African entry into government. In his correspondence with Lennox-Boyd he made no bones about his belief that once blacks had to share in the responsibilities of government the stresses and strains would be such that out of the inevitable bust-up a moderate force would emerge that could work with the other races. The question was on which side of such a line would Mboya, accounted the ablest African, be found.

TOWARDS CONSTITUTIONAL CHANGE

In London Mboya and Ngala took the position that the fifteen additional MLCs must be granted first as a precondition before any discussion of constitutional issues. In a lucid article in the *Observer*, a paper which under the guidance of David Astor and Colin Legum was a major supporter of African emancipation, Mboya warned that if the Europeans attempted to maintain predominance under pretext of multiracial government they would 'force upon themselves a racialist struggle which African leaders are anxious to avoid'. Once granted the principle of undiluted parliamentary democracy with protection for individual but not communal rights, he declared that Africans would be reasonable about the transition – 'a phased programme of reforms towards internal self-government and ultimately towards independence'.

In July 1957 when the Africans were in London, so too was the Governor and the three European settler Ministers. The latter, with Blundell as the chief spokesman, had shifted their position quite considerably. Instead of arguing, as hitherto, for parity with all non-Europeans, they now were talking out of the hearing of their constituents in terms of safeguards for a white minority. Not long before, Lord Radcliffe had recommended means of safeguarding the rights of Turkish Cypriots in a future self-governing Cyprus, and Blundell drew on this analogy when he was in the Colonial Office, saying that it was unrealistic to think that, by simply saying there was multiracial government, race would be eliminated from politics. Either on all subjects or on certain reserved subjects legislation should be supported by at least one-third of those members of each group who were communally elected. Surely, the Men of Whitehall asked the Kenya Ministers, the Europeans in Kenya did not equate themselves with Turkish Cypriots? To which the answer was: not at present, but if they were set on the road to undiluted democracy, 'the end of that road was clear, however vigorous they might be'.[36]

The idea of manufacturing a multiracial government out of a qualitative common roll franchise had been subjected to Whitehall analysis and found seriously wanting. It was estimated that 400,000 Africans already qualified for a vote under the Coutts formula that had just been used, and though far fewer than that had actually voted, even the figure of those that had was too high for a system designed to protect the minorities from being swamped. Thus fancy franchises would not work. On the other hand, if there were to be a common roll but with certain seats reserved for the minorities, the way would be open for what Blundell termed 'white-skinned Africans' to ingratiate themselves with the African voter.[37] One of the Ministers, Walter Havelock, went on about having an Upper House as protection but the others lacked enthusiasm. This discussion was to be of critical significance at the Chequers conference the following January.

THE LENNOX-BOYD CONSTITUTION

Following these preliminaries Lennox-Boyd came to Nairobi in October and attempted to forge a general consensus on the way forward. The Africans complained that Blundell and other Europeans were given far easier access to the Colonial Secretary, staying in Government House, than they had. Lennox-Boyd negotiated with each of the racial delegations separately. He was a man of conviction, who thoroughly believed in the assumptions and vocabulary of a multiracial society. His hope was that the abler Africans would forget about Ghana and see their careers in terms of a mixed government. He once told Mboya that he could foresee Kenya having an African Prime Minister in his lifetime;[38] since Mboya was only 27 at the time, the Colonial Secretary must have thought that that left plenty of time in hand.

On 6 November Lennox-Boyd cabled Macmillan that he had decided to impose a settlement of his own with minimum delay, taking advantage of a proviso in the Lyttelton plan that gave the Colonial Secretary reserve powers in case of a constitutional breakdown. That breakdown was artificially contrived by inducing the European and Asian Ministers to resign. The solution then imposed gave the Africans six additional Legco seats, thereby securing parity with the elected Europeans. After this, there were to be no further communal seats. Any later constitutional change would provide for seats to be contested on a common electoral roll. As a modest foretaste of this there were to be twelve Specially Elected members, four from each of the races, who were to be chosen by the Legco itself, thus introducing in a carefully restrained manner an element of cross-voting.

On the executive side, the Europeans were to have four Ministers instead of the previous three (thus appearing to confirm the Africans' suspicions of a gradual takeover) but the non-Europeans also were to have four: two Africans and two Asians. A Council of State would be able to act against discriminatory legislation. There was to be a standstill for ten years. The Colonial Secretary told a questioner in the Commons, 'I do not foresee a date . . . when it will be possible for the Colonial Office to relinquish control.'[39]

In Britain this Lennox-Boyd plan received a broad initial welcome across the political spectrum. The Labour Party and left-wing journals which had given Mboya such a friendly reception a few months before appeared to think it a generous arrangement so soon after Mau Mau. Mboya seems to have been genuinely uncertain at first as to the line to take. There was plenty of rejoicing at the demise of the Lyttelton constitution and it might seem obtuse not to welcome its replacement. However, when a press statement was eventually issued by the African Elected Members, drafted by Mboya, it amounted to a rejection. The basic objection was that Britain had still made no commitment about the destiny towards which Kenya was heading. Some parts of the plan, taken by themselves, might seem to carry the Africans forward but they were contradicted by other parts. The Africans were prepared to contest the extra communal seats but not the Specially Elected ones. They argued that if the official members and settler members of Legco voted together the Europeans would be deciding which Africans were to be 'specially elected'.[40]

THE TRIAL OF TOM MBOYA

In March 1958 Mboya was sent an air ticket to attend Ghana's first anniversary celebration of her independence. Having told the others that he was the only one invited, he enjoyed celebrity treatment as Kwame Nkrumah's special guest. This did not go down well in certain quarters. Odinga, who was after all the chairman of the elected members, says that this was the immediate cause of the decision, taken in Mboya's absence, to replace him as secretary by Ronald Ngala.[41] It was a warning of some of the political troubles that lay ahead.

Much stimulated by his experience, Mboya came home determined to step up the pace of political organization. He took the step he had hitherto avoided of accepting the presidency of a political party named, in deliberate imitation of Nkrumah's successful movement, the Nairobi People's Convention Party. This had been founded some months before. Since he was not allowed to start a national party Mboya began to reach out from Nairobi to penetrate the various district parties that were legally operating, so that when national parties were licensed his men would be well placed.

When the elections were held for the six extra seats they were won exclusively by candidates who rejected the Lennox-Boyd constitution. They included at last a Kikuyu, Dr Julius Gikonyo Kiano, who had spent the entire Emergency abroad acquiring an impressive string of degrees from American universities and who had now returned with a perhaps too energetic Afro-American wife. At this stage, though not later, he and Mboya were very close.

The problem was the Specially Elected seats. The African elected members had sworn to boycott this election and when eight candidates for the four African seats including two former nominated MLCs nevertheless emerged they were denounced as 'stooges, Quislings and black Europeans . . . who . . . must be treated as traitors to the African cause'. This type of language in the immediate aftermath of the Mau Mau Emergency had a very ominous ring. Particularly embarrassed by the boycott was Ernest Vasey, the enlightened Minister of Finance, who had put up as a candidate for one of the European Specially Elected seats and relied on his Asian and African friends to see him through.

The African MLCs decided reluctantly that they could not make an exception for Vasey, who was defeated in the toss after a drawn vote. The four African members (not the ex-MLCs) who were duly elected by European votes as the first symbols of multiracialism were totally shunned by their fellow-Africans. Even more abused in Tom Mboya's oratory was Musa Amalemba, an able and courageous Luhya who accepted to be Minister of Housing. ('We let him have a revolver and put police patrols around his house,' wrote

Baring.) The circumstances of his appointment would ensure that any experience that he might obtain in office would be lost to the country subsequently.[42]

It was then decided to prosecute the African MLCs for conspiracy and defamation of the Specially Elected Africans. Mboya wrote to 'Comrade Nkrumah', 'The sentences in addition to including several years' jail and/or fines may include the loss of our Legco seats and also our being debarred from voting or standing for election for at least five years.'[43] Nkrumah cabled that he was arranging legal aid and Mboya wrote back, setting out how he was applying all the political lessons he had learnt in Ghana. Two 'Sacrifice Days' had been called to coincide with the opening of the trial when all Africans would refrain from drinking, smoking and bus riding. 'We are on the verge of "positive action" and intend to prepare the country for it. We have a lot to learn from the [Ghanaian] C[onvention] P[eople's] P[arty] and my [Nairobi] P[eople's] C[onvention] P[arty] intends to go ahead with a dynamic nationalist programme for Kenya.'[44]

It was clear that at this stage Mboya was mesmerized by Ghana and its leader even to the extent of being ready to bad-mouth ICFTU in his correspondence with John Tettegah, General Secretary of the Ghana TUC. 'We do not intend to ask for financial help from the ICFTU,' Tettegah wrote, 'because it stinks and sometimes their terms are intolerable to us.' Mboya replied, 'I have noted with delight your position re. the ICFTU.'[45]

The prosecution of the MLCs collapsed. On 11 June 1958 they were acquitted of conspiracy and fined £75 each for defamation. Mboya was now riding high, having enjoyed all the glamour of starring in a show trial but not having had to suffer any, or hardly any, of the consequences.

TOM ON A TIGER

Tom Mboya was now simultaneously the General Secretary of the Kenya Federation of Labour, President of the Nairobi People's Convention Party, the most celebrated member of Legco and increasingly, as a protégé of Nkrumah, a big figure on the Pan-African scene. What he was not and what he never became was the leader of Kenya Africans. This was a fact which he did not care very often to admit. He had the manner of a leader, the charisma of a leader,

the verbal facility and the ability to absorb rapidly the most complicated of details that are the mark of a modern parliamentarian
but, although he could command love and loyalty from many, he
was never acceptable to enough of his colleagues to be acknowledged as their leader. He had little patience for endless talk. Too
often he acted and spoke as if he were the sole leader and was
encouraged to do so by those Europeans and Americans who
admired his talents, sometimes to the bafflement of Africans who
pointed out that others, like Kiano and Mwai Kibaki, had university degrees whereas Mboya had not. What his fellow-African
politicians really wanted from Mboya was his skill as secretary. Time
after time when new organizations were being founded and Mboya
was being elected to that post they solemnly resolved to restrict
him to keeping the minutes and circulating the agenda, only to
discover that he had converted these apparently humble functions
into a basis for effective control.

One of Mboya's most faithful acolytes, as it at one time appeared,
was M. D. Odinga (no relation of Oginga Odinga and, as a Maragoli,
not even of the same tribe). He served as Mboya's secretary and
was the original editor of his paper *Uhuru* (a Swahili word, meaning
'freedom', which was soon to resonate throughout the colony). But
the two men parted company and Odinga wrote in a much-quoted
article in the *Sunday Post* entitled 'Young Man on a Tiger': 'I know
Mboya sufficiently ... To him power is more precious than the
national cause ... Dictatorship is a form of rule that we cannot
tolerate. But Mboya has taken it into his head that this is the form
of leadership he has to provide to the party.'[46] This message found
many echoes in gossip-filled Nairobi over the next few years.
European friends and admirers of Mboya were reproached for wishing
to turn Kenya over to a dictator. At a time when hungry, raggedy
African politicians were spending the better part of the day filling
up yellow writing-pads with exceedingly long press releases, which
they would bring round to friendly journalists for light refreshments
and drastic editing, a disproportionate number were amazingly hostile
to the man who was doing more than anybody to dislodge the colonial power. One such, a leading figure in a party youth wing, ended
a sustained diatribe with the memorable words, 'I therefore challenge Tom Mboya to a duel.'[47]

Although the most celebrated enemy whom Mboya acquired among
the ranks of the African Elected Members (AEMs) was Oginga
Odinga, the trouble started, according to Odinga, with Masinde

Muliro, a rather cunning, quite intelligent Luhya MLC from Elgon-Nyanza who looked rather like the younger Lenin. Muliro mobilized his colleagues to complain that Mboya was monopolizing the publicity for what should have been seen as a collective effort and that Odinga was not, as chairman, doing enough to restrain him.[48] But relations between the two Luos themselves were deteriorating.

On 26 June 1958 Odinga hit upon the one dramatic move that would, he calculated, put a decisive limit on Mboya's leadership ambitions. He broke the taboo by uttering publicly the dread, the forbidden name of Jomo Kenyatta.

THE NAMING OF KENYATTA

During a Legco debate on the conditions in which political prisoners were being kept, Odinga said, 'These people before they were arrested were the political leaders of the Africans in the country . . . and even at this moment, in the heart of hearts of Africans, they are still the political leaders.' This created an uproar after which the debate was adjourned. When it was resumed the next day Odinga still held the floor. He referred to Archbishop Makarios of Cyprus who had been interned in the Seychelles but about whom there were frequent press stories on his activities and his health. He went on, 'The same should be done with Mr Kenyatta.' While he was being howled down he screamed, 'I am giving you what you should know about our feelings towards them and, before you realize that, you can never get the cooperation of the African people.' At this point he was told to sit down, and Mboya said, 'Some unfortunate statements made in the course of the debate might create a wrong impression.'[49] The unsayable had been said. A terrible *frisson* had passed across the land.

Odinga soon felt the force of the reaction. In Maseno the whites boycotted the Luo Thrift shop so that it had to close down; the African Members of Legco criticized him sharply and demanded that he apologize. The resolution they passed said that 'the statement with all its merits and demerits was inopportune and would retard other efforts'. The Kikuyu member, Julius Kiano, repudiated 'Jaramogi' at Fort Hall. But a mass meeting at Kisumu upheld Odinga and a Nairobi rally organized by Argwings-Kodhek proclaimed that, 'We solemnly reaffirm our confidence in the leadership of Jomo Kenyatta.' From this point on Odinga became identified with the return of Kenyatta to the political scene, with the subtext of reducing Tom Mboya to the ranks.[50] Mboya was for once caught without an appropriate answer. Finally on 22 September, three months after Odinga's verbal coup, he wrote in the *East African Standard* that, 'When Kenya's history is written, not only will Kenyatta's name be mentioned, but any accurate record must include the fact that he was the prisoner of the African struggle ... The question of Kenyatta's leadership is not at issue at all. The immediate question is whether or not he will be set free.' But the genie was out of the bottle. Odinga kept up the pressure: a long press release of 25 August ended stirringly, 'On an issue like this I will not flinch, I will not be moderate and I will not withdraw.'[51]

The attitude of the younger educated African politicians to Kenyatta and to Mau Mau was often at this stage an ambivalent one. Many of them, like Julius Kiano, would admit that, never having met Kenyatta, they had no idea whether he would make an effective national leader. On the one hand they felt rather ashamed of Mau Mau being considered their liberation struggle, it having been so uncivilized. Yet on the other hand they would list gains that had occurred only after the Mau Mau Emergency had begun and were arguably expedited by it: the Royal Commission on Land and Population which condemned the reservation of land on a racial basis; the East African Salaries Commission, whose recommendation of 'equal pay for equal work' was immediately accepted; the easing of race discrimination in hotels and public places;[52] and the really radical Swynnerton Plan which took advantage of the Emergency to use special powers available in Central Province to enforce measures of land consolidation which vastly improved agricultural productivity there.[53] It was interesting that Mboya, who credited these gains to the Emergency in an article in *West African Worker*,[54] included the last among them, despite its coercive aspects. As a Luo he would have noticed that attempts to copy these reforms but on a voluntary basis in Nyanza Province were having no success.[55]

But the greatest gain was that afterwards expressed by the Earl of Perth, a prominent banker who in 1957, though not even a member of the Conservative Party, had been picked by Macmillan as Lennox-Boyd's Minister of State. 'The effort required to suppress Mau Mau,' he said, 'destroyed any settlers' illusions that they could go it alone; the British Government was not prepared for the shedding of [more] blood in order to preserve colonial rule.'[56]

...งง wore on there was an increasing air of expectancy of major political change. On 27 June, on Mboya's initiative, the African Elected Members Organization (AEMO) reiterated their demand of the previous year for a round-table conference of all interested groups to be preceded by the appointment of a constitutional expert and to be presided over by an independent and impartial chairman. In July a motion for such a conference was defeated in the Legco, with the voting on racial lines, the African and Asian members together with one European voting in favour, all the other Europeans voting against.[57] Argwings-Kodhek aimed to make a comeback with a shadow national political party in the form of a 'Convention of Associations' but he was a barrister in financial difficulties and a word from the Attorney-General was enough to put him off.[58] The slogan *Uhuru* came more to be heard. More and more, in Kikuyuland and also in Kisumu, *Uhuru na Kenyatta* would be shouted.

Evelyn Baring decided to reply. Kenyatta and the others were coming towards the end of their terms of imprisonment, but there had been provision in the sentence for indefinite detention thereafter. In his speech to the Legco on 4 November 1958 the Governor warned those who would develop a cult of Jomo Kenyatta, 'The Government has no intention of allowing him at the expiry of his sentence to return to any place near the scene of his former activities.'[59] Another passage in his speech was interpreted by AEMO members as a rejection of their demands for a constitutional conference; at a signal from Mboya all fourteen rose and walked out of the chamber.

Mboya was then despatched to London to confront Lennox-Boyd, who told him that sufficient progress could be made under the constitution as it was. Mboya spent some time justifying to his natural constituency in Britain – Africa Bureau, Fabian Colonial Bureau, Labour MPs – what would appear to be his intransigence and then flew off to Accra for the triumphant celebration of the first All-Africa Peoples Conference.

For all of his having now become the chairman of ICFTU's regional committee for East, Central and Southern Africa, the warmth of Mboya's reception by Nkrumah was by no means diminished. On the contrary, he was made chairman of the whole conference and in a notable keynote speech that mocked the nineteenth-century

'scramble for Africa', he called on the colonial powers to 'scram
from Africa'. The conference discussed the 'adjustment of existing
artificial frontiers', an ambition which was soon to be reversed, the
amalgamation or federation of neighbouring territories and the
federation or confederation of these territorial groupings into a
Pan-African Commonwealth. The attendance was a Who's Who of
African nationalism. Mboya and his Kenyan colleagues – Kiano
(who recanted his opinion about Kenyatta while in Ghana),
Mathenge, Khamisi, and Muimi (a Kamba) – returned to Kenya
greatly inspired at having seen the future.

LENNOX-BOYD AND TIMETABLES

In January 1959, on Lennox-Boyd's initiative, a meeting assembled
at Chequers on the future of East Africa attended by the Colonial
Office Ministers (Lennox-Boyd, Lord Perth and Julian Amery) and
the Governors of Kenya, Uganda and Tanganyika and the Resident in Zanzibar. In one of the preparatory minutes William Gorell
Barnes, the Assistant Under-Secretary of State, acknowledged the
bankruptcy of the multiracial project as it had been designed. The
Colonial Office had been hoping, he said, to construct throughout
East and Central Africa common roll systems which would have
the effect of 'reducing the importance of race in politics', and allowing
gradual African advance without destroying 'responsible government'. 'This hope may yet be fulfilled in Central Africa,' he observed
with strained optimism, but, 'in East Africa we must face the fact
that there is no prospect whatsoever of its being fulfilled.' With
the qualitative franchise now seen to be a broken reed, the only
remaining hope of rescuing something from the ruins of the multiracial idea was to make 'a firm statement underwritten by the
Opposition' that Britain intended to maintain 'full ultimate control in all East African territories for fifteen or twenty years'.[60]

Both Lennox-Boyd and his Minister of State, the Earl of Perth,
were clearly unhappy at the way the pace was being forced. Indeed, on the eve of Chequers Lord Perth had written, 'The basic
issue, as I see it, is "Are the Africans of the Eastern territories
capable soon of governing themselves?" The answer: No, owing to
inadequate education, inadequate economic development and inadequate African civil servants. That being so, we have got to
govern ... I am in favour of putting my foot down.'[61]

Yet the feeling was also present that, in the previously quoted words of Sir John Macpherson, with African nationalism one must 'roll with the punches'.[62] Because the Governor of Tanganyika, Sir Richard Turnbull, had urged that Julius Nyerere be accommodated, it was decided that the beginning of 'responsible government' for Tanganyika could come in 1965 and that it should last at least one five-year Legco before the possibility of independence would arise. Lennox-Boyd said that 'this programme would probably set the seal for a similar programme in Uganda and possibly in Zanzibar'. But 'it is impossible to judge the consequences in Kenya, which must to some extent be treated as a separate problem'.[63]

Gorell Barnes's reference to fifteen to twenty years and the absence of the usual inhibition on the discussion of targets must explain the subsequent reports that at Chequers a date of 1975 was pencilled in for Kenyan independence. But Baring, according to his biographer who had also been his ADC, certainly considered himself as uncommitted by such a date.[64]

After the conference, Lennox-Boyd told the Cabinet's Colonial Policy Committee, which had its first session for 1959 on 13 April under the chairmanship of Harold Macmillan that, 'As regards Kenya, I have maintained the line that I do not see any prospect in the foreseeable future of HMG relinquishing control.' African nationalists were trying to break the present balance between Europeans, Asians and Africans so as to pave the way to an African-dominated country. There might well be a civil disobedience campaign which, in the atmosphere created by Mau Mau, 'is bound to lead to violence'. 'Mboya's main card,' he said, 'is probably a long continued political war of nerves designed to cause Europeans with roots in the country to lose their nerve and of their own accord to leave.'[65]

But five days later, reversing his previous position, he announced that before the next Kenya election due in 1960 there would be a round-table conference if it seemed that such a course was the best way to carry things forward towards an agreement 'within the general ambit of the present Constitution'. The principal request of the Africans had been met: whether Lennox-Boyd realized it or not, the Lennox-Boyd constitution was soon to be as dead as that of Oliver Lyttelton.

5 The Bridge-Player

'I believe that the Colonial Secretary is a very fine bridge-player...
It is not considered immoral or even bad form to outwit one's
opponents at bridge... It almost seems to me as if the Colonial
Secretary, when he abandoned the sphere of bridge for the sphere
of politics, brought his bridge technique [with him].' (Marquess
of Salisbury, House of Lords, 7 March 1961)

'Are Europeans Planning an Uprising?' The press release thus headed
came from Tom Mboya, as President of the Nairobi People's Convention Party, on 10 February 1959. It spoke of contacts between
the settlers, Group Captain Llewellyn ('Puck') Briggs in particular,
and Sir Roy Welensky, the Prime Minister of the Central African
Federation, 'in preparation for a showdown with the Colonial Office in the event that they accede to African demands for a greater
voice in the Government of Kenya'. The ghosts of 1923 were not
laid. 'We remember 1923 when the settlers threatened to kidnap
the Governor.... Not only have the circumstances changed but
there is no hope of settlers winning a shooting war in Kenya without the support of British troops.' Mboya went on to warn his
followers not to give any excuse to any European faction to resort
to violence. 'Our struggle will be positive but NON-VIOLENT.'[1]
    The Europeans were going through one of their periodical moods
of nerves and despondency, Baring told Lennox-Boyd in January.
They were upset by three things: the All-Africa People's conference
at Accra, which had shown America to be on Mboya's side; the
UN economic conference in Addis Ababa, where Dag Hammarskjold,
the Secretary-General of the United Nations, had endorsed Mboya's
linking of economic to political progress; and, finally, events in the
Belgian Congo.[2] This was a reference to a violent riot on 4 January outside the YMCA in the Congolese capital of Léopoldville
(Kinshasa), which had administered a traumatic shock to the com-
placent Belgian rulers who had been contemplating a thirty-year
transition to independence.[3] Hitherto the Belgian Congo had
appeared to be among the least politically disturbed regions in the
continent. The panic-stricken reaction of the metropolis was
unnerving to colonial rulers everywhere and was a foretaste of what
was to befall the Congo eighteen months later.

On 6 March 1959 thirty-four leading members of the NPCP, including Josef Mathenge,[4] the General Secretary, and six members of the General Council were rounded up and the party paper *Uhuru* was banned on the ground that it had imported and republished forbidden literature from India. Mboya was not arrested, a point noted with suspicion by Omolo Agar, who was Organizing Secretary of the Party and Editor of its newspaper and who was charged with seditious intent and possession of prohibited documents.[5] In the rumour factory that was the Nairobi political world it was beginning to be said that the colonial power was playing a double game, that while Mboya might appear to be extremist he was in fact the first choice of those whites who had decided that African rule of some kind was inevitable. Most importantly, Oginga Odinga was starting to share that view despite the fact that on the issues that divided 'extremists' from 'moderates' in African politics the two men were still almost invariably on the same side.

Mboya had achieved the immunity of international celebrity. He carried on coolly but energetically activating all his networks, British, American, Pan-African, trade unionist, to bring guns to bear against political repression.[6] He was refused permission to go to Cairo, which, following Nasser's victory over Eden at Suez, was even more than before regarded by the British as the epicentre of subversion. But he could not plausibly be refused permission to go to the United States, where he renewed his communion with an adoring public. Most significantly he also did productive business with high-profile figures including John F. Kennedy, who was chairman of the Africa subcommittee of the Senate Foreign Relations Committee, whom he had enlisted as sponsors for a scheme, which was to win him huge popularity, to airlift large numbers of Kenya African students to North America to obtain higher education.[7]

Other aspiring African politicians had attempted before to deal with this urgent demand. Specifically Mboya's late political opponent Clem Argwings-Kodhek had, by his own account, passed nearly two hundred potential students through Uganda to the Sudan, whence his fellow-barrister who was now Sudanese Foreign Minister arranged for them to go by boat to Cairo. Once there, the Kenya Office under Were Ambitho, which handled the subversive broadcasts to East Africa that were so detested by the British, saw to their being flown to colleges in East Germany, Bulgaria or Moscow.[8] But no one had achieved anything so spectacular as Tom Mboya's airlift: that and Solidarity House supplied the firm underpinning to his political career.

THE FORMATION OF POLITICAL PARTIES

African politicians, led by Odinga and Muliro, decided at this stage to make use of a thin multiracial cover to advance their cause. While Mboya was absent in the States, they came together with the Asian and Arab members of Legco and one ultra-liberal white member, Shirley Cooke, an ex-administrator, to form the Constituency Elected Members' Organization (CEMO) and send a mixed delegation to London. It is true that they got nowhere on ending the Emergency or releasing Kenyatta; but the really important outcome was that Lennox-Boyd promised a Constitutional Conference before the end of the year and, in the meantime, agreed to appoint a constitutional expert, Professor W. J. M. Mackenzie, to work out options for change. On their return to Kenya the MLCs announced the abandonment of their boycott of Legco.

At the same time Michael Blundell resigned his position as Minister of Agriculture in order to lead a new multiracial party, the New Kenya Group (NKG) backed by forty-three MLCs of every race, through which he hoped to manage political change. This was not, however, quite as impressive a line-up as it might seem – the African members involved were all either nominated or Specially Elected under the circumstances previously described, a point to which Masinde Muliro called attention in a letter to the Africa Bureau, the anti-colonialist lobby in London. 'Mr Blundell's group,' he wrote, 'is struggling to strike the mark as an organization but they have no hope of going to the country as a National organization.' It was his opinion that Lennox-Boyd's latest statement had run into no serious opposition except from Mboya's Nairobi party, which could be discounted now that the rival Nairobi African District Congress, over which Argwings-Kodhek had re-established his hold, had come out in strong support. Lennox-Boyd's granting of the round-table conference he described as the first political success ever achieved by Africans in Kenya.[9]

Muliro told the Rev. Michael Scott, the austere ex-missionary at the head of the Africa Bureau, that the CEMO was turning itself into a national political organization under his presidency, 'and by next week a policy of which I have been the architect will be announced'. The result would be 'some intensification of political activity . . . between now and the time of the conference'.[10] Muliro's party, which included a majority of CEMO members, was duly accorded registration under the title of the Kenya National Party (KNP) because it appeared on the surface to be multiracial. One person who was not to be invited to join was Mboya. Odinga quotes Muliro as telling him at this time that there was no room in one party for Mboya and himself; 'he had had enough of Mboya's habit of over-ruling our decisions'.[11]

But Odinga's flirtation with the image of multiracialism was not a lasting one. He complained that the Asian members were hankering for a qualitative franchise; he would have nothing less than universal suffrage which would highlight the overwhelmingly African character of the country. He joined with Mboya and Kiano in issuing a declaration that 'For the time being our struggle is an African struggle.... Agreement on slogans of non-racialism does not mark any advance in the position of the African people.' The African Elected Members split – eight going with the KNP and the remaining four, representing Kikuyus and Luos, forming the Kenya Independence Movement (KIM), which being mono-racial was not registered. Of this Odinga was the president, Kiano the chairman and Mboya the secretary.[12] Its policy declaration called for the rejection of special safeguards for minorities and the abolition of nominated and specially elected seats in Legco.

Applying what he had learnt from Nkrumah, Mboya said in a memorandum sent out to district associations, 'We need simple signs and slogans to be popularized so as to express in one single word the significance of the struggle ... [W]e must sometimes raise the temperature to various levels to meet every situation ... In a mass movement we cannot indulge in the platitudes of those who desire to be called "reasonable", "responsible" or "moderate".'[13]

There were many voices urging collaboration between the African-led parties and Michael Blundell's NKG. But the Africans viewed Blundell's liberalism with suspicion. His time-frame, they felt, was not their time-frame; they suspected that he saw himself as Kenya's first Prime Minister, at the head of a rainbow coalition. However Julius Nyerere told the press in June 1959 that there was more in common between Blundell and Mboya than most people imagined. Following this, despite Odinga's strong disapproval, the two men met at Blundell's Nairobi home on 1 July. Afterwards Blundell said, 'We found we disagreed on many points', and Mboya that 'both of us came to the conclusion that there is a very wide difference between us'. Both at various times were described as moderate but they were never able to get on.[14]

EXIT BARING AND LENNOX-BOYD

The cast of characters was about to change in a
side of the colonial power. Lennox-Boyd, tiring of politic
ing that the managing directorship of his wife's family firm, Arthur
Guinness, Son & Co., would shortly be available, told Macmillan
that he would serve only until the next General Election. He had
believed passionately in Britain's imperial mission and had held
the same office for five years. The last months of his tenure were
clouded by two simultaneous crises starting in March 1959 involving the arrest of Dr Hastings Banda and other nationalist politicians
in Nyasaland and the massacre of eleven hard-core Mau Mau prisoners at the Hola camp in Kenya. In regard to the latter a cover-up
was attempted, subsequent findings by a resident magistrate exposed the reality, and what might in other circumstances have been
dismissed as an unfortunate and distressing incident became a scandal
on a scale that seemed (like the Amritsar massacre of 1919) to
indict colonialism as a whole. Since Suez, British morale had been
in a poor condition to outface such disasters.

To place Hola in its context, it is only fair to recall the huge
task with which the authorities saw themselves faced in attempting
to undo the black magic of Mau Mau. Some 80,000 suspected activists and adherents had been arrested, nearly one in three of adult
male Kikuyus, while the rest were made to live in the 'protected'
villages. Those arrested were subjected to a process known as 'rehabilitation', a systematic attempt to purge individuals of the evil
spells and their psychological effects until they were deemed fit to
be received back into society. It is not difficult to predict that in an
operation of this scale, supervised by European officers but largely
carried out by Africans and which often called for skilled and sophisticated judgment, there were errors and abuses on the part of
both. Books like *'Mau Mau' Detainee*[15] have recorded what some
of them were. 'I do not like using strong words,' wrote Josiah Mwangi
Kariuki of one European officer, 'but he was nothing more nor
less than a cruel and vicious sadist.'[16] It would be very unreasonable to describe all or most of those involved in this harrowing
work in these terms. Nevertheless Michael Blundell quotes the very
successful head of one of the screening teams which carried out
individual interrogations as saying that, 'Since Mau Mau was built
on fear, we had to create a greater fear of our camp than that of
Mau Mau.'[17] The desired climax of this effort was the individual

·onfession, which was thought to have the effect of breaking the spell. The Christian missions through the deployment of African elders were given a chance to 're-establish Christian values'.

The massive task had by 1957 reduced the numbers behind the wire to nearly 20,000 men and a few women, but these were the obstinately resistant ones. Fearful of a situation in which 'tens of thousands of people [would be] on our hands who would be dangerous to release but whose retention would gradually become a political impossibility',[18] the Kenya Government ordered that a fresh effort must be made to reduce this total to 6,000. The task was entrusted to Terence Gavaghan, as Officer-in-Charge of Rehabilitation, who has written in *Corridors of Wire* a thinly fictionalized account of his experiences, prefaced by an 'Historical Note'.[19]

In 1958 Sir Evelyn Baring reported to Lennox-Boyd that 'I recently visited the Mwea camps [where the emphasis was on obtaining confessions] and was enormously impressed by the remarkable work done during the period of exactly one year by Mr. Gavaghan. It is his work in these camps that has been the key to the flow out of the detainees.'[20] The essence of Gavaghan's method was the 'recovery of physical control' over the detainees through strict enforcement of discipline and compulsory rehabilitation work. Dumb insolence was to be met by the 'controlled use of compelling, as opposed to punitive force'. Two key Ministers of the Kenya Government were given a demonstration of what this would mean in practice and gave their tacit approval but not in writing. It was the ghastly misplaying of this idea after it had been used to reduce the final 'hard core' down to under a thousand that brought the whole otherwise successful method and beyond that the moral basis of colonial government into disrepute.

Gavaghan had been moved on to become D. C., Kiambu, by the time of Hola. He said afterwards that there was no longer any need to deal with this 'gritty sediment' in any dramatic way – 'at worst they could have been left almost unnoticed for an independent government to decide their fate'. Instead, everything went wrong. Specialists were not to hand, misunderstood orders were passed down orally to local officers. Eighty-five Kikuyu – too large a group for the 'compelling' technique to succeed – were repeatedly struck with batons by unsupervised non-Kikuyu warders when resisting orders to work. Eleven died.[21]

When the truth finally emerged in an enquiry by the Senior Resident Magistrate in Mombasa it gave rise to ferocious attacks by Labour, led by the former Attorney-General Sir Frank Soskice in the Commons on 16 June 1959, and major doubts inside the Cabinet. The Minister of Labour, Iain Macleod, and the party chairman, Lord Hailsham, were particularly severe in their questioning of the Colonial Secretary. In the debate Lennox-Boyd, who had been reluctant to speak and was inclined to resign, was persuaded by Macmillan to answer the motion of censure and frankly admitted mistakes and scandals. James Callaghan wound up for the Opposition, speaking, Macmillan wrote in his diary, 'in his usual Irish corner-boy style'. According to the diary entry, 'The Attorney-General had difficulty in getting his speech listened to, but it was very good', and the following day, ruefully surveying an unfavourable press, the Prime Minister noted that, 'Naturally it seems terrible that eleven men should die in this way and no prosecutions or resignations. The Colonial Secretary has been supported by the Cabinet after, at one time, I feared a split. So he owes us something. I feel there must be a "re-shuffle" in the Kenya Administration.'[22]

Over the following weekend, Lennox-Boyd, being, so Macmillan wrote, 'a highly strung, sensitive and rather quixotic character', insisted that, having admitted mistakes and muddles to the House, he must take responsibility and resign. Although Macmillan told the Queen that 'the Hola incident was by no means satisfactorily explained or excused by the Government',[23] he set about persuading Lennox-Boyd to stay until the coming election. Otherwise, if he went, the Governor and two Kenya Ministers would certainly have to go as well. The Prime Minister saw the political damage at home of resignations in the months before an election and, together with Baring whom he had called to London, set about choreographing a succession of moves by which he hoped the crisis might be defused.

A second White Paper on Hola spoke of major administrative reforms and there was a further debate on 27–28 July. It gave rise to one of the most remarkable parliamentary occasions. After midnight on 28 July without notes and with taut features deathly pale, Enoch Powell, the logician from the right wing of the Tory party, shook party and country profoundly by his expression of horror at the murder of men in custody. 'We cannot say we will have African standards in Africa and Asian standards in Asia and perhaps British standards at home . . . (I)t is a fearful doctrine, which must recoil on the heads of those who pronounce it, to stand in judgment on a fellow being and to say, "Because he was such-and-such, there-fore the consequences which would otherwise flow from his death shall not flow."'

The overlapping colonial debates, over the Devlin Report,[24] over the Hola murders, and also over the establishment of the Monckton Commission that was to report on the future of the Central African Federation, brought African affairs into unusually sharp political focus. An election victory for the Labour Party under Hugh Gaitskell, who, Macmillan thought, had 'an intellectual dislike of and contempt for British settlers',[25] was thought to be quite possible, even likely, by those for whom the combination of Suez and Hola was enough to send the Tories to perdition. In Kenya consternation was felt at the prospect both in administration and in settler circles, where Tom Mboya's easy access to senior Labour figures like Barbara Castle was regarded with dread. He had been known to boast that the National Executive Committee of the Labour Party never acted on Kenya matters without consulting him; Reginald Paget and Fenner Brockway had been spoken of as Labour politicians who frequently gave him advice.[26]

Seeing that an election was not far off and knowing that Baring's term was approaching its end,[27] Lennox-Boyd was determined to appoint the new Governor before there was a danger of that responsibility passing to Labour. He had heard alarming rumours that Labour meant if they won to send Reginald Paget, the Old Etonian fox-hunting Labour member for Northampton, to Nairobi. Since Lennox-Boyd considered that Paget, 'a delightful man and always a great friend', simply would not do in Nairobi, he must be pre-empted. His first thought was to make an unorthodox appointment of his own, the South Africa-born author, adventurer and mystagogue Sir Laurens Van Der Post. He afterwards rather wished he had stuck to his instinct but, he admitted, 'it would have been a blow to the Colonial Service and it would have been a terrific gamble'.[28]

With little enthusiasm Lennox-Boyd decided to accept the strong office recommendation that the job should go to Sir Patrick Renison, who was considered to have done well in the West Indies as Governor, first of British Honduras, then of British Guiana. At 49 he was relatively young, burly with a florid countenance. Lennox-Boyd thought he had 'the sort of presence that would impress Africans in Kenya', but it was noted in No. 10 that 'In his public pronouncements there is sometimes a risk that he may appear to be talking down.'[29] To the Chief Secretary, Walter Coutts, the appointment was a surprise because the word from Whitehall had been that it was going to be a political choice. Afterwards Coutts expressed disappointment because Renison failed to 'click' with Africans and did not go out of his way to get to know them informally by having them to Government House in the evenings.[30]

Not only the Governor was going to be new. Sir Patrick was coming in with Lennox-Boyd's successor, his arch-critic in the Cabinet, Iain Macleod.

ENTER MACLEOD

Macleod was small, intense, highly intelligent, very ambitious and a brilliant orator. He had a good command of the House and although it turned out he was just right in talking to Africans – Odinga called him 'an excellent choice'[31] – he could be abrupt, almost to the point of rudeness when dealing with Cabinet colleagues. He was a bridge player of the highest calibre, who in his time had played and wagered for high stakes and for many years contributed a bridge column to the *Sunday Times*. As will be seen in this chapter, this reputation was later to be turned against him in one of those parliamentary moments that stand out in the memory. He was physically handicapped, suffering from ankylosing spondylitis, a progressive and incurable arthritic condition which gave him frequent pain in the back and a progressive stiffening of the neck, but he never allowed this to impede the relish with which he approached his work and his politics.[32]

Macleod had had no previous experience of the colonies. The appointment of this brisk, radical man would not have taken place had not Macmillan intended to mark a definite change in the pace of decolonization. Lennox-Boyd had become aware of an alteration in Macmillan's attitude to colonial matters as the election approached. This Prime Minister was never an imperialist, Lennox-Boyd reflected. Like a good publisher, his general instinct was, 'Well, that is a chapter closed. Now we go on to the next chapter.'[33] That did not mean, as Macleod was to discover, that Macmillan would be indifferent to any party political backlash that might result from the new Colonial Secretary's radicalism. 'I think the difficulty with Harold Macmillan in relation to Africa,' Macleod once said, 'was that he had all the right instincts . . . he was more than prepared for a rapid move towards independence . . . But from time to time he wanted the best of both worlds, he didn't want to fall out with his good friends either at home or in Central and East Africa, whereas I took the brutal but, I think, practical view that this was an omelette that you couldn't make without breaking eggs.'[34]

With the experienced assistance of his banker-deputy, the Earl of Perth, whom he inherited from the Lennox-Boyd regime, the new Colonial Secretary immediately addressed himself to the problems of Kenya, which he decided to visit before the constitutional conference, now fixed for January 1960. Even before leaving for Nairobi he had decided that 'if you give independence in West Africa you cannot deny it in East Africa just because there is a white settler community there'. But he also thought that any pretence of linking the rate of advance of the various East African territories should be abandoned: in Tanganyika where there had been no violence it should be shown that one could move more quickly than where violence had occurred. Believing strongly in the importance of the right type of national leader, he swiftly accepted the assessment of the new Governor of Tanganyika, Sir Richard Turnbull, that Julius Nyerere was such a leader. But where were they to be found in the other two territories? If one had only emerged in Uganda, Macleod said privately, he could have solved that problem right away.[35] Because of the complications Kenya would take him longer. He was critical of the *Economist* for expressing a different view.[36] Nyerere would be rewarded straight away by the grant of 'responsible self-government' to Tanganyika, just one stage short of independence.

Macleod's reconnaissance of Kenya was preceded by the announcement in November that the State of Emergency was to be lifted and 2,500 prisoners would be immediately released. He was also able to announce the decision taken by his predecessor that for the first time a pilot scheme would be started that would make possible some African ownership of property in the Highlands. By the time he confronted the African leaders in Nairobi, the two political parties, Muliro's KNP and Odinga's KIM had agreed to form a joint delegation for the constitutional conference. Both party presidents were members of it but neither was to be its leader: this was to be Ronald Ngala, a Giriama from the Coast, the least controversial candidate. The secretary was to be Tom Mboya. Beforehand, Muliro had got rid of the four Asian politicians who had given the KNP its multiracial respectability. The delegation was to represent African nationalists and no one else.

Macleod told the African politicians that he came with an open mind but that the pace of advance must be geared to the conditions of Kenya, not linked to developments in other territories. Ngala replied clearly and simply that what was needed to make the constitutional conference a success was a categorical declaration of the aim towards which they were working. There must be no more talk of partnership or multiracialism. They wanted democratic self-government, one adult one vote, and power in the hands of the majority. Macleod promised to include a declaration of intent in his keynote speech, whereupon Mboya crisply warned him that it had better not be like Lennox-Boyd's speeches which each group could interpret in its own way.

Oginga Odinga complained that whereas Kenya Africans were the forerunners of nationalism in East Africa and believed themselves to be more efficient than the others, it would be most unfair that they should now be left behind by Tanganyika and Uganda. On Macleod pressing the Africans to say something about safeguards for minority groups, he was told that this could be arranged but only on a temporary basis. The Africans tackled the Minister about Jomo Kenyatta, Odinga saying that it was not possible to start afresh with so many leaders in detention, but Macleod declined to discuss individual cases.[37]

At a later meeting on 23 December solely with the KIM members of the Legco, Macleod participated in a rather confused discussion about the ban on colonywide political movements; Mboya declared that it was plainly discriminatory because both parties were now mono-racial and he resented the innuendo that only KIM represented a threat to law and order. When Macleod would not give way on this point, Odinga joined in. 'Speaking,' as the usually impassive official notetaker put it, 'with some heat and considerable incoherence', the KIM president gave it as his view that he had been misled in thinking that there had been any genuine change of heart.[38]

Macleod told the Cabinet on his return that 'It is now very urgent to reach a decision . . . in relation to Kenya.' Macleod felt that some risks should be taken by reducing the security powers to the absolute minimum; Kikuyus for example should no longer be prevented from moving from one district to another; and, overriding the new Governor's serious doubts, he was going to risk a free Press by withdrawing the right to ban publications like Mboya's *Uhuru*. At the same time 'stringent controls' were to be exercised over meetings and associations – he had been told that attendance addressed by a local MLC would go up from a normal 300 to 3,000 when Mboya was the guest speaker – and the ban on colonywide parties would remain.[39]

LANCASTER HOUSE

On 18 January 1960 the Lancaster House conference assembled and almost immediately came near to breaking up. Those present were the elected members of Legco but provision was made for some delegation advisers. Macleod firmly rejected a request that Jomo Kenyatta be brought to London as an adviser. The Africans swallowed that and the rejection of a further plea that the Specially Elected Members be not admitted. They were not, however, prepared to back down on Odinga's proposal that Peter Mbiyu Koinange should receive credentials as an adviser. He had been living in exile in London and in Accra, having been declared a prohibited immigrant in Kenya. The Europeans indicated that, as an originator of Mau Mau, Koinange's presence was completely unacceptable to them.

A frantic search was initiated by 10 Downing Street for rather more specific evidence against Koinange. All that Philip De Zulueta, the intelligence man on Macmillan's staff, could come up with was a note saying that it had been reported that Mau Mau oath-taking had taken place at Koinange's house nine times between 1949 and 1951 and that his name had cropped up in Mau Mau songs. 'I do not think that it makes a very good case for treating Mr Koinange as a pariah,' De Zulueta wrote, 'because the question would at once be asked why he was not extradited and the answer really seems to be that the evidence against him was not strong enough.'[40] 'Could his *curriculum vitae* be made to look more vicious?', the acting Prime Minister, Rab Butler, enquired. 'We doubt whether this can usefully be done,' came the answer. No specific incident could be effectively 'written in'.[41]

Eventually a face-saving formula was discovered. An adviser's pass without a name was issued to the African delegation. They could fill in Koinange's name, allowing him to be in Lancaster House but not in the main conference room. The conference was at last on its way, with Macleod being guided by two decisions he had made in advance: that he should announce at the outset that Kenya was destined to be governed by its African majority, and that, in the decisive behind-the-scenes negotiations, Blundell's New Kenya Party (formerly Group) would matter and Briggs's United Party would not. Fortunately for Macleod, it had been Michael Blundell and his associates like Wilfrid Havelock and Peter Marrian, not 'Puck' Briggs, who had taken the trouble to develop excellent contacts in the Conservative Party and with the lobbies interested in East Africa.[42] It was clear that, whether or not Blundell spoke for the majority of Kenya settlers, a settlement which Blundell accepted would pass muster with Tories.

Macleod's technique was first to let everyone round the table make his prepared speech and then to get down to highly practical exchanges with small groups of delegates or even individuals often in the informal atmosphere of his flat. The African demands appeared at first sight to be unnegotiable: an African Chief Minister and universal suffrage to a legislature of seventy-one seats, with no special provision whatsoever for minorities. Odinga has described how Macleod 'called us in one by one, sounded us out, talked to us as man to man . . . We should assist him in dealing with the settlers who were not prepared to give an inch of the way. He conscripted us into looking at the problem from his point of view.'[43]

Two external events influenced the atmosphere of the conference as it proceeded. The first was the tour of Africa undertaken by the Prime Minister. It had started off in Ghana where Macmillan first used the phrase 'The wind of change is blowing through this continent' before a noisy and inattentive after-dinner audience in a country unaccustomed to handling such occasions.[44] Though carried by Reuters the phrase had zero impact. On 3 February, he repeated himself before the South African Parliament and the world was electrified. 'Whether we like it or not,' the British Prime Minister had also said, 'this growth of national consciousness is a political fact. We must all accept it as a fact and our national policies must take account of it.'

Secondly, on 27 January the Belgians at the Round Table conference at Brussels, which was taking place concurrently with the Kenya conference in London, agreed that, 'As of 30 June next the Congo, with its present frontiers, shall become an independent state.' Suddenly at one blow the second largest territory in Africa, centrally located having common frontiers with seven neighbours in all manner of colonial relationships with European metropolitan Powers, was to leapfrog all usual preliminaries. From the back of the self-government queue it was in six short months to reach the front ranks of ex-colonial states alongside the Sudan and Ghana. The news galvanized the Second All Africa People's conference which was meeting in Tunis. Since Tom Mboya, although the retiring chairman, was unable to be there, the Kenya delegation was headed by a Kenyatta relative, Dr Mungai Njoroge, the first qualified Kenya African physician, and included leading figures in the Nairobi People's Convention Party, Josef Mathenge and Denis Akumu. For them and for their colleagues, the Brussels message meant a great surge in the momentum of African freedom. They felt Mboya should be there and urged him without success to make a flying visit from London, where they feared he would get himself involved in political compromises out of keeping with the new spirit.[45] Back in London, Blundell, to his mystification, found Macleod anxiously scanning every report coming in on the Congo.

When everyone in Lancaster House had been delivered of his speech, Macleod produced his own plan. The Legco was to be reduced to 65 members (unless the Governor chose to use his remaining option of nomination) and of these a bare majority – but a majority nonetheless – of 33 MLCs were for the first time in Kenya's history to be elected for open and not communal seats and on a wide though not universal franchise. There were also to be 20 seats reserved for members from the minorities – ten European, eight Asians and two Arabs – but for them also the votes would be cast by mainly African electors on the common roll. In order that the seats reserved for minorities should not be filled by completely unrepresentative friends of the Africans, the Lancaster House settlement provided that the candidates for these seats must show that they had 'the effective and genuine support of their own communities'. It was decided to hold primary elections to ensure that this should be so but it was not until the following December and after long and heated debates that the relatively low figure of 25 per cent support from a candidate's own community was established as enough to qualify him (or her) to face the whole electorate. The remaining twelve places would be for National (formerly Specially Elected) Members, four each for Europeans, Africans and Asians, to be chosen by the rest of the new Legco.

The entire scheme might just be represented as consistent with the Lennox-Boyd constitution – the reservation of seats and the cross-voting for National seats were holdovers from multiracialism – but the crucial difference lay in the weighting of the numbers. The balance would be with the Africans. The Governor, however, would still appoint the Council of Ministers, in which officials would be reduced from seven to four. There would be no Chief Minister, but four Ministers would be African, three European and one Asian. Macleod said afterwards, 'My objective was quite a simple one: it was to get Michael Blundell's group and the Africans to agree. I never thought I could carry the right-wing Europeans with me.'[46] Briggs said, 'This is a victory for Mau Mau, a death-blow to the European community.'[47] Blundell was the key and he was under great pressure from all sides, especially since his ability to swing the votes of the other members of his own delegation was by no means certain. Leaks of the Macleod scheme had appeared in the Kenya press and settlers' feelings about the Colonial Secretary can only be described as poisonous. 'Is Macleod mad, a complete double-crosser or plain brainless?' wrote one of them in a letter which Blundell reproduced in his posthumously published memoirs.[48]

Blundell's own opinion was set out in a memorandum for his party colleagues. 'The proposals,' he said, 'will completely change the political scene in Kenya.' On the one hand, 'Mr. Macleod's decisions are far from being in line with the principles for which the New Kenya Party has stood' – the principles, that is, of multi-racialism. On the other, 'the second point in our policy – the association of all races in the government of the country – may be gained, and this will, we hope, set the pattern through which our goal of non-racialism may eventually be attained'. The Europeans could resist the changes, but, if the resistance were successful, the African people would never forget; if unsuccessful, the Europeans would suffer enormously from economic pressures.[49]

Macmillan had arrived back from Africa in time to see the New Kenya Party (NKP) delegates twice, on 17 and 20 February 1960, Macleod briefing him in advance that 'they are really very small people and are particularly sensitive to the criticism that . . . comes to them from their constituents'. The message must be '*Courage, mes braves*'. Macmillan, who was particularly good at this sort of thing, 'then delivered an oration on the general theme that change is inevitable in human affairs and is often less disagreeable than it seems in anticipation'. This, it was reported, seemed to have a marked effect on the delegates.[50] With whatever misgivings, they as well as the Africans (but not Briggs) put their names to the Macleod plan. Cuthbert Alport, the Minister of State at the Commonwealth Relations Office, told Blundell after it was all over that if he and the NKP had not been able to accept the new constitution the main body of Tory MPs would not have done so either.[51]

'This is certainly a great triumph for the Colonial Secretary,' noted the Prime Minister.[52] But Oginga Odinga on leaving warned Lord Perth that 'You will have to deal with Kenyatta.'[53] What Perth chiefly had in mind was that, while Kenya had a particularly efficient civil service, there were no Africans in the upper echelons. Following Lancaster House he insisted on bringing over the most promising of them in the lower ranks to Britain for intensive courses to make up for lost time.[54]

For one community the settlement was truly paradoxical. The Kenya Asians had always stood for a common electoral roll. Now that, at last, this is what they had, they faced political irrelevance. The great majority of them, it is true, had taken little interest in politics, though a few, mainly Hindus influenced by Nehru and Gandhi, had made a notable contribution to African political awakening. The Muslims had always been represented in politics by Independents. Deeply divided among themselves as to whether to embrace wholeheartedly the African national cause, fearful of the effects of African self-rule on their trading prospects while not daring to oppose it, Indian political leaders (who, since the partition of India, had been clumsily referred to as Asian Non-Muslims) were unable after Lancaster House to stay together under the rubric of the Kenya Indian Congress. Those who thought there was no time to be lost in throwing in their lot unambiguously with the Kenyan majority now broke off from the Congress and formed the Kenya Freedom Party under Chanan Singh and Fitz de Souza.[55]

The Europeans in the NKP team went back to face excoriating criticism from their friends and neighbours. Blundell, who was surprisingly thin-skinned for so commanding a figure, did not dare show his face in any of the clubs. He wrote fairly cheerfully to Macleod, 'People who do not like . . . the changes that are taking place are no worse and no better off than a man who liked hackney cabs and was unable to tune in to the modern taxi cab.'[56] But he adopted a totally different tone when writing to Sir Roy Welensky, the Prime Minister of the Central African Federation, to warn him about what he would be up against when dealing with Macleod in the critical negotiations about to take place over the political future of Northern Rhodesia and Nyasaland. 'He is an aggressive, tough and ruthless character, very ambitious with a first-class brain and very close to the Prime Minister. Not a likeable personality and not a straightforward one.'[57]

It was this assessment, passed on no doubt by Welensky, that the Marquess of Salisbury, no longer in office but still a powerful figure in the Tory Party, had in mind a year later when he launched his extraordinary attack on Iain Macleod in the House of Lords. The occasion was 'the acute tension between HMG in this country and the Federal Government in [Central] Africa', and his theme was that 'the main responsibility must rest on the present Colonial Secretary . . . [who] has adopted, especially in his relationship to the white communities of Africa a most unhappy and an entirely wrong approach. He has been too clever by half.' Salisbury went on to illustrate his argument by reference to the Lancaster House conference on Kenya:

I believe that the Colonial Secretary is a very fine bridge-player. Now bridge is a game where two players are matched against two other players . . . and the aim of each pair is to outwit their opponents. It is not considered immoral or even bad form to outwit one's opponents at bridge . . . It almost seems to me as if the Colonial Secretary, when he abandoned the sphere of bridge for the sphere of politics, brought his bridge technique [with him.] . . . The first occasion on which [this] became apparent, in view of these European communities, was at the Lancaster House conference on constitutional reform for Kenya . . . [A]fter not very lengthy consultation, the Colonial Secretary plonked down on the table a Constitution of his own which, particularly in the very wide franchise which it granted to Africans, went far beyond anything that any of them, even Mr. Blundell and his supporters, expected or thought safe . . . [A]fter the laying of the Macleod proposals further negotiations took place but they were only on the basis of his scheme. No others could be considered. Now that, I think, we shall all agree was extremely clever. The Europeans found themselves completely outwitted and they were driven to the conclusion . . . that it was the nationalist African leaders whom the Colonial Secretary regarded as his partners and the white community and the loyal Africans that he regarded as his opponents in the game he was playing.[58]

It had taken the Tory right a full year for its resentment over Kenya to come to the surface. When it did, the bitterness in some quarters resonated perceptively.

Talking to *The Economist*'s editorial staff shortly after Lancaster House, Macleod said that he had aimed 'a little to the left of Michael Blundell', and, having since observed ruefully that Blundell seemed aggrieved, he would have to be more circumspect over Northern

Rhodesia.[59] Economically there was an immediate crisis in investor confidence in the colony. Nearly £900,000 in assets were transferred out of the territory in one week; by the end of July the figure had risen to over £5 million. The three chief building societies in Kenya were threatened by the financial panic and one of them, the First Permanent, had to be bailed out by the Colonial Development Corporation. The word had gone out that Kenya was shortly to be under black rule and until reassuring statements would be forthcoming from the future black rulers confidence was gone.[60]

WHAT TO DO WITH MBOYA

There could be no doubt that the star turn of the Lancaster House conference as far as the media were concerned was Tom Mboya, whose role was supposed to be confined to that of secretary of the African Elected Members delegation headed by Ronald Ngala and including the two party presidents, Odinga and Muliro. Once more Mboya's quickness of mind, his fluency, his mastery of detail were on display at the conference and in the corridors and it was he whom the news organizations wanted to interview.[61] He was not one to miss any opportunity. It was not a surprise when a book published as recently as 1995 stated baldly that 'In the absence of Kenyatta Tom Mboya led the African delegation.'[62] He did not but he behaved in public as if he did.

Macleod told the Africans in London that, the State of Emergency having been lifted, colonywide political parties would be allowed. As most of the Africans were staying at the Bloomsbury Hotel (but Mboya was not) Odinga summoned these to a meeting in Daniel arap Moi's room. They decided to form a single political party called the Uhuru Party of Kenya and the firm intention of many of those present was that it would not include Tom Mboya.

At the same time Mboya's erstwhile supporters in the Nairobi People's Convention Party, such as Mathenge and Akumu, were coming back from Tunis, fired up by the mood of the All-African People's Conference and of a mind to condemn the failure to secure Kenyatta's release and the retention of remnants of multiracialism. The intellectual tone of Tunis had been set by the francophone delegates, with whom Ghana, equipped with an ideology called Consciencism expressed in the algebra of mathematical logic, was also closely aligned. They were much concerned to conceptualize the Africans' predicament. The analysis was that once the imperialists had left an African state ceremonially by the front door, they would then 'by devilish colonialist tricks' endeavour to creep in again by the back door. Three such tricks were: neo-colonialism (disguised as economic aid), balkanization (playing 'divide and rule' between states or by splitting them) and the affiliation of African institutions to international organizations. On the latter point, the anti-communist ICFTU, of which Tom Mboya was such a notable advocate and beneficiary, was the body most especially in mind. *The Economist* reported from Tunis that,

> There was an underground campaign of disparagement of Mr Mboya at the conference for being too moderate in his demands, too interested in making a hit with the imperialist press, which had built him up beyond his real significance, and too ready to sell out to the Americans.[63]

Though, like Mboya, Kwame Nkrumah had not been present at Tunis, he was clearly the man behind this campaign. The mutual admiration society between the two men was at an end. It had not survived a year of exchanges of very long telegrams and the chafing of two egos while seeking to erect a transcontinental system on a shoe-string. To Nkrumah and other Ghanaians, Mboya's American connections were deeply suspect; his explanations that he needed the ICFTU affiliation for what he could get out of it for the African cause fell on unsympathetic ears. Nkrumah was now bent on setting up an All-African Federation of Trade Unions which should be affiliated to nobody; and he was not above attempting to undermine his ex-protégé's base in the labour movement of Kenya. After Odinga, Argwings-Kodhek and an anti-Mboya trade unionist called Arthur Ochwada had visited him, he thought he knew how to do it.

Odinga now got onto the socialist circuit – Guinea, East Germany, Chinese People's Republic and the Soviet Union. He preached the absolute necessity for Kenyatta's leadership and questioned his hosts about the nature of communism. The pioneer African capitalist was on his way to becoming the prime representative in Kenya of communist interests. Where Mboya had his airlift to America, Odinga would develop Argwings-Kodhek's original idea of seeking opportunities for Kenyan students in the Soviet bloc. Kenya politics was on the way to becoming a branch of the cold war.

In view of the opposition to him that was building up it is not surprising that when Mboya arrived back in Nairobi to share with Kiano a hero's welcome at the Nairobi Stadium, all his emphasis was on the transient nature of the arrangements to which the Africans had agreed. The new Legco would not last its four-year term, Kenyatta would be released, and a fresh constitution would rapidly succeed the one agreed at Lancaster House. Nothing could be more disobliging for Michael Blundell and the New Kenya Party, who were enduring vicious attacks and needed to show that they had brought some stability.

Sir Charles Markham, who was about to leave the New Kenya Party, wrote to Blundell on 2 March, 'If Mboya and Kiano succeed in winning a majority of the common roll seats pledged to break the new Constitution, then we are indeed in a most dangerous position which could result in the total elimination of the European.' The solution, he argued, was to create a strong opposition to the extremists, attracting support from 'the unlimited number of tribes who do not wish to be ruled by the doctorate' (a reference to Kiano's string of degrees and Mboya's one honorary one). Markham believed that 'coalition [of the whites] with Muliro and the pastoral and nomadic tribes might well result in us obtaining an absolute majority in Legco'.[64] This was a will-o'-the-wisp that was to be pursued energetically for the next three years.

6 Kenyatta Released

'There were some people who thought Kenyatta was an old man with old ideas and perhaps old brains. This is a false view which ought to be completely forgotten.' (Jomo Kenyatta at Lodwar meeting of political leaders, 23 March 1961)

The new Governor, Sir Patrick Renison, set about trying to re-order his Council of Ministers in keeping with the Lancaster House formula without waiting for the Legco elections which would take over a year to organize. It proved more difficult than the Africans' acceptance of Lancaster House might have led him to suppose. The first obstacle was Renison's refusal to dismiss the existing African Minister, Musa Amalemba, who was regarded as a quisling by the elected members. But in the end, although Odinga would not accept office without Kenyatta and Mboya found himself obliged to follow suit, it was agreed that Kiano, Ngala and Muimi (a member of the Kamba tribe) should become Ministers with Taita Towett (a Kipsigis, one of the Kalenjin group of tribes) as an Assistant Minister of Agriculture.[1]

Odinga and other African Elected Members pressed ahead in secrecy with their plans to launch the Uhuru Party without notifying Mboya. They decided to launch it on 27 March 1960 at a meeting of 150 leaders from thirty local political organizations at Kiambu, under the chairmanship of James Gichuru, who of course had once before fulfilled the function of holding open a chair for Kenyatta. The draft constitution of the party was published only two days in advance of the Kiambu meeting. 'It is particularly disturbing,' said Mboya, 'that some person or persons saw fit to exclude some African leaders even from being consulted.' He announced that he would be there.[2] He was lucky in the chairman; Gichuru did not go along with the idea of excluding him.

When Mboya turned up at Kiambu he was able to play a holding game. By now the party name had been changed to KANU (Kenya African National Union) and Mboya gleefully proclaimed in an interview when the meeting was over, 'Odinga went to the meeting with a list of KANU officers and other documents and at the end of the meeting went away with them still in his pocket. It took hours to persuade the delegates not to rubber-stamp his

111

proposals.'[3] The meeting ended with a resolution to appoint a committee, of which Mboya was a member, to discuss the formation of KANU and to report back. However he had made it plain that the Nairobi People's Convention Party (NPCP) was keeping its shadow branches throughout the country in being and that if KANU was not to his taste he would be in a position to offer it powerful competition.[4]

Realizing that he had only a short time to broaden his popular support beyond Nairobi, Mboya then sought to put himself at the head of the release-Kenyatta movement. But for once his usual concern for efficiency was sacrificed to his habit of perpetual motion. He had no sooner launched a petition for Kenyatta's release, to be backed up by a strike, a boycott and a procession than he left to keep engagements in West Africa. When the campaign went off in his absence at half-cock, Mboya, never happy unless he held the initiative, declared from Monrovia, the capital of Liberia, that, since every lawful demand for Kenyatta's release had been refused, the Africans would have to proceed to organized non-cooperation. It was a breathtaking assumption of the right to commit a whole people to an open struggle with authority, made a thousand miles away from home, without any preparation, and it horrified the African political leadership. Gichuru, though an Mboya admirer, administered a magisterial rebuke.

When Mboya arrived back at Nairobi airport on 23 April fighting broke out between his supporters and those of Argwings-Kodhek's African National Congress. The latter's placards read, 'On whose authority did you give orders in Liberia?' Mboya muttered rather feebly, 'When I talked about civil disobedience I had planned to work something out on my return to Kenya.'[5] Yet Mboya's campaign, however flawed in its execution, had the effect of putting the wind up the British at the thought that, so soon after Mau Mau, civil disobedience was on the agenda and it placed the Kenyatta issue at centre stage.[6]

In London the *Daily Mail* came out with a report that the Government was contemplating Kenyatta's release. This alerted the Prime Minister. He had already had one scare with his 'emotional, Celtic' Colonial Secretary. Only two days after congratulating Macleod on the Kenya conference, he had been confronted with his resignation, after the Cabinet, under pressure from Sir Roy Welensky, had decided not to release Dr Hastings Banda at once in Nyasaland. ('Is it a plot? Is it nervous strain? . . . Is it 'Bridge'? (or perhaps

Poker) or is it emotion?', the worried Prime Minister asked him-self.[7]) This particular crisis was overriden without a word of it ever reaching the papers. But now, two months later, came this further alarm. 'What is the position about Kenyatta?' Macmillan demanded anxiously. Pointing to the press-cutting he asked, 'Is this really so? Does it rest with the Kenya Government or with you?'[8] The Colonial Secretary was reassuring. 'There is not and never has been any intention of releasing Kenyatta.'[9] There could be no comparison, Macleod declared, between the cases of Banda and Kenyatta.[10]

THE 'LEADER TO DARKNESS AND DEATH'

Renison told Macleod on 20 April, 'I think we must face up to the fact that the release of Kenyatta is the critical issue confronting us and it is impossible to avoid it . . . We are inevitably coming to a trial of strength on the main issue.'[11] A retired civil servant, F. D. Corfield, had been hired by Evelyn Baring in 1957 with the special title of Government Commissioner (History of Mau Mau) to compile an historical survey of the origins and growth of the movement, including 'the circumstances which permitted [it] to develop so rapidly without the full knowledge of the Government'.[12] On taking over his duties Renison found this long report duly completed and studied it carefully. It is quite well written and contains much valuable material from the archives but is fatally marred by a heavy bias from the outset against Jomo Kenyatta, whose actions and motives are invariably characterized in the most loaded possible language. 'Corfield is not a trained historian but an administrative officer,' Ian Buist, a Colonial Office official with intimate recent knowledge of Kenya, minuted. All the evidence had been collected 'but many will say he has not sifted or analyzed it sufficiently and the result is an obvious bias towards the Government sources in question'.[13]

Renison, who plumed himself on the quality of his prose and his skill at baring his soul in such a way as to put himself on the right wavelength with Africans, had drafted an address which he wished to broadcast to the people of Kenya. It took its inspiration from a speech by the Archbishop of Canterbury in the House of Lords in which the Primate had referred to 'the African struggle between light and darkness, life and death'. What Renison wanted to say, after 'searching my own conscience' and 'with the great assistance of Corfield', was that 'Jomo Kenyatta was the recognized and implacable leader of the non-cooperation movement which originated Mau Mau . . . Here was the African leader to darkness and death.' He liked the last phrase so much that he used it twice more in his script. He asked that the Corfield Report should be made public.[14]

Macleod was alarmed at this indication of the way Renison was proposing to inaugurate his relationship with the African public. He was not in favour of the Governor's wrestling with his conscience in public or of his giving detailed reasons for security decisions. Especially did he want him to take out the too-memorable phrase 'leader to darkness and death' – 'for the obvious reason that we would sooner or later have to deal with Jomo Kenyatta and this didn't really seem a very promising introduction'.[15] He told him not to make the speech before his coming visit to London.

Renison then consulted his African Ministers individually about what to do with Kenyatta. Disclaiming any personal knowledge of the old man, Kiano gave the advice that was eventually followed, that Kenyatta be restricted in a more accessible place than distant and unhealthy Lodwar and the world's press be allowed to interrogate him.[16] The question was then put to the complete Council of Ministers. The Minister of Tourism, W. E. Crosskill, argued that among the new generation of African politicians there were leaders who had more ability than Kenyatta ever had. They must have courage and stand on their own merits as new men of a new era and not rely on invoking the myth of a savage, bloodstained past. To this Kiano made the spirited reply that without convictions it was difficult to have the courage of them and in his heart he did not believe it was right to continue to keep Kenyatta under restriction. If Kenyatta were released, said Anthony Swann, the Minister of Internal Security and Defence, loyalists would probably try to murder him and he would not fancy having to prevent them from doing so by providing Kenyatta with a guard and taking responsibility for his life.

In view of the parts they were to play in the years to come two other contributions to this ministerial debate deserve notice. The Legal Affairs Minister, Eric Griffith-Jones, said that he for one could not remain in a Government that would be weak enough to release Kenyatta. His release would destroy every vestige of European confidence in the Government and would virtually bring European agriculture, which was still the mainstay of the economy, to a standstill. The Minister of Agriculture was Bruce McKenzie, a much-decorated war pilot from South Africa, a stout, bluff man with ample RAF-type moustaches who seemed forever engaged in an unavailing battle to hitch his belt around his trousers. In 1946 McKenzie had taken over completely undeveloped land and turned it into one of the best farms in the Rift Valley, with a pedigree herd of Friesian cattle. His reputation as a model settler had been acknowledged by election as President of the Royal Agricultural Society of Kenya. On this occasion his advice was that Kenyatta's release would force all Europeans into a single hostile bloc, that racial cooperation would break down and that outside investment would cease. He warned that it might not only be Africans who would want Kenyatta dead.[17]

Fortified by these opinions, the Governor pleaded in vain to be allowed to make his personal pitch before going off to London. 'I as the man on the spot in more than one sense am quite sure a personal statement such as I intend is more likely to hold the position . . . I am unhappy that you do not feel able to leave such a judgment to me.'[18] Rebuffed, Renison then flew to London and, with what his Chief Secretary termed his 'bulldog tenacity', engaged Macleod in rather fraught dialogue. 'I regarded him,' Macleod said afterwards, 'as a rather silly man. And he offered his resignation on it [his text] and said that unless he was allowed to use this particular phrase ['leader to darkness and death'] he would have to resign.' Faced with this prospect Macleod backed down. Politically, he reckoned he could not withstand a crisis in which Renison would have been seen as championing the rights of the Europeans on such a raw and sensitive subject.[19]

On 5 May Macleod announced in the Commons that Corfield was to be published and that Kenyatta would be kept in detention. The Report was issued as a Command Paper (covered by parliamentary privilege) specifically in order to avoid the danger of Peter Mbiyu Koinange suing for libel.[20] Renison went back to Kenya and was delivered of his speech, slightly toned down, which made a dim impression on those who saw the pattern of the future.

THE BIRTH OF KANU

Meanwhile African politics was crystallizing fast. On 14 May 1960 there was a two-day conference of political leaders, the first day at Kiambu and the second at Nairobi, attended by representatives from each of 29 District Associations and nine of the African Elected Members. They launched the Kenya African National Union, the party which has ruled independent Kenya to this day. They elected Jomo Kenyatta as President, James Gichuru as Acting President and Oginga Odinga as Vice-President without difficulty. The filling of the other offices took place 'in a contentious and noisy manner'. No one seems to have been satisfied by the results. The real battle came over the post of General Secretary. Mboya's position had improved since the previous Kiambu meeting but he was still strongly opposed for the job, among others by Arthur Ochwada, the candidate of Odinga and, indirectly, of Kwame Nkrumah. 'You are no doubt aware of the campaign against me that is being conducted from Cairo, Accra and Nairobi,' Mboya had written on 2 May to the Secretary-General of ICFTU.[21] In the end, he won by one vote. Nevertheless members of the Nairobi People's Convention Party who thought they had sufficiently penetrated associations across the colony were disillusioned by the extent to which their claims were thrust aside.

But then, to go by Special Branch reports, scarcely anyone emerged contented. Neither the Kikuyu nor the critics of the Kikuyu sounded happy at the outcome. Gichuru was the sole Kikuyu (apart from Kenyatta) among the new political leadership. There was much dark murmuring among members of the tribe because Dr Mungai Njoroge, Kenyatta's nephew and hopefully his surrogate, had been nominated for each office except the Presidency and had not been elected to any of them. Yet to the enemies of the Kikuyu the party seemed dominated by the Kikuyu–Luo alliance.[22]

At Nairobi on 15 May, the second day of the conference, Mboya made a strong pitch for a campaign of civil disobedience, on the grounds that constitutional means were of no avail. But his oratory fell flat; the majority of delegates shouted him down and, instead, the radical cause was represented by a resolution that unless African Elected Members were allowed to visit Kenyatta within one month the African Ministers and members of Legco should resign. But even this was by no means endorsed by all the Elected Members.[23]

On the evening of the same day the Kikuyu leaders from Central Province caucused and were reported to the Special Branch as expressing disappointment and condemnation at Mboya's election as secretary. They came out strongly against a campaign of civil disobedience as the only result would be a second State of Emergency.

It was stated that the Kikuyu would never be led by a Luo and that Mboya was trying to mislead the illiterate masses. It had not escaped the Kikuyu plotters prominent among whom was his former ally Julius Kiano that Mboya sat as a Luo for a Nairobi seat thanks to the disfranchisement of the Kikuyu majority and that in the approaching election this condition would no longer prevail.[24]

At a private meeting on 4 July attended by the Elected Members from Central Province, plus Gichuru and Mungai Njoroge, Gichuru was told that unless he disciplined Mboya there would be a split in KANU. The party leader must ensure that no statement was issued by Mboya without his approval and that he must be kept fully informed about what money was being collected in the name of KANU and what was being done with it. A post of Organizing Secretary should be created and filled by a Kikuyu; Mboya should then 'concentrate on the day-to-day correspondence'.[25]

Mboya was not being idle. He was busy organizing the merger of his NPCP and Argwings-Kodhek's Nairobi District African Congress, whose continued rivalry had resulted in members of both being up in court after engaging in a bar-room brawl. The aim was to form a Nairobi branch of KANU strong enough to stand up to these Kikuyu intrigues. Since the highly politically conscious Kikuyu tribe, for the first time since Mau Mau, was re-entering legitimate political activity, much attention was now devoted to Central Province. The new educated political leadership did not find it as simple as they had thought to control the formation of the branches. True, it all went well at Thika when the election of branch office-holders was held in Mungai Njoroge's medical clinic, with Mungai being elected as chairman and only one of eleven officers having a Mau Mau record. At Fort Hall, too, Kiano just succeeded in engineering the elections so as to keep out the staunchest Mau Mau adherents though leaving the defeated candidates, some of whom were very influential locally, 'extremely embittered'. But it was very different at Kiambu, where Special Branch noted that of the four chief officers three were ex-detainees and at Nyeri where, after a procedure that was 'both chaotic and disputatious and the subject of much acrimony', three-quarters of the winners were connected with subversion.[26]

In Mombasa, where there were three rival political parties already operating, the attempt to group them all under the KANU flag was not without elements of farce. The up-country Coast Pan-Africanist Party, being an ally of Tom Mboya's Nairobi party, was initially against KANU because it had assumed that Mboya would keep the NPCP going after being thwarted at Kiambu. The Mombasa African Democratic Union, being anti-Mboya, was initially pro-KANU because it too was confident that Mboya would get nowhere at Kiambu. When Mboya was elected the two parties changed sides.[27]

THE BIRTH OF KADU

Mboya's most irreconcilable opponent, Masinde Muliro, boycotted the conference altogether and declared his opposition to KANU. Ngala and Moi were both abroad. They had been elected respectively Treasurer and Assistant Treasurer. When they came back they found their constituents highly critical of the new party. To Ngala's Coastal supporters it spelled up-country dictatorship, so that he quickly declined his party office on the grounds that he was a Minister. Moi was more inclined to go along with KANU, but when he saw to what extent the combination of Gichuru, Odinga and Mboya at the top was poison to all the Kalenjin tribes, he took part in meetings at Eldoret on 21 May and Chepkorio on 11 June of the Kalenjin Political Alliance (KPA), which brought together that group of tribes.

Moi told the Chepkorio rally of over 6,000 Kalenjin that political organizations that started at the top did not flourish democratically. The right way was to start at the location and district level, where moves towards dictatorship could be curbed at source. On 25 June representatives of the KPA met at Ngong with six other tribal organizations under Muliro's chairmanship to form the Kenya African Democratic Union (KADU) to challenge what they considered the danger of Kikuyu–Luo dictatorship.

The pastoral tribes among them were especially alert to the danger that, now the first Africans were to be allowed to farm on the Highlands, land which they believed should revert to them would be seized by the Kikuyu. The Kalenjin laid reversionary claim to large areas of the White Highlands; the Maasai had their special treaties signed with the British which now looked as if they could be under threat. KADU went on to choose Ronald Ngala as leader, Masinde Muliro who had wanted the leadership as deputy leader and arap Moi as chairman.[28]

STUDENT AIRLIFTS AND THE COLD WAR

Much of the energies of Mboya and Odinga were occupied during 1960 in organizing the selection, funding and despatch of students to their respective sides of the Iron Curtain. They both obtained funds from abroad to acquire four-wheel-drive trucks and printing presses for their politics. The fact that they were in the same party but on opposite sides of the cold war meant that party discipline was often breached by attempts to undermine each other in their respective strongholds.

Odinga gained financial and other material support from the communist world, which he visited extensively in the summer of 1960. On 12 August, accompanied by Were Ambitho, who was perhaps the single most hated African in Britain's books because of his Cairo broadcasts in celebration of Mau Mau as a national liberation struggle, Odinga arrived in Beijing. They were both received in audience by the Chinese Premier Chou Enlai and attended a banquet held in their honour. Afterwards Odinga addressed a mass rally at which he said, 'We have NATO bases in our country supported by the USA. We have US infiltration in our trade union movement [a reference to Mboya's links with the ICFTU and the American AFL-CIO] and we have their intelligence services all over Kenya. Indeed the threat of US imperialism in Kenya is greater than that of Britain.' Odinga went on to Moscow and was received by Deputy Prime Minister Mikoyan.[29]

Tom Mboya, hitherto labelled as 'extremist', came to be seen by the establishment in a more kindly light. 'Throughout his career he has had to contend with colleagues and assistants whose lack of principle, unreliability, dishonesty and narrow outlook make his achievements all the more remarkable,' wrote M. C. Manby, the Director of Intelligence and Security in November 1960. 'So long as Kenya's destiny runs parallel to his own ambitions there is no one on the prevailing political scene more ruthlessly competent to direct its course than Tom Mboya.'[30] And in the following month Blundell wrote, 'Although Mboya makes truculent, aggressive and negative speeches, I am increasingly coming to the conclusion that he is a moderate.'[31]

Mboya was adding to that impression by his cultivation of the white business community with important effect in steadying nerves and by his trip to London with Gichuru (always a reassuring personality) in September to talk with investors about economic stability,

recognition of titles to property and just compensation for any ex-
propriated land. The radicals in KANU were not at all pleased at
what they heard. Led by Josef Mathenge and the Mombasa trade
union leader Denis Akumu they formed the Ginger Action Group
(GAG) to keep the party up to what they felt to be the mark.
They were encouraged though not actually joined by Odinga, who,
being now for the first time in receipt of substantial funds from
the east, was in a position to give appropriate politicians some relief from the financial embarrassment which at that period was their
constant lot.[32]

SHOULD KENYATTA BE RELEASED?

Since July 1960 all concerned with Africa had been watching with
horrid fascination what was happening in the former Belgian Congo.
On 30 June, as promised, King Baudouin of the Belgians in his
own person handed over sovereignty to the Republic of the Congo
and to a most diffuse coalition government. It was headed by an
uneasy dyarchy, President Joseph Kasavubu, who in the presence
of the monarch made a proper and respectful speech, and Prime
Minister Patrice Lumumba, who made an improper and insulting
one. Neither had much relevant experience.[33] Lumumba invited Dr
Julius Kiano, who headed the Kenyan delegation for the ceremony,
to attend a Cabinet meeting. Kiano who had by now grown accustomed to the orderly procedure of Renison's Council of Ministers
was scandalized by the complete absence of system or decorum
that prevailed. There seemed to be no agenda. The Prime Minister answered phone calls throughout the meeting, and on spotting
the press through the window would jump up and go to talk to
them.[34] A few days later the Congolese Army, the former *Force
Publique*, mutinied and the Congolese state began rapidly to unravel.
    Kenya was thus confronted – as was Britain – with the spectacle
of what could happen if the transition to independence was abrupt
and not sensitively handled. The man who saw this most clearly
was the second ranking civil servant in the Colonial Office, the
Deputy Under-Secretary of State Sir John Martin, who had been
Churchill's Principal Private Secretary during the war. His advice
to Iain Macleod in December was that, in respect of Kenya, 'the
momentum of internal political forces and the influence of events
elsewhere are such that the only hope of avoiding disaster à la

Congo is to go extremely fast and recognize that as from now (i.e. after the election) the tune is to be called by the Africans.'[35]

But what was perplexing Harold Macmillan, as he confessed to Lord Kilmuir, the Lord Chancellor who sat on the Colonial Policy Committee, was that, 'People are not yet accustomed to the idea that, sooner or later, we shall have to accept independence in Kenya.' The two men worried that this was a big problem from the Party point of view. 'We might even split on it. Lord Salisbury and Lord Lambton could easily rally a "settler" lobby here of considerable power.' Macmillan reflected that the Kenyan settlement had always been aristocratic and upper-middle-class and 'has strong links with the City and the Clubs'.[36]

In mid-December Macleod learnt that Renison had drafted another long statement about Kenyatta. Taking up Kiano's suggestion he was proposing to move him from Lodwar to a more accessible and attractive residence at Maralal, still 180 miles from Nairobi but cooler, where, though still under restriction, he could be visited by politicians and also the world's press. In a top-secret and personal letter to Macleod consciously modelled on a standard military appreciation ('Information, Intention, Method. . . .'), the Governor underlined the importance of the British still being in charge when Kenyatta finally came to be released. But first, said Renison, he must be 'de-bunked' and his 'legend' allowed to diminish through press publicity and the opinions of visitors. 'I know you don't much like my personal approach to policy statements of this nature,' was Renison's way of softening up Macleod. 'I am sorry to inflict another on you . . . I know what it meant to you to let me do it my way [last May] and I was proportionately grateful. I know my way is too personal, too naive for England, but I think it is the best way so long as we govern in countries such as this.'

'I cannot see how a thirteen paragraph statement helps to debunk a man,' snorted Max Webber, the Kenya desk man, on the receiving end. But Sir John Martin differed from Webber and other officials and indeed, in respect of timing, from Renison. He thought that the decision about Kenyatta should be taken in the light of advice from the new Ministers who would emerge from the election which was to take place in February. If this were to be in favour of immediate release it should be accepted. 'If we are now to have an African Kenya, it is clearly impossible to keep the African national leader behind bars.'[37] If this advice had been followed much of the remainder of this story would have been very different.

Macleod decided to go along with Renison rather than with Martin. After a conference with the Governor at Chequers he notified Macmillan that the release would not take place until enough time had passed, probably fifteen months, for the de-bunking to take effect and for a new Government under the Lancaster House constitution to be thoroughly grounded. 'The press would quickly get bored with him,' Macleod told Macmillan. 'We would like to see an African Chief Minister established in Kenya before Kenyatta is finally freed from restriction.'[38]

FEDERATION RE-BORN

There was another reason for Macleod's wishing to find Chief Ministers swiftly both for Kenya and Uganda. Julius Nyerere, in a speech in July 1960 had come out in favour of an East African Federation and had offered to delay Tanganyika's independence for a short while to allow time for the other two territories to catch up. He had made the very sensible point that it would be far more difficult to persuade a state to abandon its own flag, anthem, postage stamps, seat at the UN, once it had begun to enjoy them. Federation should, therefore, take place either a little before or at the same time as independence from the colonial Power.

British lips began to salivate at favourable African reference to federation. East Africa seemed a much more viable unit for independence that any of the individual territories; and it also for some reason seemed to be thought that a Federal Government would be much easier to deal with over matters like defence. Now that the Suez Canal base had been denied to Britain in rather dramatic circumstances,[39] Kenya had been identified by the generals as the most suitable location for a theatre reserve. A base had been for some years in process of being constructed at Kahawa and the air force facilities at Eastleigh were being expanded. They would be used, for example, if Iraq were to develop its threat to annex Kuwait. But at the end of 1960 red lights started flashing in the Defence Ministry when Mboya, under attack because KANU's draft election manifesto was not radical enough over land, chose to emphasize the commitment that 'KANU will press for the immediate closing down of the base.' Surely, said Harold Watkinson, the Minister of Defence, Britain should cut her losses and stop spending the remaining £5 million on Kahawa.[40]

Macleod did not find it easy to reply and deferred doing so until after the conference between the Colonial Office Ministers and East African Governors in January 1961. The big question there was how best to cherish the boon of Nyerere's initiative on federation, which was clearly designed to hasten independence all round, while playing for time in Kenya, where there was still so much to settle. After talking with the Governors Macleod thought he had found a clever way of squaring this circle. The important thing, he said, was not to confuse federation with independence. First, let Tanganyika be promised internal self-government in mid-May. Then let Nyerere convene talks in East Africa in August with the two other Chief Ministers on federation (on no account must the initiative appear to come from Britain). That meant that there must be Chief Ministers for Kenya and Uganda by then.

Macleod asked Renison whether, if it was the price of Federation, he could get a Chief Minister in place by June. Renison thought it possible but it would depend who the Chief Minister was. It was his hope that KANU would win the election because it had more able politicians, as compared with KADU which was 'a politicians' 2nd XI'. Mboya was the most forceful personality but was very young; perhaps he might be willing to work under Gichuru 'but the problem is that Gichuru has no personality'. Macleod however had formed a favourable impression of Gichuru when he had been over in London. He thought that the existence of Chief Ministers was Nyerere's touchstone. Given that, he would be ready, Macleod surmised, to accept 'regional independence' for Tanganyika, leaving the federal level still dependent on Britain until Kenya and Uganda had been sorted out. Moreover a federal government could be expected to take a less extreme attitude towards the military base than KANU in election mode.

With Renison and the local general pleading the bad effect on civilian and Service morale of any abandonment of the building programme at Kahawa, Macleod succeeded in overcoming Defence Ministry's worries. The only change was to be that the word 'base' would be dropped in favour of 'facilities'.[41]

THE KENYATTA ELECTION

But first there must be the election. The primary elections to qualify candidates for the reserved seats took place between 18 and 23

January 1961. Gathered together under the title of the Coalition Party and under the leadership of the ex-Speaker Sir Ferdinand Cavendish-Bentinck, the unreconstructed white settlers determined to make their last stand. Since the decisive vote in the main election would be African the Coalition's only hope of electing its candidates in the reserved seats (except for Nairobi West, which was a two-member seat) was to knock out the more liberal opposition in the primaries by denying it a quarter of the white vote. There would then be no choice for the common roll electorate.

The most spectacular campaign was the one that saw the Coalition's leader pitted against Michael Blundell for the Rift Valley seat. Cavendish-Bentinck was portrayed by his supporters as the man of integrity who had descended into the political arena to defend the interests of those whom he had encouraged to come and settle in Kenya, as contrasted with Blundell, the 'man of many voices' who had shifted from one expedient to another and who was now completely compromised by his acceptance of Macleod's constitution. Blundell, somewhat taken aback by the ferocity of the attack on him, held that only by working with Africans could European interests be preserved. In the event Coalition candidates won two seats by knock-out and one of the two seats in Nairobi West. These did not include Cavendish-Bentinck who received 1,545 votes to Blundell's 542, which, much as it disappointed Blundell, was just enough at 26.7 per cent to keep the latter in the race. Blundell then went forward to defeat his adversary by 20,009 to 2,051 in the main election and was thus committed to the service of an overwhelmingly African constituency, loyal to KANU and to Kenyatta. Altogether Blundell's New Kenya Party won four seats to the Kenya Coalition's three, the remaining two European seats being held by Independents.[42]

Before the African candidates faced the voters between the 19 and 27 February there was a sharp confrontation between the two wings of the KANU party. The one constituency in which the KANU theory that national politics should not relate to tribalism would be put seriously to the test was Nairobi East, the only seat in the capital that was not reserved for a minority candidate. With the ending of the Emergency and the removal of any residential or voting disqualifications from the Kikuyu this tribe would provide 27,000[43] out of the nearly 40,000 registered voters. In those circumstances could Mboya hold the seat? Or, to put the question the other way: was it right that after the Kikuyu had endured so much during the Emergency they should now be denied the high-profile representation that was their due?

Argwings-Kodhek had taken himself off to Luo country after the controversial merger of the two Nairobi parties. Central Nyanza had become a two-member seat and he was duly nominated there to run with Odinga as the official KANU candidates. In Nairobi there was persistent plotting by Kiano and others to find a really prominent Kikuyu challenger to take on Mboya, who was after all the General Secretary of their own party.[44] After various names such as Gichuru and Dr Mungai Njoroge had been canvassed in vain, the Independent candidate for Nairobi East turned out to be none other than Dr Munyua Waiyaki, a Kikuyu brain surgeon whom Mboya had trusted to be his branch chairman.

The rumour that Mboya had been marked down to be Chief Minister by the British, desperate to cut out Kenyatta, was now being assiduously promoted. Odinga issued a press statement on 16 January accusing Gichuru and Mboya of holding 'furtive meetings' with Macleod with that object in view and on 24 January Odinga, together with Mungai and Margaret Kenyatta, Jomo's politically active daughter, openly supported Waiyaki's nomination. Kiano, somewhat more covertly, was attempting to organize the Central Province against Mboya.[45] Odinga was determined to make the contest 'the Kenyatta election' and in this he largely succeeded. Under pressure, Mboya and Gichuru felt obliged to undertake not to take office until the release had taken place.

Some of Mboya's counter-moves were not well conceived. He announced a strike to force Kenyatta's immediate release. But workers were not prepared to come out simply at his say-so. Next he tried, through Gichuru, to drum Odinga out of the party. Following Waiyaki's nomination the party president on 30 January 1961 suspended Odinga as vice-president and summoned a special meeting to effect his dismissal. The party, said Gichuru, must rid itself of destructive elements and not appear to be influenced by Russia or China. 'We are determined not to allow another "Congo" to develop in Kenya by inviting foreign interference from either East or West.'[46]

Addressing the Governing Council of the party on 3 February about 'this non-compatibility of the officials . . . which has led many to think that KANU is a mere house of wax', Mboya accused Odinga of not being motivated by 'anything else than the wish to eliminate me from political life'.[47] Odinga proved strong enough to repel this attempt to cast him out. The meeting lasted twelve hours, for eight of which Gichuru, Mboya and Odinga had to wait outside. At the end Odinga was reinstated and Gichuru and Mboya were warned to 'do their jobs more conscientiously'.

Only one thing could rescue Mboya now: his ability to reach out to the people. He put on a spectacular campaign, in which his slogan of 'ndege' – aeroplane – symbolized the student airlift to the United States. When the votes were counted on 27 February Mboya had received 31,407 against Waiyaki's 2,668. It was a stunning success and ensured his unchecked prominence up to and beyond independence. It did not end, however, the intrigues against him.

In the colony and protectorate as a whole a remarkable 84 per cent of the electorate voted in the 44 contested seats. KANU received 67.4 per cent of the vote and 19 seats. KADU polled 16.4 per cent and got 11 seats. Outside Nairobi tribal loyalties were paramount. Many results were of a highly lopsided nature as between parties. In such cases the party indiscipline which resulted in an official candidate being challenged and in some cases (such as in Kisii) being defeated by a fellow party member did not really matter. But in at least two cases (Nakuru Town and North Nyanza) KANU lost seats because its vote was split. Three African members were unaffiliated to either party.

Because of the constitutional provision for twelve National Members (four of each race) to be elected in the Legco, it was necessary for the new legislature to meet before it could be fully constituted. Here the alliance between the New Kenya Party and KADU was fully revealed. By superior discipline and careful manoeuvring they extracted nearly the maximum possible advantage: three out of four additional members in each of the four categories. The only KANU-backed European who got in was Derek Erskine, a former MLC who had had to resign his seat because of the extreme unpopularity of his pro-African views. In physical appearance Erskine might have been taken as a typical cavalry officer, but he was a personal friend of Jomo Kenyatta and had done much to support the Kenyatta family during his long incarceration. He would not be quite alone, because in a dramatic switch Bruce McKenzie, though elected a National Member on the NKP ticket, was shortly to identify himself with KANU.

KENYATTA UNVEILED

Because of the KANU candidates' pledge not to take office without Kenyatta – each candidate had also pledged himself if elected to be ready to resign to create a vacancy for his leader – the questions of Kenyatta's freedom and of the composition of the new Government were inextricably linked. Macleod's plan was, first, to install African Ministers; then later to advance one of them to the post of Chief Minister; and, after a period in which he had been fully run in, to release Kenyatta who would by then it was hoped be a back number. It must be remembered that no one had seen Kenyatta for many years. He was thought to have grown old and exhausted by long detention in a hostile climate; he was said to be a heavy drinker; it was not known whether he was in touch with political developments. It was increasingly felt by the authorities that his complete silence was giving him a spurious prestige.

Renison invited four party leaders – Gichuru, Mboya, Ngala and Muliro – to Government House to listen while he delivered his latest thoughts on radio about the Kenyatta question. These were that Kenyatta was to be allowed to see political leaders, that he would be moved from Lodwar to Maralal and that he could there hold a press conference. But for the time being he could not be released from restriction. The four African leaders expressed disappointment but not anger and asked for permission to see Kenyatta, which was immediately granted. Renison added to Macleod, 'Their plans entirely exclude Odinga who is anathema to us all.'[48]

However their respective party colleagues were not having that. Their suspicion was that if just those four went they would persuade Kenyatta to authorize them to take office. It was left to KADU alone to breach the barrier that so long separated Kenyatta, Kaggia, Ngei and the others from Kenyan political life. When they got to Lodwar Kenyatta struck them as being surprisingly robust. He had recently been allowed a radio and newspapers. He showed impatience over the party divisions and asked to see representatives of both parties.

On 23 March a mixed delegation came – Gichuru, Odinga, Mboya and two others from KANU and Moi, Khamisi and four others from KADU. 'The immediate impression of the delegates was the dust and heat', recorded Mboya's minutes. Kenyatta took the chair for a three-and-a-half-hour meeting. 'There are some people,' he said, 'who think Kenyatta is an old man with old ideas and perhaps old brains. That is a false view which ought to be completely forgotten.' He was told of the bitter disputes within the KANU branches between ex-loyalists and ex-detainees and he vigorously denied that he was for either one or the other. He said that he had read the party policies and could see no difference between them and he berated the political leaders for contributing to his continued restriction because of their disunity and quarrels. He wanted the meeting to pass a resolution 'that from now on KADU and KANU work as one body on all national issues'.

This was blocked by Moi who wanted it to be known that under no circumstances would KADU consider a merger with KANU. The real problem, he said, was within KANU; it was there that the personality problems and lack of discipline were to be found. It was Bildad Kaggia who resolved the matter by suggesting they concentrate on two essentials: Kenyatta's immediate and unconditional release and the achievement of full independence in 1961. Mboya produced wording that committed both parties to work together for these objectives; it was endorsed over Moi's strongly expressed objections.[49]

PRESS CONFERENCE AT MARALAL

Kenyatta was shortly thereafter moved to Maralal, a pleasant hill station halfway between Lodwar and Nairobi. On 11 April sixty-five newspapermen, television commentators and cameramen, including a handful of Africans, travelled the 180 miles from Nairobi either by an alarmingly primitive road or tiny Piper planes to meet him. Renison's 'de-bunking' operation was to begin. The Governor had, in the present author's contemporary account, 'left no doubt that he was deliberately using the press as an instrument of government', to prise open the mystery of 'whether Kenyatta was mentally and physically capable of taking part in politics, whether he was aware of recent developments and in what frame of mind he looked to the future'.

The man who appeared was vigorous and in complete command of himself. He was bearded and wore a leather jerkin and corduroy trousers, red tie and multicoloured shirt. He was carrying a staff with a circular handle and an ornamental fly-whisk. He had a deep voice and spoke slowly in generally fluent English, with an occasional searching for a half-remembered word. The contemporary account went on:

The press conference started slowly and in almost too velvety a tone; all the necessary questions were courteously put and conscientiously answered during the course of three hours . . . Kenyatta, so he says, has always believed in non-violence and will never change; he has dedicated his life to African nationalism but any resident of any colour can, if he wishes and obeys the laws, become a citizen of independent Kenya with equal rights; and he ungrudgingly acknowledges the need for an African Government to have outside advisers and capital . . .

He had denounced Mau Mau in the past – what more could he say? He was against violence and illegal oathing. The findings of the court at Kapenguria and the more recent Corfield report were 'a pack of lies' supplied by paid informers. But he bore no grudge. The two sides in the Kikuyu civil war – those in the forest and those in the Home Guards – should be equally accepted now as 'brothers and sisters' . . .

The one thing he declined to do was to rescue the Governor from his constitutional crisis by telling the other African leaders to take office without insisting on having him released first . . .

Despite the quite touching faith which politicians and civil servants sometimes display in the ability of journalists to lay bare the inner man, I seriously doubt whether the Governor is any better off as the result of our journey.[50]

This conjecture was accurate. 'His performance at the press conference, Renison reported to Macleod, 'gave every indication he has not changed materially since the evil days of 1952',[51] and Macleod told Ngala and Derek Erskine, who were together in London, that he had not gained much comfort from the press interview.[52]

MACLEOD BACKPEDALS

Macleod himself was at this time going through a wrenching experience in connection with the Northern Rhodesian constitution whose shape would determine the future existence of the Central African Federation. His relations were exceptionally tense both with Sir Roy Welensky, the Federal Prime Minister in Salisbury, and with his own Cabinet colleague, the Commonwealth Secretary Duncan Sandys. The notorious onslaught from the Tory grandee Lord Salisbury, which has already been extensively quoted, had taken place on 7 March. The appalled Tory Ministers in the Lords reacted according to their temperament – Lord Perth offering a short and dignified personal statement of solidarity with Macleod, Lord Kilmuir drenching Salisbury in vitriol on the first day of the debate and Lord Hailsham repeating the performance in his own fashion on the second. Many peers, feeling that it was not for this that they had come to grace the Upper House, headed for the exit.[53]

Politically the Rhodesian question was a much greater threat to the internal cohesion of the Tory party than Kenya. But the one feature of the Kenya situation which was capable of arousing emotions in Britain comparable to those aroused over Central Africa was the question of Jomo Kenyatta. 'It is worth noting,' said Macleod in mid-April after a short visit to East Africa, 'that European feeling about Kenyatta's release is much stronger in Britain than in fact it is in Kenya.'[54]

Whereas initially Macleod had unquestionably led the breakthrough over Kenya he was now backpeddling and attempting to slow down the pace. The idea of Kenyatta as Chief Minister was 'of course, unthinkable', he told the Cabinet's Colonial Policy Committee. But, if not Kenyatta, who? There was one obvious candidate; at least he seemed obvious to the Colonial Secretary and to senior Kenya Government officials such as Walter Coutts, the retiring Chief Secretary and Eric Griffith-Jones, the Minister for Legal Affairs. That candidate was Tom Mboya.

Walter Coutts, who was still declaring that Kenyatta's release 'would undoubtedly be disastrous',[55] was figuratively taking Mboya up to a very high place and showing him the kingdoms of the earth. 'Talking to him,' he recalled later, 'I remember using the expression that the clock of time had now struck for Mboya. Did he not think that it was time he seized power in Kenya?' Mboya replied firmly, 'No, I'm sorry, if these people feel they are not going to come in without Kenyatta, then I don't come in either.'[56] Coutts always regarded this failure to grasp the opportunity of cutting out Kenyatta as evidence that, for all his qualities, Mboya lacked moral courage. This does not seem right. Mboya had the intelligence to see how crucial the mood of the Kikuyu would be in the transition to independence. If he went for the office of Chief Minister while still only thirty he would fatally antagonize that able, quarrelsome, conspiratorial tribe. He had just met Kenyatta and realized that he was in vigorous possession of his faculties. He had also come to believe that Kenyatta alone had the will and the prestige to heal the wounds of the Kikuyu civil war. Unless this was done the auspices for an orderly *uhuru* (freedom) were not good.[57]

A GOVERNMENT AT LAST

During a short stop-over at the RAF's Kenya base at Eastleigh in early April Macleod met separately delegations from KANU, KADU and the NKP. He turned down both Muliro's proposal that Kenyatta be released two months after the formation of the new Kenya Government and the suggestion of Kariuki Njiri, a young Kikuyu member for Fort Hall, that, since he was so unsure of Kenyatta's intentions and personality, he and Renison should straight away go to see him for themselves. This was the kind of dramatic gesture that in other circumstances might have appealed to Iain Macleod. But he frankly told KANU that he must be permitted to exercise his own judgment about the timing of Kenyatta's release because it was of 'some political delicacy' in Britain. He had been attacked by many who believed that advance in Kenya was too rapid. Macleod told Blundell that it would be 'an utter disaster' to give way on Kenyatta. Blundell's advice was that acceptance of office by KADU would, if successful, serve to break up the KANU front; a minority Government in the first instance would after a while prove to be no longer so as it acted as a magnet for other elements, including perhaps even Mboya.[58]

At home that advice was strongly supported by Macleod's deputy, the Earl of Perth. He wrote on 13 April 1961:

> The more I think on Kenyatta the more I am convinced that we are right to bend all our efforts to get KADU and others to form a government. What you would in effect be doing is backing the Rest, who are in fact the majority versus the Kikuyu and Luo (two-thirds versus one-third). Knowing the fears of the Rest such a government might, if launched and strongly backed, last a long time. It certainly represents the best chance for European interests.[59]

In mid-April Macleod received Ronald Ngala at the Colonial Office and seems to have to put some steel into him. At any rate, Ngala went back to Nairobi and accepted from the Governor the title of Leader of Government Business. Masinde Muliro became Minister of Commerce, Daniel arap Moi became Minister of Education and Bernard Mate, a Meru who had been elected for KANU, crossed the floor to be Minister of Health and Social Affairs. There were altogether five African Ministers, one Asian, three settlers – including Blundell back at the Ministry of Agriculture – and, in addition to the Governor, four civil servants. The Chief Secretary disappeared, but the new post of Deputy Governor was filled by Eric Griffith-Jones. It was a political government of sorts but it represented minorities both of the black and the white population.

It was a government, too, without Ibrahim Nathoo, the Asian who had been Minister of Works since 1954. Macleod had urged him to carry on but he had gloomily complained of the insupportable pressures, personal and political, on him to quit. Nathoo had got used to being a Minister and wanted to hold on to his job but he was an Ismaili, a follower of the Aga Khan, and Prince Karim's blunt ruling that the sect could not be seen as standing in the way of Kenyatta's release was in the end decisive for him.[60]

The Asian community was feeling that whoever gained from the changes that were bound to take place they were the ones most likely to lose. Mostly, they had kept their heads down but their prominent figures were increasingly feeling the need to associate themselves with those Africans who seemed most likely to end up as the winners. Still, Arvind Jamidar accepted the Ministry of Works in the minority government. Renison used his power to create eleven nominated members so as to give his new democratic government a parliamentary majority.

On the very day that the new Kenya Government took office Macmillan received a note from Lord Home, the Leader of the House of Lords. He had received a minatory message from one of the major Tory grandees, Viscount Swinton, a former Commonwealth Secretary. 'You should know,' Home wrote, 'that Lord Swinton told me that if [Kenyatta] was released there would be a revolt in the Conservative Party and he would be among the rebels.' He had gone on that 'the idea of his release was utterly repugnant to decent-minded people'.[61]

Renison had asked permission to give the new Government a fair wind with an announcement that a house would be built for Kenyatta in the Kiambu area to replace the one that had been demolished, and that in due course if conditions were stable when it had been built he would be moved to it. Macmillan told Macleod that the Governor's formula was acceptable so long as the words 'in due course' meant that the necessary security conditions for Kenyatta's release would remain.[62] Macleod wanted to see the Governor's opening speech to the new Legco in advance. 'Frankly, I was disturbed by what you told me over the telephone of the draft paragraphs in your speech and I am sure we cannot go nearly as far. It is always being said that we set out to pull a constitution down before it has had a chance to work.'[63] But Renison was responding to a new set of Ministers, who in turn had the motive of proving to the country that they were no traitors. He wanted to announce that the post of Chief Minister would be created before the end of 1961 – a sure signal that independence was coming – and also that further constitutional advances were on the way, to be worked out in Kenya without need of another London conference. He was ahead of the Colonial Secretary now. Macleod responded sharply to the full draft of his proposed speech. 'I am sorry that we are not in agreement on this matter . . . the howl of triumph on the one hand and of fury on the other that would go up if, in the very first speech in the Legislative Council, you held out the prospect of the early constitutional advance that you propose would, I am sure, be most damaging.'[64]

Having won a few months' grace while Kenyatta's house was being built, Macleod now needed a Chief Minister. He wanted to give the post to Ronald Ngala well before the house was completed. But he had reckoned without the Governor, who was not prepared to recommend this because 'Ngala is not, I fear, of the necessary stature for such a post.'[65] Macleod rejoined that, 'I cannot agree to the post being created until I know definitely who should be Chief Minister.'[66] But it was a telegram from Griffith-Jones to Max Webber at the Colonial Office that had Macleod really worried. This summarized a discussion in the Council of Ministers, whose drift was that the sooner Kenyatta was released the better because that would oblige him to disclose his intentions. Macleod was exasperated that, having been urged to authorize the Maralal press conference because of the need to reveal Kenyatta's intentions, he was now presented with the same argument to justify a further concession. He was also seriously concerned at the likely domestic political backlash. 'I need not emphasize to you how explosive here this matter is and I feel that I must make it clear that HMG cannot contemplate either early release or amendment of the constitution,' he burst out to the Governor.[67]

THE RETURN OF KENYATTA

But events were advancing fast in Kenya and some people at least
were beginning to adjust their thoughts to a rapidly changing future. Members of the Central Province Advisory Council, representative of Kikuyu loyalists, said on 16 June that while they would
never themselves have sponsored Kenyatta's return to the Province,
they had come to realize that he was bound to be released un-
conditionally on the day of independence and they considered it
the lesser of two evils to do it before independence while the British
were still in charge. The Kenya Intelligence Committee recommended
that once Kenyatta had moved to Kiambu the Government should
announce its intention to free him from all restriction shortly. Blundell
went to see Kenyatta and came back with the feeling that 'he is a
man who on balance may well be now a constructive force in this
country.... I am certain that he should be released and that if he
wishes to enter politics we must allow him to do so.'[68] On 9 July
1961 Renison wrote to the Colonial Secretary:

> My considered view ... is that it is unlikely that Kenyatta's charac-
> ter has changed. He is arrogant, dominating and satanic ... That
> he sees himself in no other role than that of overall leader is
> certain as is the fact that he has the vigour and personality for
> the role ... If he is not released in the near future I think it is
> inevitable that my Government will be compelled to resign and I
> shall be unable to form another government.
>
> My recommendation, made with conviction but with a heavy
> heart, is therefore that you should make an announcement in
> the House of Commons before the forthcoming recess.[69]

There is a note in the Premier files at Kew which is a cry from
the heart from Macleod to Macmillan. It was on 26 July, the eve
of the decisive meeting of the Cabinet. 'I am deeply worried about
this matter which affects my personal position with the Party. There
is almost universal agreement in Kenya that Kenyatta should be
released ... [Y]esterday the Governor had to telephone from Nairobi
to say that the resignation of his Government was imminent unless
we could make a statement on Kenyatta fairly soon. This would be
a disastrous outcome of all our work in Kenya.'[70]

　　The announcement on 1 August was much better received than
Macleod had feared. Kenyatta's house, a standard District Com-

missioner's residence, was completed at Gatundu, in the Kiambu
district of Central Province and on 14 August Kenyatta was transferred there under restriction and a week later released. On the
day of his arrival the house was stuffed to overflowing with gifts,
many of them from Asians, all very prominently labelled and en-
graved with the names of the donors. The atmosphere was relaxed
and *en fête* with the different races mingling with each other and
some African women dancing and ululating with Oginga Odinga in
their midst. Tom Mboya, wandering around a little out of place,
observed to a British journalist, 'It is particularly fitting that Kenyatta
should have come back on the eve of my thirty-first birthday', which
seemed an odd remark to make in the circumstances.[71] When Jomo
Kenyatta arrived he struck people as looking younger and fitter
than might have been expected. The Kenya Africans had got their
leader.

7 Majimbo

'It would be in Kenya's general interests that those who are in power just before independence should be those who have a reasonable chance of continuing into independence, otherwise their period of tutelage is but a waste of time.' (Tom Mboya, *East African Standard*, 13 July 1961)

On 8 October 1961 Iain Macleod was removed from the colonial sphere in which he had made his name to become Leader of the House of Commons and Chairman of the Conservative Party. Macmillan had positive reasons for effecting the change: Macleod was, he said, a thrilling speaker, he had worked at Central Office before and both his new appointments were deliberately designed to give the party a distinctively 'progressive Tory' stamp in the two to three years up to the next election.[1] Nevertheless, one factor on Macmillan's mind was that at the Colonies Macleod had proved to be 'although a brilliant and most likeable man ... not an easy colleague'. 'He is a Highlander – which means that he is easily worked up into an emotional mood; it also means that he is proud and ambitious,' the Prime Minister had noted in his diary in June.[2] Pride now made it difficult for Macleod to leave the Colonial Office with so much work uncompleted; ambition, however, made his next two posts attractive. He was hailed in the press as having been marked out as Macmillan's most likely successor,[3] though in truth the tag 'too clever by half' was to guarantee that he never became a competitor for No. 10.

The new Colonial Secretary was Reginald Maudling. The large shambling figure with the easy-going manner seemed to offer a contrast with the taut, more combative style of Macleod. Macmillan thought that Maudling would cause him less trouble; in reality, he noted in his diary, he found his new Colonial Secretary *'plus noir que les nègres*, more difficult and intransigent than his predecessor'.[4] Intellectually he was an exceptionally gifted man, with a mind so quick as to leave his civil servants lastingly impressed.[5] His reputation for laziness could to a degree be attributed to the speed at which he worked. However, he never quite avoided the suspicion that because academic honours had come easily to him he had acquired early the habit of counting too much on his remarkable powers of last-minute assimilation.

ENTER PETER OKONDO

The same day that the Cabinet reshuffle was announced a caller from Kenya was received in the Colonial Office. This was Peter Habenga Okondo, Parliamentary Secretary to the Ministry of Finance[6] and one of the KADU Party's rare intellectuals. He had come with the party's outline proposals for the future constitution of Kenya. They were a great shock to officials; for one thing, they disabused anyone who might think that there was nothing to tell between the moderate groups in the two parties. They had been drawn up with the assistance of the leading figures in Blundell's New Kenya Party and they represented a radical departure both from the style of government Kenya had known so far and from the Westminster model towards which it had hitherto been heading.

Peter Okondo himself was the first Kenya African graduate in accountancy, having attended Cape Town University where he joined the Communist Party. He said that he particularly enjoyed the party's evening lectures on such subjects as aeronautics.[7] When he got back to Kenya in 1951, he was an embarrassment to the authorities, not on account of his being a Communist because of this they had no knowledge (and the Communist Party itself seems to have forgotten that he had ever been a member), but because of his qualifications. He wanted public employment and as a university graduate would not accept less than 700 shillings a month. His Provincial Commissioner wrote, 'I do not hold out much hope of this man ever being rehabilitated ... He is a typical example of how undesirable it is to send Kenya Africans to South Africa for higher education.'[8]

Okondo took a job with Oginga Odinga as an accountant for Luo Thrift, where he found business practices not quite up to his standards – capital treated as income, overheads not costed, no relationship between cash in till and cash sales, no provision for losses and no insurance. After trying to sort Odinga out he set up his own Okondo School of Commerce while continuing to edit Odinga's journal *Dunia Keuta*. He joined KAU in the last months of its existence and was elected its Auditor. During the Emergency he learnt that he was in danger of arrest and fled to Uganda, where the Governor employed him in the civil service. Later he got a well-paid job with Shell, but his interest in politics remained and, after failing to get a KANU nomination in Nyanza, he joined KADU and was elected as a National Member, where he devoted his energies to providing his party with a theoretical foundation for the policy named *majimbo*. This could be translated as federalism or regionalism and was intended to institutionalize the idea that Kenyan nationhood must of necessity have a tribal foundation.[9] It promised to combine the American and Swiss models (Okondo's second wife was Swiss) so as to provide something which was a complete departure from the Westminster system.

Colonial Office officials, whose aim was to promote a coalition of moderates of all parties and races, were instead faced with a KADU/NKP core of moderation which proposed to make revolutionary changes to the traditional structure of government. 'The idea of an American type of constitution is ludicrous,' thundered Leslie Monson, the Assistant Under-Secretary. 'The American Constitution, one of the most cumbrous forms ever thrust upon themselves by human beings, has only survived because the central government asserted its authority in one of the bloodiest civil wars in history.'[10] Alarmingly the approach was acquiring some political support in Britain. According to the Tory backbencher Patrick Wall, 'A Westminster-type constitution will lead to dictatorship and the exodus of Europeans and Asians . . . KADU assisted by the New Kenya Party are determined not to be out-manoeuvred by HMG as they were in 1960.'[11]

UHURU NA MAJIMBO

KADU was not confining itself to producing constitutional papers. Out in the rural constituencies were tribesman like the Kalenjin who feared that in the Highlands the Kikuyu were penetrating everywhere and would be much the quickest off the mark when it came to sharing out formerly white farms. Speeches did not always match Nairobi spokesmen's careful respect for the name and fame of Jomo Kenyatta, especially once he had committed himself to KANU. There were none too subtle reminders that the Kalenjin group of tribes made a disproportionate contribution to the armed forces on which the central government would, in the final analysis, need to rely.

Many rallies were held like that at the end of October 1961 at

Iten, a remote village in western Kenya on the borders of the Rift Valley settler country and the Eleygo Marakwet Reserve. The young warriors of the KADU Youth Wing squatted where they had parked their spears and their vividly quartered shields and chorused the newly-learnt slogan *Uhuru na Majimbo*. It had been raining and older Kalenjin tribesmen huddled in their damp animal skins or European dungarees. They had come to listen to their local member, William Murgor, the Parliamentary Secretary to the Ministry of Defence and Internal Security, who leapt on top of a trestle table. A contemporary account goes on:

Murgor, an ex-chief, resplendently attired in Red Indian-like headdress with waving plumes and beaded chin-strap, red toga knotted African-style on the shoulder, a ceremonial fly-whisk in one hand and a modern shooting stick in the other, was prancing out his animosity against Jomo Kenyatta and the whole Kikuyu tribe. 'Our people who fought in Burma, what did they fight for? Freedom!' he declaimed in a high, squeaking voice. 'Kenyatta has said that the Kikuyu are spread all over the country, but they won't come here ... I say that, if the Government cannot move the Kikuyu squatters from the Kapsabet forest, we shall have to take steps to do it. Do you support me?' [Cries of 'Yes!' 'Yes!']

The Parliamentary Secretary for Internal Security went on, 'The school opened for the Kikuyu children ... should be closed', and then he came to the heart of the matter. 'I was insulted by the Kikuyu in the Nakuru meeting.' At this the Minister raised his shooting stick and beat furiously on the table until the stick was smashed into the shape of a scimitar. Then he whipped off his plumed hat and, sawing the air with parallel movements of this in one hand and the flywhisk in the other, croaked hoarsely, 'If Kenyatta orders the Kikuyu in Nakuru to declare war on the rest of the tribes we are ready for them.'[12]

Blundell, in a letter on 1 February 1962 to Walter Havelock, the NKP Minister for Local Government, reported that he had seen Renison and informed him that KADU would insist on regionalism as a major objective. He added that 'we must hope that KANU will break and that some elements in KANU can form a broader government with KADU by which the evil elements in KANU can be defeated', because 'any constitution which is likely to end in

Jomo and Odinga on top must mean the end of everything we have tried to create in Kenya and the elimination of the European community'.[13]

KENYATTA REDIVIVUS

Jomo Kenyatta was now in a position to re-enter politics and assert his leadership. The initial impression he made was not particularly encouraging. As in 1946 his long absence from the scene caused him to be for a while hesitant and imprecise. While Mboya seemed to be marginalized, Odinga was much in evidence as Kenyatta's business manager – keeping him in Communist bloc funds, according to Special Branch reports, and organizing his attendance at Tanganyika's Independence Day in December 1961 – and he appeared in public surrounded by the 'old gang' of released detainees. Worse, he seemed to endorse, at least by his presence on the same platform, the anti-European sentiments of one of them, the rather wild Kamba leader Paul Ngei.[14] Jock Leslie-Melville of the NKP wrote to a supporter in London at the beginning of November,

KANU are trying to sell Kenyatta to the British public as 'a dear, kindly old soul, full of honest and benevolent intentions towards everyone'. Naturally our machine must be brought to bear to prove exactly the opposite – that Kenyatta is a tribalist ... that he had the thing on a plate when he came out of jug and has managed to do nothing, that he is scared stiff of the thug element and has surrounded himself with ex-detainees.[15]

But appearances were misleading. Kenyatta was feeling his way with politicians whom he scarcely knew. According to his friend Derek Erskine he showed in private 'disdain and intolerance' for his fellow ex-prisoners except for the Luo Achieng Oneko. He had his initial reservations about Mboya. He said to Bruce McKenzie, who, despite being white, rapidly gained his confidence, 'They tell me that you are the man who can control this hotheaded young Mboya.'[16] There were three questions to be settled about Kenyatta's immediate political future: whether he was going to join one or other party or whether he would form his own party,[17] whether he wanted to enter the Legco and if so who was going to create a vacancy for him, and whether the law would be altered which rendered him, as an ex-convict, ineligible for Legco service. Odinga thought he had the perfect answer. Kenyatta should lead KANU but a KANU that looked very different from hitherto, a KANU in which all the officers (except for Odinga as deputy president) were ex-detainees. Odinga reminded all KANU MLCs of their individual pledges to resign in Kenyatta's favour and argued that, the Nairobi seat having the highest profile, the ideally placed candidate for running on to his own political sword was Tom Mboya.[18]

MAUDLING IN THE SADDLE

Constitutional talks between KADU and KANU had been dragging on week after week under the Governor's dogged but uninspired chairmanship throughout August, September and October 1961, and in November a failed attempt was made to form an interim coalition government. KANU as the majority party was not willing to be a mere add-on to an incumbent government; it claimed the right to serve as an equal partner to the KADU–NKP combination. Meanwhile in the Asian camp the executive of the Kenya Indian Congress was deciding that backing a minority government was too risky an undertaking for an exceptionally exposed community and in October 1961 it switched support from government to opposition. Two of its three MLCs obeyed the decision to cross the floor but its Minister, Arvind Jamidar, clung to his office and in sympathy the Secretary-General of the Congress resigned his party post. Once more the ineffectiveness of Indian politics was on display.

Unhappily the one point on which all parties seemed agreed was that Renison was not a gifted chairman. KANU was openly demanding his replacement. But privately Government supporters were not any more complimentary. 'His bungling and ineptitude led us to the last breakdown', according to Leslie-Melville, a view that was shared by Blundell although KADU wished to avoid undermining a Governor whom they felt was basically on their side.[19]

On 28 October 1961 Kenyatta formally joined KANU and in November led a party delegation to London to press for a fresh constitutional conference. But he showed no interest in the Nairobi seat and, Maudling having insisted that his legal disqualification be removed, he accepted instead an offer (one of only four actually made) to enter the Legco in a by-election as one of the two members for Fort Hall. 'I recognize,' Maudling wrote to his colleagues, 'that

this involves some unpleasant implications, in particular the prospect of Kenyatta becoming Chief Minister and ultimately Prime
Minister but this is a problem that is inescapable.'[20]

Macmillan himself presided over the session of the Colonial Policy
Committee on 15 November, at which the Colonial Secretary said
equally bluntly that 'it is quite impracticable to contemplate ruling
Kenya for an extended period', by which he meant for longer than
another eighteen months. It was a session which was attended in
the absence of Duncan Sandys, the Commonwealth Secretary, by
his Parliamentary Under-Secretary, the eleventh Duke of Devonshire, grandson of the ninth Duke,[21] who had in 1923 declared that
in Kenya the interests of the Africans must be 'paramount'.

All were oppressed by the events in the Congo, which advanced
from crisis to crisis and which were approaching a showdown between
the UN and the Katangese secessionists. Maudling thought there
were only two ways of avoiding Congo-like disorder in Kenya: either
Britain must provide the necessary forces to enable her to impose
her rule for a number of years or she must find a constitution on
which both KANU and KADU would agree. The first option was
out; the second would be very hard to achieve. Maudling was
under no illusions that he could get away with promoting Ngala as
Prime Minister, nor had he any hope that Britain could give Kenya
only internal self-government without shortly following this up with
independence. 'Kenyatta will become Prime Minister, whether we
like it or not,' he said gloomily. He thought that 'the consequences
of this for the future of the Commonwealth are very serious', but
the only two ways of avoiding it were to delay independence or to
grant it on condition that Kenyatta did not become Prime Minister.
Neither was practicable. Macmillan, however, wound up the discussion by saying that they must try to get agreement on something
like the American constitution which did not include unfettered
parliamentary sovereignty.[22]

Kenyatta and his large delegation from KANU duly arrived in
Whitehall. It was thirty-two years since he had first sought to put
his case before a British Government. He expressed himself mod-
erately but firmly, leaving much of the detail about such topics as
KANU's readiness to guarantee property rights and the independence of the judiciary to Mboya. On one subject the KANU delegation
was explicit: the Governor, Sir Patrick Renison, had 'proved his
partisanship and prejudice against KANU'. One of his terrible broadcasts had come near to describing the party itself as subversive. He

had, it was said in no uncertain terms, committed himself to his KADU Ministers to such a degree that 'any hopes of advance from further talks under the Governor's chairmanship are entirely misplaced.'[23] Maudling declined to discuss this question but on the quick trip which he shortly afterwards made to Nairobi he began himself to doubt whether Renison was the right man to handle the next stage of the march to independence. One of the main gains of the KANU visit to London had been the beginning of a happier relationship between Kenyatta and British public opinion. In a major television interview on the BBC he had given a positive and reassuring impression.[24]

Maudling's quick mind and decisive manner when he went to Nairobi in November left a favourable first impression on hitherto frustrated politicians. He pleased them by promising a new constitutional conference in London in February to decide a framework agreement leading towards independence. KADU put much store by his conclusion that, in addition to a stable and competent central government, Kenya would need 'other governing authorities with their own defined rights which do not derive from the Central Government but are entrenched and written into the Constitution'.

But the African politicians said after he had gone that they were going to judge Maudling by the promptness by which he followed up on his promise to appoint two commissions, one to delimit constituencies, the other to set up regional boundaries. Unfortunately this was one of those matters which the Minister did not find particularly urgent.[25]

LANCASTER HOUSE REVISITED

On the eve of the second Lancaster House conference, which turned out to be a marathon running from 15 February to 6 April 1962, Maudling addressed a memorandum to the Colonial Policy Committee with brutal candour. 'It is not possible, even if we wished, to secure the continuance of European political power in Kenya,' he said. 'Nor is it likely that we shall see in Kenya a Government which is actively pro-Western in its foreign policy.' The Colonial Secretary then got down to cases:

Kenyatta and Odinga (who will not hesitate to continue to accept assistance from the Communist bloc) represent the extreme wing of the [KANU] party . . . I think it is fair to say that their approach is essentially tribal in character and if they come to power (and I would expect them to use any means of doing so) we can expect a determined effort to assert Kikuyu domination under Kenyatta's leadership throughout Kenya. Mboya is essentially national rather than tribal and genuinely anxious to build a strong and modern nation . . . I believe, therefore, that it would be very much in our interests to promote . . . a split [within KANU], especially if it resulted in a coalition between KADU and the Mboya element in KANU . . . Our ability to bring about such a split may depend to some extent on the tactics we adopt during the Conference.[26]

He told a session of the Colonial Policy Committee (CPC) on 2 February 1962 that although a federal system was the best hope for minorities it would be very costly and Kenya could not possibly afford it.

In reaching that last conclusion Maudling had been influenced by the dire report on Kenya's finances that had just been delivered. On 1 February Michael Cary, Macmillan's Deputy Private Secretary, who had been reading the same official report, briefed the Prime Minister before the CPC meeting over which he was to preside the following day in terms of eloquent despair:

Already in fact bankrupt but with worse to come, wholly lacking in political, cultural, social and economic cohesion, threatened with internal tribal strife and external attack from the north, but lacking in funds and forces to maintain adequate security services, an independent Kenya presents the least hopeful prospect of all the Colonial territories to which we have given or contemplate giving independence.

It is against such an assessment, made less than two years away from independence, that what was to be achieved by Kenyatta's Government once it had come to power can reasonably be judged. Cary went on to tell Macmillan that 'The Kenya extremists (notably Messrs Kenyatta and Odinga) are dangerous and unreliable.' 'It would be much easier for us,' he said, 'both before and after independence, to work with a government of the centre under Mr Mboya.'[27] In terms of their assessment of personalities, the British had reached a halfway point in the swing of the pendulum. They had started at aiming to separate 'moderates' like Ngala from the 'extremist' Mboya; now they were trying to split the 'moderate' Mboya from the 'extremists' Kenyatta and Odinga; in the future they were to favour the 'moderates' Kenyatta and Mboya at the expense of Oginga Odinga.

With Tanganyika already independent and Uganda due to follow in October 1962, the CPC felt that 'The best outcome would be East African Federation but, if Kenya falls too far behind the others, they may not be prepared to wait.' Macmillan repeated his admonition that 'something more like the American constitution' should be aimed at, in which guarantees should be deeply entrenched.[28] Maudling told the full Cabinet that when he had been in Nairobi he had found that independence was being widely predicted for the first half of 1963. The Provincial Commissioners, he said, had given him unanimous advice: (1) that that rate of advance was too rapid; and (2) that they could think of no way in which it could be slowed down.[29]

At this Macmillan came up with one of those characteristically daring but unworkable solutions which earned him a reputation for lateral thinking. Why not hand over Kenya to the United Nations as a trusteeship in order to stave off independence for about five years? This would have been a *bouleversement* indeed, since it had been one of the main preoccupations of British policy since the war to keep the hands of the UN Trusteeship Council off British colonies. The Permanent Secretary at the Colonial Office, Sir Hilton Poynton, had made his reputation largely as a stonewaller in New York. Because Macmillan's suggestion was Prime Ministerial, the Foreign Office felt it necessary to go through the motions of treating it seriously. The Colonial Office killed it stone dead.[30]

The constitutional conference began on 14 February in the Long Gallery at Lancaster House. Among the long succession of opening speeches, Ngala's emphasis was on democracy, pluralism and avoidance of the internal disruption occurring elsewhere in Africa. 'We wish to build a country in which dictatorship is impossible and . . . it is only if we manage to do this that we will finally be able to resist the menace of Communism. Already its agents are active in Kenya.' Kenyatta spoke of the importance of building a fully integrated nation with no racial or tribal discrimination, of the desirability of Kenya making an impact in Pan-African and international affairs, and of the overriding need to remove the atmosphere of uncertainty in the civil service. 'The answer can be found in only one decision at this conference, namely agreement on a date for full independence for Kenya.'

At first KANU, which in this conference was playing the 'conservative' role of being content to build on existing political and administrative systems, objected to the priority of treatment accorded to KADU's ideas. But observers noticed the grin that spread over Tom Mboya's face as KADU spokesmen were subjected to Maudling's sharp interrogations.[31] But Ngala, Okondo and their team were determined not to give much ground. They had worked out with the aid of a Swiss constitutional adviser, Dr Edward Zellweger, and a British MP, Frederic Bennett, their own framework for federation and, backed up by the two European Ministers, Michael Blundell and Walter Havelock, and the European Legco member from Mombasa, R. P. Cleasby, himself a lawyer and an advocate of Coastal autonomy, they defended it robustly. On 23 February, at the end of the first week Ngala wrote to Maudling:

> I feel that at this stage . . . I should leave you in no doubt as to the position of the KADU Parliamentary Group . . . [W]e have consistently made it clear that we cannot even consider, let alone accept, any constitutional proposals for Kenya which do not provide for regional governments with independent legislative powers and their own revenues, each being the effective administrative and executive authority for the region.[32]

KADU, badgered to provide more specific detail of their proposals, insisted that it was pointless to discuss other features of the constitution 'until and unless these principles, which we regard as fundamental to the future of our people in Kenya, have been agreed'. Committees on Land and Citizenship and on the Judiciary and the Public Service were set up but in early March Ngala told the Colonial Secretary that his group would take no further part in their work until satisfactory progress was forthcoming on the structure of government.[33]

Under the KADU plan Kenya would be a federal state, consisting of six regions and the federal territory of Nairobi. At the federal level there would be a bicameral legislature, with the Upper House representing the regions, with seven members elected from each region by the Regional Assembly, and the Lower House elected by universal adult suffrage in seventy one-member constituencies. The two houses would have equal powers of legislation (Peter Okondo stressing that there should be no question of a Kenyan House of Lords) and, in addition, the Upper House would have to approve a number of senior appointments, including members of the Supreme Court and senior officers in the armed forces. The Federal Council of Ministers would consist of ten to fifteen members drawn from all the regions, with a minimum of one and a maximum of three from each. After the Swiss fashion the Council would elect a chairman, who would also be Head of State, for one year only; he could be re-elected later but not immediately.

At the regional level there was to be an assembly, which would have legislative powers over listed matters as well as residual powers over all matters not specifically allocated to the centre, and an executive, headed by a President, elected by the legislature from among its members. Each region was to have its own Civil Service Commission appointed by the regional President, as well as its own constabulary and gendarmerie; only the CID and the Special Branch would be at the federal level. In addition to implementing their own legislation, the regions would be the normal body for implementing federal laws, but if a region failed to act it could be overridden by a Federal Commissioner appointed with the consent of the Upper House. A Bill of Rights should be entrenched in the constitution, dual citizenship should be permitted, and there would be no objection to land and property being owned by a non-citizen.

This KADU plan was in principle and in detail assaulted by KANU and its supporters. Derek Erskine, for instance, declared his anxiety that the Upper House would merely be a convention of regions with the consequence that the actual government would exist only at the regional level. The Prime Minister of Kenya, according to Erskine, would be no more than a Mayor whose term of office expired after a year, so that it would be doubtful if anyone would be capable of initiating policy in such an emasculated central government. Fitz de Souza, the Asian lawyer in KANU's team, wanted to know, since the civil service was to be organized at a regional level, what staff a Federal Commissioner would have to impose federal law on a recalcitrant region. That this was no academic question was being spelled out at that very time and for months past in the former Belgian Congo.[34] Mboya cited not only this fact but also the extreme difficulty the United States Government was at the time experiencing in enforcing federal decisions about civil rights on the Southern States.

KANU, too, was in favour of a Bill of Rights to be enforced by an independent judiciary and of the entrenchment of certain powers, mainly over land, but at local district level. Why, demanded Odinga, was KADU which was so against a unitary form of government at the centre so much in favour of it at the level of the region?[35] Local minority fears would not in his opinion be satisfied by *majimbo* since the majority tribe in a region would be able to dominate the others. Maudling observed afterwards that Odinga was 'the only man I have ever seen actually froth at the mouth in a moment of excitement, and his moments of excitement were many'.[36]

At the sixteenth plenary session on 19 March, when a working party produced its deadlocked report, Maudling confessed that it was disturbing that after five weeks of discussion there still was more disagreement recorded than agreement. This led Odinga to accuse the Colonial Secretary of shedding crocodile tears. KANU and KADU, he said, could easily have reached agreement if left to themselves. 'The trouble between them has been caused by the British Government placing agents among KADU.' Odinga warmed to his theme. The British were playing, he said, at 'divide and rule'. He had been called a communist but he had a great stake in Kenya. He had twelve children and was the biggest capitalist in the country with £50,000 worth of property. He was an African nationalist and no one could lure him away from a United Kenya to any form of regionalism.[37]

But it was not only critics in KADU that Odinga was worried about. He asserted that press briefings were going on behind his back about the dangers of communism; his worst suspicions were aroused by the closeness of Mboya, Gichuru and McKenzie who were staying together at the London home of the Aga Khan's representative in East Africa and he openly attacked the activities of Derek Erskine, whom he accused of joining KANU so as to sabotage it. Erskine, he complained, was going round making allegations that Odinga was training an army to usurp power in Kenya once it was independent.[38]

The Times came out with a leader, closely mirroring what is now known to have been the Colonial Office scenario. Calling for a national government in Kenya, it asserted that 'It is suggested in official quarters that there is no solution until Mr Kenyatta has been removed from his present position.' Mboya was designated as the only man who could transform the political scene by leading a substantial breakaway from KANU and forming an alliance with KADU. This judgment hugely underestimated the extent to which

Mboya was detested by leading members of KADU, notably Ngala and Muliro. For them the dictatorship which they repudiated was pre-eminently the dictatorship of Tom Mboya, though to be sure they also had in mind the idea of a collective dictatorship of the Kikuyu tribe.

In a manner reminiscent of 1923, with a switch of colour, the deadlock was accompanied by unnerving reports of the constantly deteriorating situation back in Kenya in the prolonged absence of almost the entire political class. In an open letter to Kenyatta on 13 March, the treasurer of KANU's Nairobi branch, A. M. Akech, reported that, 'The public are disturbed at such news that it is only yourself and Mr Oginga Odinga who are working hard at the conference and that the Rest of other KANU members spend most of their time in Bars. The public are also perturbed by the number of non-conference participants who are there as individual supporters . . . We demand an investigation as to how these people managed to get to London – who paid for their tickets and who keeps them in London.'[39]

The Colonial Secretary, having patiently sat out weeks of seemingly endless disputation, was ready, once most people were in a mood to accept his guidance, with a suggested compromise. But Kenyatta's role was also crucial and now saw the beginning of his exercise of real leadership. He addressed the KANU delegation, telling them that it was not possible to return with a report of failure. They might be forced to accept a constitution they did not want, but once they got independence they could change it later.[40] KANU members, many by now eager for office, accepted this advice with varying degrees of enthusiasm. Even Odinga, however reluctantly, went along with it because it came from the lips of his hero-figure.

Maudling's compromise was cheerfully contradictory though, thanks to the stubborn bargaining of KADU and their European advisers, it incorporated a good part of the *majimbo* doctrine. Subject to there being 'a strong and effective Central Government . . . responsible for a wide range of activities' (KANU principle), there was to be 'the maximum possible decentralization . . . to effective authorities drawing their being and power from the constitution and not from the Central Government' (KADU principle). The regional boundaries were, on the one hand, to be related to existing provinces (KANU), but, on the other hand, particular attention was to be paid to the wishes of those who desired to be grouped together in the same region (KADU). There was to be a second chamber, the Senate, to represent the regions (KADU) but it was to have similar powers and limitations as the House of Lords.

As well as the points decided, Maudling set up a series of commissions which were to report on regional boundaries, constituency delimitations, fiscal affairs and so forth whose mere existence created a stir during the ensuing months but which served to buy a little more time in which to press ahead with the Africanization of the senior civil service.

It was an integral part of the settlement that KANU and KADU should both hold office in the Government which was to negotiate the detail of the draft constitution. 'Reggie [Maudling], partly to obtain agreement and partly, I suspect, to persuade us to return home, framed his constitutional proposals in such a way that KADU signed them for their constitutional content whereas KANU signed them in order to participate in a coalition government,' Rhoderick Macleod, a settler MLC and KADU adviser, wrote to his brother and ex-Colonial Secretary, Iain.[41]

COALITION GOVERNMENT

The coalition government that was formed at the end of the conference was still headed by the Governor and the Deputy Governor, though it was announced that, since Renison was owed large amounts of leave, he would not be immediately returning. (This was interpreted by the Nairobi press corps that he would not be returning at all, but in this it was mistaken.) It would be Sir Eric Griffith-Jones, therefore, who would be presiding over the early stages of the attempt to agree on ways of carrying out the conference conclusions. There was to be no Chief Minister (though in his memoirs Maudling erroneously refers to Kenyatta and Ngala as Joint Premiers[42]) and two other posts (Legal Affairs and Defence) were still held by civil servants.

Kenyatta and Ngala were both made Ministers of State, Kenyatta for Economic Planning and Ngala for Administration and both for Constitutional Affairs. Of the KANU leaders, Gichuru was Minister of Finance, Mboya Minister of Labour and McKenzie Minister of Land Settlement. On the KADU side Moi took Local Government, Muliro remained at Commerce and Industry and Havelock was, after a slight delay, to replace Blundell as Minister of Agriculture.

The first notable absentee was the Vice-President of KANU, Oginga Odinga. Kenyatta had wanted him appointed Minister of Finance, but Maudling, after Kenyatta had appealed to him in private, wrote, 'I must repeat that it is impossible for me to accept as a member of the Government a man who is generally known to be in close contact with Communist Governments and in regular receipt of large sums of money from them.'[43] Maudling recorded that during the conference Tom Mboya and Bruce McKenzie used to see him frequently after meetings to assess how the work was going and to chart the way ahead.[44] No doubt it was partly as the result of this regular contact that Maudling became convinced that Kenyatta could not be excluded from the leadership. But he had at least separated him from Odinga.

The other notable absentee was Michael Blundell. He had chosen to step down after making an important contribution to the plans (shortly to be discussed) for resettling Africans on the former White Highlands. 'I do not really like some of the people who are in politics now,' he confessed to the author Elspeth Huxley. 'If Iain Macleod had left me a medium which I could have used to defeat these politicians I would have stayed but the truth of the matter is that a man like Bruce McKenzie can, largely because of his political outlook, always outflank men like Wilfrid Havelock and myself in the circumstances of Kenya today.' Blundell had been upset by the bitterness of the reaction of his mainly KANU constituents to his taking office in a KADU Government and disconcerted to discover the kind of patronage services that African voters expected from an elected Member.[45]

Over the long period of the conference Maudling had not been happy in his working relationship with the Governor. The feeling grew in the Colonial Office that it was not getting the range of imaginative advice from Renison that it was entitled to receive. Besides which he did not seem to enjoy the intimate contact with all African politicians that the situation appeared to require. 'How do you sack a Governor?' Maudling at one point asked the Assistant Under-Secretary concerned.[46] Sir Hilton Poynton, the Permanent Under-Secretary, pleaded for Renison's reputation and record and his overdue entitlement to leave. Maudling let the matter slide, allowing Griffith-Jones to take over for the time being. He did eventually tell Renison that he would have to go but there was delay in appointing a successor, so that the Governor still hoped that he had a reprieve.

Meanwhile, Blundell was dissatisfied with Griffith-Jones. By June he was writing to KADU's chief lobbyist, Frederic Bennett MP, that the Acting Governor should be replaced:

> He is out of tune with KADU generally. He is still obsessed with the idea of splitting KANU and Mboya emerging as the great national leader. This is quite impossible at the present time and I attended a meeting . . . with Mboya and Griffith-Jones in which Mboya told him this quite bluntly.
>
> Mboya's idea is that after the General Election KANU might manage to form a Government with Kenyatta as Prime Minister. Kenyatta might then feel strong enough to isolate Odinga and invite some of the KADU group to support his Government.[47]

As a prediction of how events were to fall out over time this summary of Mboya's views was strikingly sound. Griffith-Jones meanwhile was reporting to Maudling that the influence of Blundell with KADU was declining.

THE MILLION-ACRE SCHEME

Not all the time of the Lancaster House conference was concerned with constitutional niceties, though one might be forgiven for thinking so. Lord Delamere, the President of the Kenya National Farmers Union and son of the pioneer colonist, urged Blundell at the outset of the Conference not to let zeal for regionalism carry him too far. '[T]he European farmer,' he wrote, 'regards the formation of a Central Land Authority as his only hope for the future. Any thought that he would be satisfied with some extension of the present settlement schemes under local control should be dismissed from your mind.'[48]

These settlement schemes had first been launched after the ending in 1960 of the exclusively white character of the Highlands. They had started out as a means of diluting the bad impression created abroad, especially in the United States, by the European monopoly; they were not designed specifically to respond to the problem of landlessness. As the rapid approach of African independence became apparent many white farmers who wished to leave in the new circumstances were willing sellers looking desperately for a willing buyer. The British Government at first looked hopefully towards the World Bank, partly simply as a source of loan funds but also as an international body which would be more suitable than an ex-colonial power to enforce the disciplines of repayment for years after the British departure. In all these matters the Earl of Perth, with his background in international banking, played a major role.[49]

But the World Bank works to certain rules, the most important of which in this context is that loans must be for development of the economy and not mere transfer of ownership. In so far as KANU's favourite proposition about the Highlands – that there was a great deal of fertile land about that was not being properly developed by white farmers[50] – was true, it should not have been difficult to meet the Bank's criteria. It was calculated that an acre of grassland supporting sheep worth an annual gross return of less than £5 might be turned over to coffee at £130 or to tea and pyrethrum (a very effective insecticide) at £60–£90, but this was to prove very optimistic.[51]

In practice, the first two schemes – the Yeoman scheme (as in 'sturdy yeoman') and the Smallholder scheme – in which the World Bank participated in association with the Colonial Development Corporation had taken a long time to get under way. The Kenya Government had transmitted its application for a loan to the Bank in June 1960 and it was November 1961 before the Bank finally agreed. The Yeoman scheme bore fully the marks of the World Bank's criteria. The yeomen in question were to be men with farming experience, managerial capacity and adequate financial resources – in other words, members of the African middle class. And 1,800 families were to be settled on 90,000 acres of high potential, under-developed land on holdings of 50 acres.

Unfortunately this scheme soon ran into trouble. Africans able to put up the £50 required did not want to take ready-made holdings not chosen by themselves. Also some Africans, influenced by radical politicians such as Odinga and Kaggia, who argued that Kenya should not be saddled with any debts for regaining African land from Europeans, called for a boycott of the scheme. Violence was sometimes threatened to anyone who took it up. Moreover, arguments about tribal 'spheres of influence' made it difficult to find suitable blocks of land. The emphasis was accordingly switched to the 'assisted owner' approach, where the European farmer was to find his own purchaser and draw up a plan. This increased the flow of African families into the highlands but in doing so the Settlement Board departed rather far from the terms so meticulously negotiated with the World Bank which then declined to acquiesce.

The Smallholder scheme also enlisted international finance through the World Bank with a view to settling 6,000 families on 90,000 acres of high potential underdeveloped land. By the middle of 1962, 25,000 acres had been bought and 731 families were being settled on them. But by then it had become plain to the British Government that if they did not speed up the process to meet the social pressures particularly from landless Kikuyus the chances of a smooth transition to independence were slim. Already there were sinister intelligence reports of a Kenya Land Freedom Army operating in the Rift Valley with a recurrence of illegal oathing and drilling and a proliferation of shadow titles, such as 'District Commissioner', 'Senior Superintendent' and 'Attorney-General'. The oaths, as with Mau Mau, committed the takers to steal guns, to eliminate KADU, not to inform and to kill. Three instances were found of an oath to kill Kenyatta 'if he sells the country'.[52] The colonial courts convicted 736 Africans of oathing and illegal possession of arms; another 1,313 people were convicted in the African courts. The question was naturally being asked: is it starting all over again?

Concurrently with the World Bank's Smallholder scheme it was decided to start a New Smallholder scheme, which did away with the need for any agricultural experience on the part of the applicant, did not require the land to be settled to be of high potential, and provided a much smaller loan (£100 instead of £400) for developing it. Smallholders were to be given free transport to their new farms, maintenance during settling and assistance with building materials. The Federal German Government agreed to contribute to the financing.

Even this was overtaken during the course of 1962 by a heightened sense of urgency to cut off unrest. The Earl of Perth announced in July that Britain would finance a really dramatic expansion of high density settlement; Maudling himself came over to Nairobi to launch it. This was the product of a skilled lobbying operation in the margins of second Lancaster House by those European groups which had been marginalized by the political deals at first Lancaster House. Lord Delamere for the Kenya National Farmers' Union (KNFU) and Maconochie Welwood for the Coalition had for some time been agitating for a million-acre scheme. Now Welwood had mobilized support from Lord Home, the politically influential Foreign Secretary, conveying to him that without substantial land transfer there would be widespread violence and a mass exodus of Europeans.[53] A backbench deputation of Tory MPs to see Macmillan followed

with a similar message that, while large European-owned plantation could be saved, European mixed farming was largely finished.
The Colonial Office was listening to the Coalition now, and after a
tough battle with the Treasury it won agreement that Britain was
to provide Kenya with aid of £16.55 million (of which £7.5 million
was a grant and the remainder a loan), to provide 200,000 acres a
year for five years by which time 70,000 African families should
have been settled.[54]

Alexander (Sandy) Storrar, the Director of Settlement at the new
Ministry of Land Settlement that was set up by the coalition government formed in April 1962, has recalled sitting down with Bruce
McKenzie, his Minister, with one desk and one secretary to set up
the Department. 'We were given instructions to prepare a plan for
a settlement of a million acres of the European Highlands'. In some
areas they had as little as seven acres per family to work with, in
others as much as forty or fifty. Originally the idea was to select
specific people but the pressure became so great that eventually
they put the names in a barrel and withdrew them at random:

> We set these holdings at about two to three hundred families
> per scheme. It was really very much a sort of military operation.
> You had to get the land ploughed, so that the people could get
> started straight away. We usually had the [African] settler plus
> his housing material (which were uprights and corrugated iron
> roofing) all in the same tractor and trailer and he was taken out
> to his holding. Normally he set up the corrugated iron and bivou-
> acked for a few days until he could get it built.
>
> Though production of certain items, particularly wheat, dropped
> very considerably at first, within the third year of settlement the
> production levels per acre were back up to the production levels
> of the European farms previously.

McKenzie and Storrar were able to take pride in the fact that in
time some of their schemes did better than the supposedly higher-
quality World Bank ones.[55] But, as Storrar explains, not all schemes
were so successful. He tells the story of the attempt to set up at Ol
Kalou a number of co-operative farms in 200,000 acres of wet land.
At the start all went well with white settlers who had sold out acting as settlement officers. But the co-operative deteriorated, 'the
people pegged out their own land and this was done very unwisely
and unfairly'.[56]

The resettlement of landless Africans remained a highly controversial topic long after the coming of independence. Some radical
politicians continued to agitate against the system of incurring debt
by buying out white farmers. They also objected to the use of ex-
settlers to supervise the new African settlements.[57]

THE NORTHERN FRONTIER DISTRICT

Besides the central constitutional argument that dragged on so long
at Lancaster House there were other serious issues which the British insisted needed to be addressed before there could be any
question of independence. These were primarily the Northern Frontier question, the problem of the Coastal Strip and the fate of the
Maasai treaties.

The most serious and potentially threatening of these was the
problem of the Northern Frontier District (NFD). In size it formed
nearly half the land area of Kenya; it was, however, very parched
and supported only small pastoral populations. The majority of the
Frontier District's inhabitants, living in its six eastern districts, were
Somalis, that is members of a race which considered themselves to
be totally different ethnically, historically, religiously and linguisti-
cally from those whom they referred to dismissively as 'Bantu' or
'the bunch of black barbarians in Nairobi'.[58] The racial purity of
the Frontier District's Somalis could be overdone. According to
Peter Fullerton, who was District Commissioner in Wajir, 'It is ironical
that the Somali who is the worst of all racial snobs has the least
pure racial lineage.' This was on account of the large number of
alien tribes they had managed to absorb in the course of the south-
ward thrust which was halted only by the arrival of the British.
Nevertheless, Fullerton hastened to tell his successor in June 1961,
the Somali 'is nevertheless a fine advertisement for miscegenation'.[59]

The flag of the Somali Republic, whose independence dates from
1 July 1960, bears five stars; they represent what the Somalis consider to be the five fragments of their national home. Two of these
fragments – the former British protectorate of Somaliland and the
former Italian trusteeship territory of Somalia – were knitted together
to form the new Republic. There remained three others: French
Somaliland, centring on the port of Djibouti, the Ethiopian territories of Ogaden and the Haud, and the Northern Frontier District
of Kenya.[60] This last had been ruled by the British from Nairobi,

but its population had always been cut off by a security curtain from the rest of Kenya. There had been no development until after the Second World War in what was known to its administrators as a 'walled city'. Fullerton described himself as being 'on the left wing of the movement to demolish the walled city policy'. During 1960 the pass system was abolished and trade and movement was allowed between Somalia and the NFD. The impact of the first Lancaster House conference was immense. In January 1960 Wajir was politically dormant; by March, says Fullerton, 'it was seething with politics, and a political party, the Northern Province People's Progressive Party (NPPPP), was in formation demanding the immediate secession of NFD to Somalia. The state of mind can only be called Kenyaphobic.'[61]

At the time of Maudling's first trip to Nairobi in 1961 and subsequently at the Lancaster House conference in 1962 five Somali political parties put their case for the eastern part of the District being immediately separated from Kenya and prepared under British rule for subsequent amalgamation with the Somali Republic.[62] 'All Somalis are pious to the point of sanctimoniousness,' Fullerton told his successor. And, indeed, one of the Somali party leaders, Yusuf Haji Abdi, told Maudling in November 1961, 'Although the people of Kenya believe Jomo Kenyatta to be a god, we could never accept this as, in common with many other religions, Islam can never accept that an ordinary man is a god.'[63] Another, Wako Hapi, swore that if the British would not oblige they would take their case to the UN.

At Lancaster House both KADU and KANU rejected any possibility of a secession that would have drastically reduced the total area of their country. But while KADU's tone was conciliatory in proposing instead the provision of a seventh region under their scheme of *majimbo*, that of KANU was harshly ideological in dismissing the Somali case as being totally contrary to Pan-African principles:

KANU believes strongly in African unity ... In doing so KANU seeks to abolish for ever the tactics of 'divide and rule' which have kept Africans apart and have enabled imperialists to continue subverting our newly won independence through new forms of 'neocolonialism' ... The Somalis in Kenya have the right to determine for themselves what Government they want to live under ... This means they may move to Somalia any time they want.[64]

The Somali representatives did not hide their dismay at this stand. 'KANU has said in effect, "Leave your homes if you do not agree with us."'

THE MAASAI AND THE STRIP

As with the Somalis, so with the Maasai the 1962 Lancaster House conference provided an opportunity to air the problem rather than to supply a solution. The Maasai case was that up to the beginning of the twentieth century they were the natural top dogs in what was to become Kenya; that despite what they described as 'their great war-like traditions' they had not offered resistance to the British; and that they had been cajoled, sometimes roughly, into accepting treaties (of 1904 and 1911) under which they agreed to move off their fertile, well-watered land in the Rift Valley into reserves that were to be theirs for 'as long as the Maasai as a race shall exist'. The first treaty specifically stated that this was agreed for the purpose of providing opportunities for white settlers. If these settlers were now planning, wholly or in part, to leave, it followed that some land in the Highlands should be returned to the Maasai. In any case if British sovereignty was to end, the Maasai Treaties must be given a new validity.

The Maasai were much admired by some Europeans as conforming to their conception of the 'noble savage'. Slender, tough and handsome, honourable, independent, mostly illiterate and near-naked, the 'morans', as their young men were called, ate meat and drank warm blood drawn from the necks of oxen as well as a brew from berries and bark calculated to make them fearless. They were normally rich in cattle, which was their currency, but, just as on arrival the British had found them at a disadvantage because of cattle epidemics and internecine wars, so the approaching departure of the British found them in a desperate plight because a failure of the rains had been followed by a plague of army worm and then abnormal rains and flooding. Grass had then sprung up, looking from the air like scum floating on the surface of an immense lake. Starved cattle gulped down the soaking grass; it was too much for their shrivelled stomachs and they died in their thousands. Altogether it was calculated that two-thirds of the tribe's half million head of cattle had gone. Many of the Maasai, having seen their cattle destroyed, were now talking about cultivating the land, an activity that they had hitherto held in disdain, for which purpose they wanted at least some of their old fertile lands.[65] In the end they got no more than an assurance that their present lands should be guaranteed to them in the Constitution.

There remained the question of the Sultan's mainland dominions, the Coastal Strip of the Kenya Protectorate. A separate conference met in Lancaster House in the margins of the main proceedings there from 8 to 12 March 1962. In essence Sultan Seid bin Abdullah, described in the *Kenya Weekly News* as a man 'bred to be subservient to events',[66] speaking through his counsel Dingle Foot, wanted to emphasize that his legal rights were beyond dispute but that he did not wish these to stand in the way of the decolonization of the whole of Kenya. Therefore he would await reassurance from the new National Government that the institutions and the way of life of his subjects would be fully safeguarded before committing himself.[67]

As Colonial Office draftsmen took off for Nairobi to toil under the direction of the new National Government it was plain that much work remained to be done. Kenyatta and Mboya were for the first time in office as Ministers but their target of *Uhuru* in 1962 was quite evidently unobtainable.

8 KANU Triumphant

'A sound East African Federation is, of course, a dream answer to many of our Kenya problems' (Malcolm MacDonald, 7 June 1963)

'If weekends could be abolished in Kenya for the rest of the year there might be a chance of the country getting a constitution,' said a London weekly about the new 'National Government' in Kenya. On Wednesdays, the article went on, the Ministers from both parties would meet politely enough under Sir Eric Griffith-Jones's chairmanship. 'But at the fatal weekends, when political rallies [are held], the Minister of Labour [Mboya] calls for a vote of no confidence in the Minister of Commerce and Industry [Muliro] at a meeting in the latter's constituency and one Minister of State for Constitutional Affairs [Kenyatta] celebrates in advance the elimination at the polls of the party led by the other [Ngala].'[1]

Muliro retaliated against Mboya's provocation by declaring the political truce at an end and by being 'thoroughly difficult and uncooperative' over applying to his own Ministry Griffith-Jones's ruling that Ministers of one party should accept a Parliamentary Secretary of the other. Daniel arap Moi, the Minister of Local Government, was reported as 'showing little enthusiasm for political restraint'.[2] The Colonial Office clearly thought that KADU was overplaying its hand. One senior official, Peter Kitcatt, commented, 'I must admit that I am often puzzled by KADU tactics... It seems to me that KADU have got this one wrong. If all the KADU Ministers in the Council were to resign, there is not the slightest reason why the KANU Ministers should do likewise, nor could there be any justification for dismissing them.'[3] Maudling agreed and told Griffith-Jones, 'If KADU were to withdraw from the Coalition they should not assume that I should be prepared to dismiss KANU Ministers.'

Frederic Bennett, KADU's constitutional adviser, informed Rhoderick Macleod, the executive secretary of the NKP, on 29 May 1962 that he had put together a pro-KADU lobby of MPs, consisting of Sir Charles Mott-Radclyffe, Sir Tufton Beamish, J. H. Cordle, F. W. Harris, Sir Roland Robinson, Godman Irvine and himself. Their task would be to keep pressing KADU's case on the Colonial

Office.[4] On 1 June he reported that the group had seen Maudling, whose Parliamentary Private Secretary Bennett had been for the four years before Maudling had gone to the Colonial Office. Bennett wrote gloomily that he found no change in the Minister's personal conviction that KANU was going up in popular esteem and KADU was going down. He had had a crisis lunch in London with Muliro and others at which they agreed that they simply must somehow halt and reverse the trend of thinking in Whitehall about politics in Kenya. Muliro speculated that European civil servants were sending deliberately negative reports to strengthen their own case for compensation for loss of office.[5]

Rhoderick Macleod, meanwhile, was reporting to Griffith-Jones that Moi had confided to him the suspicion that a paper for the Council of Ministers on local government powers drafted for him by his expatriate civil servants would have the effect of undermining the framework agreed in London. Macleod told Griffith-Jones, 'Either there has been some carelessness or Daniel's suspicions may have some foundation'. Blundell, angry at having Moi block his last agricultural reform because regional government must be established first, grumbled, 'KADU are in a highly emotional and non-constructive mood; it is almost impossible to get them to see reason on anything. As a result of this one or two of us are in despair and Eric Griffith-Jones has definitely taken a strong dislike to them.'[6]

THE COMING OF SANDYS AND MACDONALD

To many people's surprise it became known in June that Renison was after all returning to Nairobi when his leave was over. Although KADU's European advisers were often rude about the Governor in their correspondence they were restrained by the hope that a pro-KADU bias arising from his previous experiences would counterbalance officials' preference for KANU. When he reappeared on the Kenya scene at the end of June, this did not prove entirely to be the case, since the demands of *majimbo*, when it came to defining them in detail, tended to run against the interests of what Renison habitually termed 'my service'.

Maudling came to Nairobi once again in July to announce the million-acre agricultural settlement scheme and to inspect progress on filling out his political framework. He was confronted with an address from Ngala which spoke of KADU's belief that 'there was very little honesty of purpose in KANU's undertaking to implement Regionalism'. 'I must tell you bluntly,' Ngala said, 'that if the degree of Regionalism agreed to in London is whittled down our people will not be prepared to continue in a Kenya such as KANU envisages'. Backed by Reginald Alexander, one of KADU's more intransigent white supporters who spoke explicitly about the prospect of partition, Ngala then launched into a denunciation of the expatriate civil service. 'The contention, common among senior Civil Servants, that there must be a centralized Service is unacceptable to us . . . we cannot agree that our future should be shaped in order to meet their wishes.'[7]

The Colonial Secretary was left in no doubt of the attitude of the top civil servants when he and the Governor met with the Permanent Secretaries, the Chief Commissioner and the Provincial Commissioners on 9 July. At a time, they told him, when resources of competent staff were running extremely low, the effect of attempting to disrupt the machinery by dividing it up between independently operated fragments could hardly be contemplated. Some of those present made no bones about their inclining towards the party, KANU, which offered the more practical approach. Maudling begged them to avoid harping on political and financial factors and to confine their critical advice to arguments of sheer administrative impracticality.[8]

That morning Ngala and Moi staged a walk-out from the talks about the public service, because discussion of a central pool of candidates from which regions and the central government would both draw did not match their understanding of what had been already agreed. In a letter to Renison Ngala argued that KADU's conception was one of six regionally based public services whose members would be wholly committed to the region and be drawn from its people. Hence they could see no valid reason why all recruitment should not be handled by the regional commissions. Ngala complained to Renison that Maudling had simply waved aside the opinions of KADU Ministers who were trying to explain these views.[9]

No sooner had Maudling returned to London than he became caught up in Macmillan's 'Night of the Long Knives', in which faithful standbys like Kilmuir and Selwyn Lloyd were shunted off the stage to be replaced by supposedly shinier models. Maudling became Chancellor of the Exchequer and the Colonial Office was entrusted as an additional responsibility to the Commonwealth Relations

Secretary, Duncan Sandys. Civil servants who had been accustomed to the quick-thinking style of Macleod and Maudling were in for a culture shock.

Duncan Sandys combined a slow-moving mind with reluctance to read any but very short documents. Nevertheless he was extremely conscientious over detail and he exuded a sense of joy in the exercise of power. This combination of characteristics explained his methods of work. His thorough grasp of innumerable local situations was acquired by oral briefings that were painfully prolonged. 'He asked very good, critical, searching and detailed questions,' said his Parliamentary Under-Secretary Nigel Fisher (who had also served under Macleod and Maudling). 'You saw from the questions he asked the Departmental policy gradually evolving, but terribly slowly. It was an agonizing business sometimes'. Fisher felt that most of his staff 'thought it was the nearest thing to hell on earth to work for Duncan Sandys', and the Duke of Devonshire, his Minister of State, recalls his reducing two of his civil servants to tears.[10] 'He was a natural bully', one of his skilled constitutional draftsmen said afterwards. 'If you let him he would be all over the room and you would be broken.'

It was notorious that when a conference occurred or a major crisis sprang up anywhere in the Commonwealth Sandys would 'work right round the clock and expected all of us to do so too'. He would favour starting work at 10pm and going on until four in the morning or later till dawn on the principle that no one else needed sleep. Three hours later he would phone up his staff to convey his latest ideas. Once he got hold of an issue (and he would never concentrate on more than one territory at a time) he was incapable of delegating, even to the point of insisting on doing the Department's specialized work himself – such as drafting statutory instruments – which caused him to became known as 'the Abominable Draftsman'.[11]

Emerging from one such occasion the Duke of Devonshire told Fisher that 'I have never before known a man who could cram four hours' work into twenty-four.'[12] Harold Macmillan thought highly of him; he was 'a very tough man – he wouldn't have any nonsense . . . and was – quite simply – good at any job you gave him to do.'[13] The Cabinet gave him a great deal of freedom in dissolving the Empire and he used it with gusto. When the new young Sultan of Zanzibar showed a reluctance to become independent if that meant that he would lose the Coastal Strip, Sandys burst out, 'What do you mean that I can't make him independent? It makes a mockery of imperialism!' A civil servant summed him up: 'He was a nit-picker but he insisted that the nits that were picked should be his own.'[14]

With the new Colonial Secretary came in a new Governor, not because Renison's term had been completed but because Sandys, having come to the same conclusion as Maudling had once done about his unsuitability for handling the last stage of decolonization, started immediately to act on his judgment. He did it rather gracelessly as Churchill had done with General Northey forty years before. Renison came to London in November and was told abruptly that he was to be replaced in favour of somebody with political experience. It was a premature and to him deeply disappointing end to his career. His African Ministers, some of whom had been bitterly critical of him in the past, felt that he had latterly pushed energetically for early independence. The KANU Ministers in particular had realized that his fight for 'his' service was a fight for their kind of Kenya. When he flew back sadly to Nairobi to say his good-byes they turned up in force at the airport to greet him.[15]

Duncan Sandys knew whom he wanted as the new Governor, but he had to press hard with his well-known implacability to get him. He wanted his predecessor as Colonial Secretary from the 1930s, Malcolm MacDonald. After a stirring year fighting the Battle of Britain on the home front as Minister of Health, MacDonald had been despatched to the periphery by Winston Churchill as High Commissioner in Ottawa and thus had begun a remarkable second career of Commonwealth diplomacy and political guidance, taking him subsequently to India and South-East Asia where he had earned a unique prestige among large portions of the Third World.[16] He was, however, little known in Africa, though, to be sure, thirty years before he had handled Kenyan matters among others at the Colonial Office.

The immediate reaction of Milton Obote, the former political activist in the Nairobi of the 1950s who had been Prime Minister of Uganda since May 1962 and of an independent Uganda for just over a month, was highly negative. Ignorant of MacDonald's reputation for empathy with nationalist politicians, his conclusion was that Britain was using the unexpected change of Governors as one more device to protract the march towards Kenyan independence.[17]

EAST AFRICA FEDERATION

Obote considered himself directly involved in Kenya affairs because the issue of East African Federation was once more on the table. 'Federation became a totally different proposition once the period of *uhuru* began,' as Oginga Odinga observed. Once African rule in all three of the East African territories appeared certain, Africans besides Nyerere saw that 'the united strength of the [twenty-seven] millions of Uganda, Tanganyika and Kenya would make East Africa a force to be reckoned with in international affairs.'[18]

Macleod's clever calculations at the beginning of 1961 had unravelled. Nyerere had argued that since there was no assurance that Kenya and Uganda would advance sufficiently swiftly his offer of delay was no longer valid. He wished to press ahead with the independence of Tanganyika, which occurred on 2 December 1961.[19] This meant that Communist bloc countries were able to set up embassies in Dar es-Salaam, with which Kenya politicians had little difficulty in establishing contact. Journalists would notice that raggedly dressed political friends who had disappeared suddenly from Nairobi had returned a few weeks later clad in the smart dark blue suits which went along with their eastern trips. In October 1962 Uganda followed. There remained only Kenya.

Sincere advocacy of Federation was combined with its disingenuous use by some politicians as a device for hastening the end of the last East African colony. With Tanganyikan independence a new organization, the East African Common Services Organization (EACSO), came into existence in December 1961 to replace the High Commission, which had since 1 January 1948 provided a degree of commonalty to the management of the region's infrastructure. The EACSO, which could only operate by unanimous decision, controlled the railways, airways, posts and telegraphs, customs, income tax collection (though not rates), university, research institutes and radio communications of East Africa. It also attempted ineffectively to rationalize economic planning. It was headed by the three senior ministers, which in the case of Kenya involved after June 1962 the awkwardness of the alternating attendance of Kenyatta and Ngala. There was a Ghanaian Secretary-General but, unlike the European Economic Community with which it was sometimes compared, there was no equivalent of the independent European Commission with exclusive powers of initiative. There were, however, four functional committees, each headed by the three appropriate ministers, and a

Central Legislative Assembly with limited powers.[20] If a Federation were to be built there was in existence a foundation on which to build.

One major obstacle, inherited from past attempts to pool the economies of the three territories, was the general awareness that Kenya, though for the time being the most politically laggard of the three, had much the strongest economy. Of the 474 companies registered in East Africa, 404 were in Kenya. The federal cause might, then, be vulnerable to charges of promoting Kenyan dominance. The headquarters of EACSO was located in Nairobi, many of its employees were Kenyans, and the suspicion was easy to engender that an East African common market was being run to service the Kenyan economy.[21]

In a minute of 12 December 1962 the Duke of Devonshire, who was just back from Dar es-Salaam, argued that both the efficient working of EACSO and the desire for Federation were being frustrated by the fact that Kenya was still a dependent territory and suffered from divided leadership. Nyerere and his deputy Rashidi Kawawa had talked of the need for a quick election so as to provide Kenya with an acknowledged leader on a footing with Obote and Nyerere. The Duke observed, 'I fear that they regard it as a foregone conclusion that such a leader will be Kenyatta.'[22]

THE ROLE OF OBOTE

Devonshire's report was written in the knowledge that Obote and Kawawa, both now representing independent countries, had decided to come to London together to confront Macmillan and Sandys about their supposed footdragging over the next Kenya election. The personality of Apollo Milton Obote, who was now to make his first appearance on the Whitehall scene as a Commonwealth Prime Minister, was to be a key factor in determining whether or not there was to be an East African Federation. He was a member of the Lango tribe in the north of Uganda, whose supposed primitivism had been so cruelly mocked by Clement Argwings-Kodhek during the sharp political infighting in Nairobi in 1957. After his return to Uganda in that year he began organizing what in February 1960, with the merger of two existing parties, became the Uganda People's Congress. A slight figure, in those days appearing undernourished, he was nicknamed 'Gandhi' as he pedalled around the country on a bicycle stirring up political activity.[23] With his image of radical nationalism he only managed to defeat his more conservative rival, Benedicto Kiwanuka of the Roman Catholic Democratic Party, in May 1962 by virtue of a highly improbable coalition with the monarchist Kabaka Yekka movement in the kingdom of Buganda. This was followed in October by independence.

'Obote is a complex, even a schizophrenic character,' wrote Sir David Hunt, the newly appointed first British High Commissioner to Kampala, in briefing Macmillan about his approaching visitor. 'At one moment he can be the most moderate and courteous of individuals and at the next he can be violently discourteous and unreasonable.'[24] Obote had come back from a conference in Léopoldville spitting hate in his usual quiet voice at British policies throughout Africa and saying he felt ashamed to be talking English at a Pan-African meeting.[25] 'I am not sure,' warned Sir David, 'that there would be an advantage in [our] giving a boost to the idea of an East African Federation . . . If . . . we give too much encouragement Obote and Kawawa may suspect an ulterior motive.'[26]

'I have had to spend several hours being reproached (and almost insulted) by two very unprepossessing characters,' Macmillan confided to his diary when Obote and Kawawa had been to see him. 'However it all ended amicably and they accepted a very harmless communiqué. I must say that Duncan Sandys handles these people with extraordinary patience.'[27] Their demand had been for an April election so that a proper government on Kenya's behalf could take part with them in EACSO's budget session in May. Sandys laid out in detail all that he and his department were doing to expedite Kenya's independence. He explained the complexities of the new constitution, which enshrined novel principles. He was doing everything he could think of to speed things up.[28] Kawawa asked for time to be saved over the two months allowed for challenging the voting register and Sandys was able overnight to get MacDonald to cut the period down to two weeks. When answering Prime Minister's Questions on these talks Macmillan was urged to press ahead with the project of an East African Federation both from the right – F.W. Harris, one of Bennett's group – and from the left – Fenner Brockway, of the Movement for Colonial Freedom.[29]

SANDYS'S PLANS

Sandys's actual intention, spelled out in a note written to himself before his visit to Nairobi at the end of February 1963, was to hurry on with internal self-government at 'a very early date' and then to postpone actual independence for as long as possible thereafter. 'It would appear,' he jotted down, 'that any timetable leading to independence should in fact be governed by the speed at which it is possible to Africanize the higher branches of the administration. This will obviously take time if it is to result in administration of an acceptable standard, and the longer the final goal of independence is delayed the more sure and firm will the basis for it be.'[30]

Contrary to the impression left by MacDonald's later oral history account at Rhodes House the new Governor did not persuade Sandys after ten days in Nairobi that he must speed up independence. At that stage and for several weeks afterwards MacDonald still shared Sandys's view.[31] It is true that on 14 January, in his first assessment of the Nairobi scene, he urged rapid elections in order to limit the damage being inflicted by electioneering speeches. These should be followed immediately by the introduction of the new constitution. 'But after that,' he wrote, 'we can perhaps play the problem rather longer, watching how the political situation develops and . . . also how much time it will take to make the new constitution work effectively before considering a date for independence.'[32]

Although he was to admire Kenyatta, Mboya and even Odinga, MacDonald came to have few illusions about the African political class as a whole. 'Most of their minor politicians and some of their major ones act rather like children playing at being statesmen,' he once wrote to Sandys. 'They strut and shout and express their Egos vehemently and their emotions are always on the tips of their tongues.'[33]

However, the important fact was that the new Governor had made an immediate difference to the tempo of life at Government House. Receptions ceased to look like a parade of the European community, African politicians slipped in and out constantly for informal talks and the working practices of the Council of Ministers were radically altered. Before, it had been meeting one morning a week to consider the constitution and even then achieving very little. MacDonald proposed that it should meet under his chairmanship for three days every week in morning, afternoon and evening sessions with nothing on the agenda except the constitution. In breaks between meetings Ministers could look in at their Ministries to find out what was happening. Officials objected that the Africans would not want to work so hard and that if the Governor served drinks during the evening session they would drink too much. The Governor persisted and, except for one occasion involving one Minister, all was well. In particular MacDonald found Kenyatta to be very abstemious.[34] 'Since MacDonald took over,' wrote Rhoderick Macleod to Bennett, 'the pace at which we have been discussing and deciding matters of vital constitutional interest has been fantastic.'[35]

This rate of progress prepared the way for Sandys on his late February visit to make twenty-five key decisions on matters that had been deferred to his ruling. He decided, for instance, that there were to be seven civil service commissions but that the chairman and three other members of each were to be the same people. 'All has gone well up to now in difficult and tedious talks with Kenya Ministers, who have agreed to abide by my decisions,' he reported to Macmillan and his department, but went on to explain how, nevertheless, a sudden crisis had blown up on the subject of the sleepy town of Kitale. 'At the last minute KADU Ministers are threatening to resign and provoke riots and bloodshed.'[36]

Kitale is in the Trans-Nzoia, in the north-west, not far from Mount Elgon and the Uganda border; it was the railhead of the northernmost branch of the East African railway built to serve (at a considerable loss) a Soldier Settlers' scheme started after the First World War in the lush and gently sloping grassland that reminded them of Gloucestershire.[37]

Talk of riots and bloodshed had arisen out of the report of the Regional Boundaries Commission, chaired by Sir Stafford Foster-Sutton, which was one of the five commissions appointed by Maudling after the second Lancaster House conference. The members had conscientiously toured the country and heard representations from 210 deputations before drafting recommendations of how Kenya was to be divided up between six regions. They had the baffling task of reconciling the twin directives they had been given: the one to stay as close as possible to existing administrative boundaries and the other to pay heed to people's preferences. 'It is clearly established,' they found, 'that there is a compelling and sincere desire on the part of many of the peoples of Kenya to be associated with some and not with others.' The Kamba, for instance, were adamant in their desire not to be in the same region as the Maasai. No one wanted to be left in the same region either with the Kikuyu or with the Luo. The Embu (conditionally) and the Meru (absolutely) wanted to be no part of the first nor did the Luhya of the second. On the other hand some tribes, drawing on memories of their pre-colonial past, asked to be linked to a particular neighbour, the Marakwet supplying as evidence of such mutual traditional harmony with the Maasai the fact that when they used to go to war with each other they were able, when they realized that they were beaten, to raise their hands in surrender. The Maasai would, obligingly, not insist on fighting to the death.[38]

The attitude of the Luhya towards the Luo made it inevitable that there would have to be a new Western Region, separate from Nyanza. Without waiting for the report to be completed, Masinde Muliro dashed into Kitale's Sports Stadium to lay with a flourish the foundation stone for the Region's headquarters. When the Foster-Sutton Report was published, however, it emerged that Kitale had been assigned instead to the Rift Valley. The Council of Ministers had agreed in advance not to change any of the recommended boundaries except by unanimity. Ngala and Moi demanded that Kitale be switched, not to mention Muliro, who was by now going ballistic. However, Mboya sensed the opportunity to exploit tribal divisions in his opponent's camp, with the Pokot from the Kalenjin group and the Maasai favouring the report's verdict and the others opposing it, and vetoed any alteration. Sandys at the last minute managed to prevent the talks breaking up and Muliro resigning by inventing a quick method of transferring territory by mutual agreement from one region to another during the first six months of the constitution.[39] The truth was that neither party wanted to be stuck with the responsibility of causing delay in the country's independence. It was this that gave the British still a certain leverage on events.

The Colonial Secretary had no such luck with what he had described in advance as 'the most urgent matter'. This was the Somali demand for secession. 'If we do not settle this before independence the Somali will no doubt settle it with the sword when we are gone,' he had written. 'Once again – as in the case of the "Queen's Chinese" – we are getting prepared to turn our backs on loyalty.'[40] Kenyatta, who was otherwise obliging throughout, was on this matter emphatic and unyielding. 'We cannot over-emphasise,' he said, 'our strong feelings and determination against secession.'[41] The best that Sandys was able to do was to establish a seventh region in the North-East and to appeal to the Somalis to give the regional system of government a fair trial in the interval before their fate came up for settlement in the discussions on independence.

In early April MacDonald's health collapsed under the strain he had been under and for nearly eight weeks, accompanied by a beautiful Chinese female photographer, he wandered throughout the wilder parts of Kenya, communing 'with more or less dumb animals who never made speeches and never gave a thought to Kenya's politics'.[42] Griffith-Jones carried on in his absence and he was back for the election.

THE 1963 ELECTION CAMPAIGN

Everything in Kenya was now being directed with an eye to the election. Aware of KADU's strength in the security services, a problem heightened by the decision of the leading Kamba politicians, under Paul Ngei, to break away from KANU and form a separate African People's Party, KANU was preparing itself for a post-election struggle. It was convinced that a new election would establish decisively its democratic credentials. It was not so certain that its opponents, inevitably strong in certain areas and eager to exploit 'regionalism', would be disposed to respect these credentials and accordingly it was taking precautions. Special Branch kept the Governor informed of what was going on.

It was reported that eleven Kikuyu students had returned from Israel on 12 November 1962 after undergoing a five-month course in security and intelligence at Tel Aviv. Their spokesman, Josiah Mwangi Kariuki, the ex-Mau Mau detainee whose political role once independence had taken place was not to be to the comfort of the KANU leadership, had arrived with an Israeli offer to Kenyatta of forty-five scholarships, twenty-five for military training and twenty for instruction in intelligence and security. Kenyatta delegated the choice of candidates to Julius Kiano who was expected to pick the potential intelligence officers only from the Kikuyu. Dr Mungai Njoroge was also in Israel and came back with offers to train Kenyan pilots. The Israeli consul was given the task of preparing these students' papers so that they should appear to be going for agricultural training.[43] The Israelis' purpose was to 'break the Arab barrier' and to establish friendly governments in sub-Saharan Africa with whom they could do trade through the Gulf of Aqaba.[44]

Odinga was busy preparing his own candidates for the new Kenya with funds from communist sources. Twenty-five Kenya Africans were reported in February 1963 as having received military training behind the 'Iron Curtain', thirteen in Bulgaria and twelve in the Soviet Union. Eighty-three more had been interviewed. Altogether 342 Kenyans, students of one sort or another, were in the East. Kenyatta, it was reported with some relief, was no longer dependent on communist funds.[45] Largely through the travels of Joseph Murumbi, the efficient Goan (and part-Masai) treasurer of KANU, he was now furnished with considerable sums from Morocco, Egypt and Ghana. A portion of the Ghanaian funds, of which Mboya was specifically to be kept uninformed, was supposed to be devoted by Kenyatta to detaching Kenya trade unions from ICFTU; indeed, much of Mboya's time and energy as Minister of Labour were diverted into wrestling with a series of strikes, some of which were clearly politically motivated.[46]

Murumbi also brought about a very necessary tightening up of party discipline and central control – there had been several times when the telephones at KANU's headquarters in Jeevanjee Street had been cut off because the bills had not been paid.[47] Things were different now. Files were in order; bills were paid; appointments were kept; instructions carried out. The Director of Intelligence told the Governor that 'although the final electoral battle will be fought on ground of KADU's choosing, the KANU forces have the inestimable benefit of the truly massive financial, material and moral assistance of the "Casablanca" [i.e. radical] group of African states, to say nothing of the help accorded to the party indirectly through Oginga Odinga and his associates by the Communist embassies in Dar.'[48]

It was estimated that, largely through Murumbi's efforts, Kenyatta had some £160,000 available for the campaign, while Odinga had been promised £75,000 from the Russians and, independently, Mboya had another £30,000 to £40,000 to spend from friends abroad. He was reported as having paid the £50 deposits of a substantial number of independents or representatives of small parties where their appearance would be damaging to the chances of KADU. KADU's total fighting fund, on the other hand, was not thought to exceed £35,000.[49] KANU was going all out to achieve a crushing victory.

The main disorder of the campaign took place in Kamba country, because of the defection from KANU of Paul Ngei, who enjoyed the prestige of having been, with Kenyatta, one of the accused at the Kapenguria trial. He had charisma but little else to commend him. He had scant regard for Kenyatta's efforts to create an inclusive society and to reassure the white minority. At one press conference, after descanting on how Africans blew their noses more hygienically than Europeans, he visualized a world in which white men had eliminated each other in a nuclear war, leaving supremacy to the blacks.[50]

Most Kamba politicians followed Ngei in the formation of the African People's Party (APP) and he managed to rally some individuals from other tribes, mostly disillusioned ex-allies of Tom Mboya, like M. D. Odinga and Omolo Agar. But it was soon apparent that Ngei had no idea how to set about organizing a political party. His listing of party candidates was arbitrary and not very intelligent and even the more educated among the Kamba were reported as having considerable reservations about his ability and innate extremism.[51] Nevertheless Ngei retained considerable backing in his home ground, where the threats by the KANU Minister of Works, Mwinga Chokwe, that if the Kamba voted for Ngei no roads would be built in Kamba country and that if Kamba tribesmen living at the Coast did not back KANU they would be 'dropped into the sea', were not well received.[52] But despite Ngei's stream of vituperation against KANU in general and Kenyatta and Mboya in particular and his desultory series of negotiations with Ngala for a political alliance with KADU, he never attracted a wider following.

It was announced that polling for the three separate elections – for Regional Assemblies, Senate and House of Representatives, in that order – would be staggered over a week from 18 to 26 May, with the voter having to appear at the booths on three different days. There were 117 single-member constituencies for the House, with twelve Specially Elected members to be chosen by the new elected MPs. For the Senate there was to be one member each from the 40 administrative districts irrespective of wide differences in population plus one from Nairobi. All told, the Regional Assemblies were to contain 211 members, 26 of them Specially Elected.[53]

'KANU is assuming total victory,' reported the *Spectator* on the eve of the vote. 'Its plans for the country pour forth from the ever-chattering typewriters in the National Headquarters . . . Primarily they are meant for the European civil servants, professional men and large farmers whom KANU does not wish to see leave the moment Kenyatta becomes Prime Minister and to the controllers of international credit on whom the new Kenya Government must absolutely depend for development.'[54] For the same reason Kenyatta sent one of his most impressive intellectuals, Mwai Kibaki, who had a first-class degree in economics, to campaign in the Highlands. One British journalist received an excited phone call from a settler who had almost certainly only met Africans before as servants or farm hands, to say, 'I've just been to hear Mwai Kibaki. He is the first person I've ever heard talk sense about the economy of Kenya.'[55]

Although KADU could claim to be the party which championed the new constitution it was only able to nominate 59 candidates. KANU, with its greatly superior resources, was from the start on the offensive. With A. J. Hughes, the former political correspondent of the *East African Standard* and author of the Penguin *East Africa: The Struggle for Unity*, in charge of its publicity, it poured out a generally up-beat stream of releases, emphasizing the chances of foreign investment, ambitious programmes for education, the prospect of achieving East African Federation and the pursuit of Pan-African ideals.

The Kamba, though sometimes privately sneered at by the Kikuyu[56] were regarded as ethnically close to them, so Paul Ngei's revolt was a particular annoyance to the KANU leadership, which wanted to make an example of him. That it signally failed to do so, yet that this failure made scarcely any difference to the overall result, is a measure of KANU's success elsewhere. However, the drive against Ngei in his home district of Machakos gave rise to the only serious incident in the whole campaign apart from the murder of two party workers in Nyanza in isolated inter-clan feuds. On 10 May KANU mobilized about fifty car-loads of supporters to bring them in to a rally at Kangundo, in the Machakos district. Since they then complained that they were under threat from Kamba tribesmen they were given a General Service Unit escort of para-military police, who did not hesitate to set about Ngei's backers with their batons once general jeering had opened up.

Not far away at Tara Market Ngei himself was holding a rival meeting. A KANU van drove into the village by mistake and was subjected to ruthless stoning. The driver in a panic tried to turn it round; it crashed into a tree, then into another. Someone dashed for cover into an innocent baker's van full of bread and the rocks smashed down on it too, as it crashed out of control into the back of a stationary lorry. That there were no fatal casualties was due to the fortuitous presence and interventions of the BBC.[57]

Despite what one account described as 'the Montague-and-Capulet forays by the youth wings in the streets and in the blackness of the bush',[58] the election went off remarkably peacefully. There was, to be sure, violence of language in the simplified code-messages signalled to the people at meetings. 'Wait and see when I blow the whistle,' declared Moi in menacing tones.[59] 'If Mboya misbehaves after we have formed the Government we know where to put him,' asserted Ngala. 'He is completely unacceptable to KADU under all circumstances. We honestly, sincerely and firmly reject Mr Mboya as a person. For seven years I was a member of Legco. The one man I have learnt never to trust is Mr Tom Mboya.' Ngala then alluded none too subtly to the security forces. 'If you want security I have given you security in my policy. All the armed forces are behind you.' This unhelpful remark prompted Mboya's instant retort that if the armed forces misbehaved themselves under a KANU Government they would be dissolved and replaced by a fresh recruitment.[60]

When he spoke at Mombasa, a centre of regionalism, Mboya was provocatively open about KANU's intention to amend the 247-page constitution, which had taken over a year to draw up. As soon as the election was over he proclaimed, 'Regionalism is buried.' 'Big money often goes to the heads of little men,' declared Joseph Murumbi scornfully in the pages of the Aga Khan's organ, the *Daily Nation*. KANU would not 'stand by and watch the country go to ruin because a few people want to carve out little kingdoms for themselves under the guise of protecting tribal interests'.[61] Certainly the KADU campaigns gave much evidence that tribalism was not dead. A Luhya candidate was not alone in giving as the reasons for not voting KANU: 'The Kikuyu take oaths at night; Kikuyu women have abortions; Unity with the Kikuyu is unity with death.'[62]

In the effectiveness of its discipline KANU was strikingly more successful than in 1961. Then high party officials had campaigned against each other, official candidates had been defeated by 'KANU Independents', and at least two seats had been presented to the opposition by a split in the KANU vote between several competing personalities. Now any constituency that started behaving the same way was swiftly brought into line. In Kericho East, for instance, the urban vote was mainly cast by Kikuyu and Luo workers from the big tea estates, while the countryside around was solidly KADU. The local KANU party was so badly split that it had two sets of rival officers and no agreed candidate. The national party headquarters lost patience and imposed its own candidate, Christopher Kiprotitch, who alone would be allowed to use the national party symbol, *Jogoo* – the cock. The local papers were full of press releases loudly protesting against Kiprotitch's nomination and he was challenged by a prominent trade union leader, O. O. Mak'Anyengo, running as an Independent. It looked like a repetition of 1961, more especially in that Mak'Anyengo was a more effective campaigner than Kiprotitch, and there seemed to be a real prospect of the KADU man pushing past both of them. The result, however, was that Kiprotitch was elected with 11,193 votes, the KADU candidate came second, and Mak'Anyengo received a derisory vote of 351.[63]

The KANU campaign ended on the eve of polling for the House of Representatives with a mass meeting at Nairobi addressed by Jomo Kenyatta. By then it was obvious to all that he was going to be the first Prime Minister of Kenya. Only the margin of victory was uncertain. A new era was about to begin. As he finished speaking the heavens opened and the monsoon struck. The crowd scattered to obtain shelter. Some of the press found refuge in the nearby Muthaiga Club, at that time the sanctum of the white settler. The rain was flooding in, putting much of the ground floor under water. In the one corner of the reading-room where there was still a small patch of carpet not yet saturated, deep in his newspaper and paying no attention to what was going on around him sat the ancient Colonel Ewart Grogan, due to become 89 on Uhuru Day, the man who walked from Cape to Cairo, epitome of the original settler. And the water was still rising.[64]

THE ELECTION RESULT

The result was a decisive victory for Kenyatta and for KANU, more complete than Special Branch had predicted. On the basis of the Constituencies Delimitation Report which had been published in mid-January the Government's assessment for the House of Representatives was: KANU 45, KADU 42, Independents 30. The eve of poll prediction was KANU 62, KADU 38, APP 9. The actual figures were KANU 72, of whom seven had run as Independents but identified themselves immediately as KANU and another, elected as KADU, had instantly crossed over, KADU 32, APP 8, Independents 2. In Kamba country all the seats were captured by Ngei; in Mombasa Mwinga Chokwe was the only KANU Minister to lose his. KANU took care that it should not suffer this time from indiscipline in the Special Elections. It won 11 of the 12 seats, with successful candidates on the KANU slate including its two prominent European farmers, Bruce McKenzie and Peter Marrian. The complete boycott of the election which had been proclaimed by the Somalis in the North-East region operated successfully. No candidates presented themselves and no voting took place.[65]

In the other two elections for the institutions which, according to the advocates of the *majimbo* constitution, were supposed to exercise a mighty restraint on KANU's ambitions, KANU did unexpectedly well. It had an absolute majority in the Senate, with 20 seats (including two Independents who declared themselves for KANU) out of 38 against KADU's 16 and APP's 2. KANU and KADU won three Regional Assemblies apiece, KANU the Central, Nyanza and Eastern Regions, KADU Western, Rift Valley and Coastal. Daniel arap Moi and Ronald Ngala were then duly elected the Presidents of the Rift Valley and Coastal Assemblies to make of those Regions' powers what they could. Since nobody stood for the North-East, the Governor had to assume legislative control.

On 1 June the victors formed the Government which was to lead Kenya into independence. Jomo Kenyatta became Prime Minister, Oginga Odinga Minister for Home Affairs, Tom Mboya Minister for Justice and Constitutional Affairs, Joseph Murumbi and Peter Mbiyu Koinange Ministers of State, and Bruce McKenzie, the only European in the Council of Ministers, Minister of Agriculture. Kenyatta was careful to distribute portfolios as broadly as possible – there were four Kikuyu Ministers besides himself (Gichuru, Kiano, Mungai Njoroge, Mbiyu Koinange) and four Luos (Mboya, Odinga, Ayodo and Achieng Oneko) but each region found itself represented in the fifteen-member (and soon to be sixteen-member) Government. Other than Kenyatta himself, Oneko was the only former defendant at the Kapenguria trial to be included, though both Kubai and Kaggia were among the junior Ministers, as were Argwings-Kodhek, Mwai Kibaki and Peter Marrian. Kenyatta, rightly suspecting that Kaggia would be a future source of radical discontent, had tried hard to deny him the party nomination for his home constituency at Kandara. But Kaggia having engineered the defeat of this attempt, *Mzee* made the best of it by including him in his team.

Malcolm MacDonald then made a decisive move that endeared him to Kenyatta and ensured his influence with the new masters of Kenya for as long as he remained on the scene. The constitution provided that so long as internal self-government lasted the Governor should retain responsibility for defence, external affairs and internal security, including all matters relating to police forces, but he was empowered to delegate these responsibilities to any Minister. Immediate alarm had been expressed at Odinga's obtaining the Home Affairs portfolio. MacDonald responded by employing his powers of delegation to assign the entire range of functions to Kenyatta.[66]

Sandys, who had not been informed in advance, was taken aback. 'Do you consider we should have been consulted by the Governor before taking this important decision?' he asked his Permanent Secretary, Sir Hylton Poynton. 'Does this mean that Kenyatta will be able (a) to engage in acrimonious arguments with the Government of the Somali Republic about the future of the Kenya Somalis; (b) to decide upon the use of the King's African Rifles for suppression of Somali or other disorders; (c) to invite communist countries to send so-called trade missions to Kenya or establish consulate there?'[67]

MacDonald responded that this was his way of keeping Odinga's hands off the police and intelligence without making it too obvious by handing over only these powers. 'I also had it in mind that it would give [Kenyatta] and his colleagues a chance to become familiar with the practical problems touching external relations.'[68] Sir John Martin advised Sandys that although the Colonial Office could not entirely swallow MacDonald's arguments there was something to be said for them. In the end Sandys found it prudent not to transmit even the mild and carefully qualified rebuke Sir John had drafted for him.[69]

The three East African Governments were now determined to waste no more time in converting KANU's victory into action. On 5 June Kenyatta, Obote and Nyerere, meeting in Nairobi, issued a statement pledging themselves in the most emphatic terms to the political federation of East Africa. 'We believe,' they said, 'that the day of decision has come and to all our people we say: there is no more room for slogans and words.'

9 Uhuru na Harambee

'One of our main objects was to avoid forcing a split between the moderates and the extremists in the Government which might have strengthened Odinga's hand.' (Commonwealth Relations Office guidance on last Kenya constitutional conference, 14 November 1963)

In his inaugural speech as Prime Minister Jomo Kenyatta launched a new slogan: *Harambee* – 'All Pull Together' – to link up with *Uhuru* – 'Freedom' – which had long been the popular cry. Since his days as a journalist on *Muigwithania* in the late 1920s and the 1930s the need for hard work and unity had been his theme. He had admired the British when he had lived among them and now that he was in power he hastened to reassure the white farmers about their future. His speech to them at Nakuru had a remarkable impact in turning round their opinions of him and in winning their confidence. Men who would have regarded him a year or even a few months back as Satan Incarnate were saying, 'It'll be all right so long as the Old Man is still around.'[1]

The trouble was that most people in late 1963 did not expect Kenyatta to be around for very long. His actual age was unknown but he was almost certainly nearer 70 than 60 (many thought well over 70) and he had been forced to live in a physically hard climate.[2] The gossip in Nairobi was already about who was to succeed Kenyatta – would it have to be another Kikuyu or would a Luo be acceptable, and, if a Luo, which one? Seldom indeed was heard the notion that a representative of that third element in Kenya politics, the miscellaneous collection of tribes that made up 'the Rest', would be considered. Still less was it plausible, after the 1963 election, that the heir would come, as he eventually did, from the ranks of the KADU leadership.

Just as remarkable as Kenyatta's new stature among the European settlers was the way in which, all past hesitations dropped, he moved to take command of his administration and to make it clear that, as Malcolm MacDonald wrote, 'he is . . . the supreme maker and pronouncer of policy'.[3] Almost overnight Kenyatta-watchers dropped the habit of contrasting his prestige as a 'Freedom Fighter'

179

in the world outside with his supposed ineffectiveness as a domestic politician. MacDonald was to tell how, before he took up the Governorship, he was briefed by the Colonial Office that Kenyatta was elderly, drinking himself to death and failing rapidly in mental and physical powers.[4] In office he created a very different impression – and after 1 June the ability of these two men to work smoothly together played a very major role in easing the transition. MacDonald told Sandys in November that 'In all this the personality of Kenyatta towers above every other individual element. Without him . . . we should be in a mess.'[5]

On 7 June MacDonald wrote to Sandys, 'It is true that when you were in Nairobi I thought it might be possible to carry on with internal self-government until well into next year and possibly until the middle of it.' But he had changed his mind. Julius Nyerere had been staying with him in Government House and he and Tom Mboya had just dined with him. They had persuaded him that now was the hour for the East African Federation if they were willing to seize it. It was admitted that the initial public support had waned but, with KANU's triumph, it was growing again. It was true also that Uganda had been making some difficulties but now she was once more on track. There would be a crucial conference of the East African Governments about the federation in the third week of August; consequently, Mboya said, the Kenya independence conference must be planned for September. MacDonald excitedly cabled, 'A sound East African Federation is, of course, a dream answer to many of Kenya's problems.' Mboya had said that independence and federation should be established on the same day or within a few days of each other.[6]

Sandys soon realized that for this prize he would have to pay a price. He was expected to get his Cabinet and his party to agree not only that Kenya should be independent before the end of 1963 but that, once more, a brand new constitution should be significantly changed. He had not forgotten the reproaches levelled at his predecessors that the ink was never left to dry on a Kenya Constitution before Britain was giving way to the demand that it be scrapped. His junior Ministers found him curiously unsure of his ability to cope with opposition from his own camp in the Commons.[7] He had already had forewarning in May of what might be in store. While Kenya was actually voting, Frederic Bennett had put down a parliamentary question for written reply on 22 May, asking Sandys 'whether he remains satisfied that the present constitution will be suitable in all respects for independence'. Sandys replied that 'the British Government do not contemplate making any basic alterations'. Bennett was in Nairobi by the time the reply was published and he took great care that it received the maximum local publicity.[8] This was followed up on 2 July by a similar question from Patrick Wall, by which time Mboya had been to London and also made public statements deriding regionalism. Sandys again went on record against 'basic changes in the Kenya constitution which would upset the arrangements arrived at with so much difficulty between the parties'.[9] It seemed as if the British Government's hands were tied: Kenya was to be committed to KANU men and KADU measures.

Yet there was the Federation factor. Nyerere followed up the Nairobi summit by sending a message to Macmillan on 7 June, reminding him that

> Britain was advocating a federation on [economic] grounds when we, for political reasons, were opposing it . . . In its election campaign KANU brought out clearly its desire to change the present constitution of Kenya, to attain independence immediately and to become part of an East African Federation. I am asking now that Britain should agree to give independence to Kenya on the basis of a constitution determined by the elected government of that country. Furthermore I am asking that this should be done immediately so that a Federation can be inaugurated this year.[10]

As if to confirm that Federation was not on offer otherwise, Sir Ralph Hone, a constitutional lawyer and former administrator, warned the Colonial Office that he had been hired to draft a constitution for the East African Federation and that his brief was of such a nature as to 'involve the Secretary of State in great political trouble over safeguards in the Kenya Constitution for minorities'.[11]

To Sandys's initial irritation,[12] Kenyatta decided immediately after the Nairobi summit to send Tom Mboya, newly installed as Minister for Constitutional Affairs, to London with Murumbi and Mbiyu Koinange to instil urgency into the drive for Federation and to fix a definite date for Kenya independence. Sandys told Mboya, 'We are 100 per cent behind Federation', while expressing distress at that part of the Nairobi declaration which had been worded as if Britain had wanted to place obstacles in the way. Mboya brushed this aside as having been put in (presumably by Obote) merely for domestic consumption and immediately got down to laying out substantial plans for a Federation. It was to be introduced in two stages, so that the interim institutions, being built on the existing legislatures, could take over straight away while direct federal elections would follow after a year. The Central Government would have real powers in defence and foreign affairs. There would be uniform rates of federal income and company tax. External borrowing would be an exclusively federal subject, while economic planning would be a concurrent one. It would be necessary in consequence, he said, to rethink the provisions for amending the Kenya constitution in order for it to fit in this new federal structure.

Mboya asked for 20 October – the eleventh anniversary of Kenyatta's arrest – as the date for *uhuru*. Macmillan and Sandys were both undoubtedly moved by the rapid progress being made over Federation. But Sandys told the Kenyans that it would be rushing things if the end-of-colony conference were held before the Federation had been definitely settled. He was frank with Mboya about his own political problems. In normal circumstances, he said, it would have been impossible to justify to Parliament an independence date earlier than mid-1964. A 1963 date was open to criticism of indecent haste and could only be justified as facilitating Federation. Strictly for private information he said he had a December date in mind.

But private information was not good enough for Mboya. Not being able to deliver on Kenyatta's anniversary, he did not relish going home unable to proclaim any date at all. If that was to be the case, he indicated, nor could he give a pledge that the British military could stay around for a year after independence to run down their Kenya base. He would rather represent their talks as having failed to reach any kind of agreement. Sandys adjourned the meeting, whereupon Mboya rang up Kenyatta and told him that only the question of the date stood in the way. *Mzee* went straight round to Government House and persuaded MacDonald to cable Sandys, urging that a date be given. The Governor suggested 30 December but in the end Macmillan and Sandys took Mboya's point that, if the new Federation was going to apply for UN membership during the current session of the General Assembly, Kenya must be free by 12 December. The communiqué announced that date.[13]

MILITARY CONSIDERATIONS

A paragraph of the Sandys–Mboya communiqué of 20 June 1963 recorded that 'the retention of a British military base in Kenya after independence was not desired by either the British Government or the Kenya Government'. It went on to say that the withdrawal of British troops should take place over twelve months, although there was some mention of the possibility of defence facilities which Britain and Kenya might be able to offer each other after independence. Thus finally perished the doomed post-Suez project of basing Britain's Middle East reserves on Kenyan soil. The costly buildings at the Kahawa Base were, as *The Economist* had predicted when they were started, just completed in time for them to be handed over at independence – when they were used to accommodate the new Kenyatta University.

A last attempt at a permanent military presence had been made by Sir Patrick Renison on his fateful visit to meet Sandys in November 1962. Renison had hoped to trade the indefinite presence of British troops for the underwriting of Kenya's ambition to build up its army from the present three battalions of King's African Rifles to a more balanced force of Brigade Group strength. Sandys replied unsympathetically that he wondered whether this made sense. It was no good giving sizeable economic aid only to have it squandered in building up an army. Renison tried the argument that, failing a British response, Odinga might fill the vacuum by bringing in communist help. But this had no effect on Sandys either. His officials put it to Renison that he was assuming that no solution of the Northern Frontier District problem was possible that did not leave behind a *casus belli*. Renison retorted, realistically enough, that he doubted whether a peaceful solution was possible and that, even if it were, one Brigade Group would still be needed.[14]

The speeding up of the final rush to independence meant that the chances, never bright, of avoiding a *casus belli* with the Somalis were snuffed out. In March, after Sandys had announced the creation of a seventh region in the North-East, Somalia broke off diplomatic relations with Britain. The Americans, who were worried by active Soviet efforts to gain control over the Horn of Africa, were not impressed by the British handling of the issue. 'UK ineptness has added to this mess,' Robert Komer of the National Security Council reported to President Kennedy. 'The British have long encouraged the Somalis to think the UK would give them

Somali Kenya before granting independence. But Sandys, in nego-
tiating the Kenya constitution . . . reversed the field and triggered
off the Somalis.'[15]

MacDonald flew to Wajir, in the North-East region, hoping that
his legendary ability to get on with unsophisticated people would
work for him again. It did not. All thirty-four chiefs from the six
districts had resigned and no one would talk to him. He came back
very dispirited.[16] The boycott of the elections was completely effective. The one attempt, at Isiolo, to keep the polls open in the hope
of being able to elect somebody, however small the vote, produced
an angry riot on the second day which was suppressed by police
shooting that killed four people.

Meanwhile, in the course of five speeches in the House of Lords,
vigorously delivered if a little spoilt by an excess of historical discur-
siveness, the Earl of Lytton, a former Northern Frontier administrator,
strove to bring home Britain's obligation to settle the matter finally
while it still had the power.

Despite the absence of diplomatic relations with Mogadishu a
conference was assembled in Rome in August between the British
and Somali Governments. There was no meeting of minds. The
Somalis had insisted as a condition of the meeting that it must
be bilateral. Mboya, Gichuru and Koinange, not being allowed to
represent the Kenya Government, were therefore included in the
British delegation. When the Somalis had completed expounding
their case the Minister of State who headed the British delegation
soon yielded the floor to Mboya, who disposed of the Somali case
with panache in line with Pan-African principles. The British then
made the statement that they could not take a unilateral decision
to change the frontiers of Kenya on the eve of independence against
the express wishes of the Kenya Government.[17]

Just as in 1962 the policy of discovering the views of the people
of the Northern Frontier District (NFD) had turned out not to
mean that decisions were to be made 'in accordance' with these
views, so in 1963 there was scarcely any transition between treating secession as premature and its being treated as too late. It was
scarcely surprising that already in the weeks just before independence there were no fewer than nineteen instances of *shifta* (guerilla)
action in the barren north.

EUROPEANS AT BAY

Politically the Europeans in Kenya were concerned in 1963 with whether the land settlement schemes would restore a real market in land, whether the British Government could be pressured into bailing out those who wanted to leave but could not afford to, whether they would accept any continuing moral responsibility for Europeans who opted to stay, and whether the new Kenyatta Government, shortly to be sovereign, would respect the guarantees which had been offered.

An incident in the House of Commons that occurred in May 1963 just before the Kenya election illustrated the possibilities for political pressure. At the end of April, with Sandys away, Nigel Fisher, the Colonial Under-Secretary, had been battling alone in answer to some close questioning from the Tory backbenches and by Sir Anthony Hurd in particular. Hurd wanted to know what was being done for various categories of white settlers, some of whom had fallen on bad times and were unable to extricate themselves from the rapidly changing situation. Hurd cited a bitter article in *The Times* by Maconachie Welwood of the Coalition Party, now the most effective spokesman of the European minority, on the theme that 'our pledges to Europeans will never be fulfilled'. Fisher stonewalled as he had done before, adding that, 'I think it only right and fair to say that the schemes are African settlement schemes; they are not European compensation schemes.'[18] The reason he had to say this, which caused great offence to his own party, was that the Treasury bridled at the word 'compensation' as opening the way for limitless claims from British subjects who had believed official promises and seen them not fulfilled.

On this occasion, the Tory Chief Whip, Martin Redmayne, informed the Prime Minister that 'some of our more responsible members' had been to see him about their worries. He had, consequently, taken Fisher aside and 'asked him to tell me what his problems were'. Fisher listed the compassionate cases, over 300 in all, where 'the difficulty is that the element of compensation is very obvious'. The Colonial Office was trying to get the Kenya Government to help it work out a scheme that would contrive to obscure that element. The million-acre settlement scheme was going well but only covered 800 farmers and there were 2,000 more, many of whom wanted to leave Kenya. The Treasury would not allow another £1 million capital for the Kenya Land Bank to help these farmers unless the sum was docked off the £4.1 million grant promised to independent Kenya for development aid. Fisher said that this was inviting African Ministers to say, 'You are cutting down on our schools, hospitals and agricultural development and giving money instead to the settlers. They are your problem and your responsibility.'[19]

Macmillan sent a minute to the Chief Secretary, John Boyd-Carpenter, telling him that there was strong feeling about this among their supporters[20] and that 'I believe that we have a moral obligation to these people.' Boyd-Carpenter showed willing to help with some of the compassionate cases but was still adamant about avoiding payment of compensation. It should be possible for the Bank of England to rustle up some help for the extra settlers from commercial banks. A week later the Chief Secretary gave in: the banks would not help, so the Land Bank had to have the extra million.[21]

THE FATE OF FEDERATION

'My conclusion is that Federation by the end of this year is a near certainty,' wrote Sir David Hunt from Kampala on 1 July. 'The three countries are so committed and there is such a wave of popular enthusiasm that I cannot see now what is to stop it.' Yet in the course of the same letter Hunt listed some indicators that might have seemed to point to an opposite conclusion. Kenya's intention, he had been told by MacDonald, was that the Federation would be a tight one; there was a general consensus that Kenyatta would be the first Federal President. But the Kenyans also assumed Mboya would be Foreign Minister. Would the Ugandans really be satisfied with Obote being only a Vice-President without portfolio? Hunt thought he would want to be in charge of foreign affairs, while Nyerere would be the Vice-President in charge of internal matters. 'What is unclear to me,' he reflected, 'is what powers would be left to the Governments of the three Regions. KADU's idea is that there should be no Government of all Kenya, all the powers given to that Government being taken over by the Federal Government. I don't think that is likely.' But then, he argued, something like this would surely have to happen over Buganda since 'once Uganda surrenders to the Federation the minimum powers which must be necessary, it will have very few powers left vis-à-vis Buganda'.[22]

Another bad omen, little noticed at the time, was a speech on

21 June by Kwame Nkrumah, who still entertained dreams of developing sufficient leverage from his little western republic of Ghana to make himself President of Africa. 'Regional groupings of any kind are a serious threat to the unity of Africa,' he declared. 'Only by fomenting and nursing regional and sectional political groupings in Africa can the imperialists and ex-colonial Powers be sure of retaining their rapidly waning influence in Africa ... It is for the same reason that the British Government also is reported to have fervently supported the idea of political federation in East Africa.' Milton Obote was becoming notorious for his echoing of the language of Nkrumah; indeed on 8 June he had received a dressing-down from Sandys for the un-Commonwealth language[23] he had just used about Britain at a Pan-African conference at Addis Ababa. There were worrying reports about the machinations of the Ghanaian High Commissioner in Kampala, Busumtwi Sam.[24]

At the beginning of July the British noted the 'caginess' of Obote's references to Federation in the Uganda Parliament. Later, referring to Nkrumah's dismissive remarks, the Opposition leader said, 'Pan-Africanism can be thought about later but we in East Africa are in a hurry.' To this Obote's powerful cousin[25] Akbar Nekyon, the Minister of Information, made a direct reply. He denied that Uganda was fully committed to federation; the negotiations for it he compared to the endless saga of the Geneva Disarmament conference. 'But we Africans are brothers,' a member interjected. Nekyon riposted, 'Brothers we may be, but we have our interests to protect.'[26]

Despite such straws in the wind, Britain was in July clearly of the opinion that East African Federation was as good as done. On 9 July Sandys had written to Sir Geoffrey de Freitas, who after a career as a Labour politician and junior Minister, was serving as High Commissioner in Ghana, to offer him the post of the first High Commissioner to the new East African Federation 'for which we need someone with political nous and experience of Africa'. De Freitas accepted a week later. 'All the indications are that the East African Federation will become a reality,' the Permanent Secretary to the Commonwealth Relations Office wrote.[27] The CRO had sufficient delicacy to stipulate that only Sir Geoffrey's formal appointment as first High Commissioner to Kenya be mentioned in the public announcement but De Freitas took very good care that correspondents were heavily briefed about the bigger intention that lay behind it. The hint was widely picked up and did not escape the suspicious eyes of Milton Obote.

In mid-August Mboya and Murumbi produced a memorandum which found its way into the British Cabinet files. It was the first overt sign that the Federation project was in serious trouble. Though the Heads of Government had been supposed to meet in Dar es-Salaam on 10 August this had been cancelled and the working party had met on its own, with Zanzibar present for the first time as a fourth member. The two Ministers were quite blunt about the problem. 'Whereas Kenya and Tanganyika are in complete agreement in their interpretation of the Nairobi declaration of 5 June, Uganda and Zanzibar hold completely opposed views and would not agree to discussion of any other issue unless and until their views were met.' Mboya and Murumbi traced the difficulty back to the working party's meeting at Kampala on 29 June when Uganda had changed its representative and had started querying all the instructions to the legal draftsmen. 'The point was reached . . . when the very personality and existence of the proposed Federation was, in our view, questioned by Uganda, i.e. the suggestion that such matters as foreign affairs, citizenship and foreign borrowing be excluded from the federal list of subjects.' They concluded that, apart from the problems of the Kingdoms inside Uganda, there had been very strong external pressure against federation.[28] For Obote, the right-wing objections of the Buganda monarchist movement on whose votes he depended were being reinforced by leftist suspicions that Mboya and Nyerere would align themselves with the West.

This was bad news for Tom Mboya who had invested a great deal of political capital in the notion of Federation which he had been driving forward in his own imperious way. In Kenya the most popular new song to be belted out in the *bundu* was one in praise of union with Uganda and Tanganyika. There was also widespread support in political circles in Kenya for Mboya as East African Foreign Minister. The motives for this were mixed. Some Kenyans who were apprehensive of a Mboya dictatorship after Kenyatta would have been glad to see him diverted from domestic politics to a sphere in which his country could safely take pride in his undoubted talents and in foreigners' recognition of them. Some projected his career structure further and saw him eventually as the first African Secretary-General of the United Nations.

At the beginning Odinga also was in favour of Federation, even going to Kampala in an unsuccessful attempt to persuade Obote as a fellow-radical that it would strengthen Africans' international hand. He was also, it was believed, influenced by the consideration that if Kenyatta became Federal President, he, Odinga, would stand an excellent chance of becoming Kenya's next Prime Minister.[29] However, when Odinga had been to see Nkrumah, he began to tell a different tale, which had President Kennedy counting on Nyerere taking over the East African Presidency from Kenyatta before long and steering the Federation into the Western bloc.[30]

By the time that the conference assembled in London in October to wind up Britain's sovereign connection with Kenya, even Nyerere's last minute offer of the Federal Foreign Ministry to Obote was proving insufficient.[31] In an interview with the *Uganda Argus* on 8 October, Obote came out publicly against Federation. He employed the main elements of the Nkrumah case, although he did say (for what it was worth, which was very little) that he would be happy with a Federation provided that it also included the Congo, Rwanda, Burundi, Northern Rhodesia, Somalia and Ethiopia. Anything less was an example of neo-colonialism, as witness the De Freitas appointment, which the British had no right to make to a Federation which did not exist.[32]

It was apparent that so far from Kenyan independence being followed by Federation within the hour or at most within the week this was not going to come about in the immediate future, if ever. Nevertheless Kenya's independence had been slotted into the time-table of decolonization for 12 December and it was no longer practical politics to halt the process.

END-OF-COLONY CONFERENCE

At the last London conference on Kenya in October 1963, which was supposed just to tie up loose-ends and only to make modifications in the *majimbo* constitution where its implementation had been shown to be impractical, Duncan Sandys was confronted with a Government backed by an impressive mandate asking for major changes. The opposition, controlling three of the Regions, still backed by most of the Europeans, was calling for the confirmation of the regional safeguards that were still in process of being erected. As President of the Coastal Region Ngala was already complaining about Nairobi's interference and threatening that if he did not get what he had been promised he would proclaim full autonomy for his region. Sandys told the Cabinet committee beforehand that it would be impossible to get Parliamentary approval for an independence bill which took away safeguards from the regions.[33] There were, he said, three points at issue: control of the police, control of the public service and provision for constitutional amendment. Although KANU's demands were excessive, experience had shown that in respect of the first two points it was fair to say that safeguards for regional interests had unduly complicated efficient and economic administration. The third point was the one where there was least hope of agreement. The Kenya Government demanded that Britain change the requirements for amending the constitution, which currently stood exceptionally high – a 75 per cent vote of the House of Representatives and a 90 per cent vote of the Senate, where KANU only commanded a bare majority. Sandys said there was a danger that KANU would withdraw from the conference before a settlement was reached. Then KADU would go for partition, the Somalis would probably secede and tribal war would break out.[34]

When the conference began Sandys started out, in that manner likened by the Duke of Devonshire to 'the mills of God', to grind his way through the material. At one point he summoned the Inspector-General of the Kenya Police Force from Nairobi and in the presence of the delegations asked him very slowly and in great detail about his establishment. Odinga's patience with this method of proceeding finally ran out. 'You are the Secretary of State,' he shouted. 'You are expected to know these things.' Sandys said calmly, 'You must be patient. It is the way I work.' Odinga screamed, 'I'm sick of the way you work. Your officials are sick of the way you work. They will not tell you, but we will tell you.' The officials present could scarce forebear to giggle.[35]

On 13 October a KADU delegation waited on Sandys and MacDonald. Bearing news from Martin Shikuku, the excitable General Secretary of KADU, who had just got back to London from a trip home to Kenya, Ngala told them that tension was high and rising in the KADU regions because of fears that Sandys was going to re-arbitrate issues that were regarded as already settled. The regions saw themselves being left with no power of their own. Their worst fears about a KANU Government were already being realized – an order had been signed for the arrest of KADU leaders and only countermanded by the Acting Governor. The paramilitary General Service Unit had been sent into KADU regions to intimidate the people. They, therefore, had no alternative but to request Sandys to arrange for the partition of Kenya.[36]

Intelligence reports were coming in telling of instructions sent by the KADU delegation in London to all KADU members of the House and Senate to congregate at Nakuru. Party members in the Coast, Western and Rift Valley regional assemblies were said to have been supplied with copies of a draft resolution, which would 'declare to the world that as from 1 November this region shall be part of the Sovereign Federal Republic of Kenya, consisting of those regions which desire independence from the tyrannical rule of the Nairobi Government'. Action would be triggered when Muliro would fly back to Nairobi and go straight on to Nakuru and the waiting politicians there.[37]

It was obvious that the conference would not achieve consensus. Sandys told the first meeting of Sir Alec Douglas-Home's new Cabinet that there had been a real danger that the KANU Government, if frustrated, would have made a unilateral declaration of independence on 20 October. 'In that event it would not have been realistic to seek to hold the country by force.'[38] At this juncture, the decisive judgment was that made by Malcolm MacDonald. To be sure, he had himself expressed anxiety ahead of the conference about the danger of the Kalenjin and the Maasai with their warrior traditions reacting violently against decisions that they rejected.[39] But, when it came to the crunch, he advocated siding with KANU on the ground that the chances of civil war would be greater should it be that party that was turned down.

Late at night, Sandys sent for Nigel Fisher, whom he considered more sensitive to the mood of the House of Commons than himself. After they had both listened to MacDonald eloquently presenting his case and after Sandys had asked 'his usual terrible questions', he turned to Fisher and asked him, 'If I did what Malcolm wants, could we get away with it in the House of Commons?' Fisher asserted that he could and that he should, provided he first explained his reasoning 'upstairs' in party committee. 'Duncan sat for a long time in total silence and said, "It's very difficult for me. I don't often call in aid as an excuse for indecision my own conscience, but . . . I feel we are letting down KADU." MacDonald responded rather formally, "Secretary of State, I do well understand the difficulties for you. This is one of the most difficult decisions that in my experience I have seen a Secretary of State have to take since I sat in your chair thirty years ago when I was Secretary of State and had to deal with the Palestine problem.'" Duncan Sandys again sat silently for a long time and then stumped off to bed. The next morning he decided in favour of KANU.[40]

MacDonald thereupon cabled his deputy in Nairobi admitting flatly that KADU would be embittered by the new amendments, which most importantly would permit changes to be made in the constitution, except over questions of land and human rights, by a two-thirds majority in a national referendum. They would provide for a single Public Service Commission and a single police service for the various regional ones (while permitting recruitment to the junior ranks within the regions). He admitted that 'some of [the changes] are contrary not only to previous agreements reached by Secretaries of State in various Nairobi talks but also to the Lancaster House framework itself'. After acknowledging in unvarnished language that they might have violent trouble, particularly from the Kalenjin, he concluded, 'In our judgment prospective damage to British and Kenya interests is far less dangerous than the damage which would result from the alternative.'[41]

MacDonald's assessment of the odds proved correct. Muliro did not fly home ahead of the rest. There was no rebellion by KADU tribes. To the contrary, three of the most verbally bellicose Kalenjin figures in KADU, one of them William Murgor of the Iten rally, crossed the floor and joined KANU, complaining to their new colleagues that Frederic Bennett had been giving KADU poor advice about the decisive effect that tribal threats such as the blowing of whistles, the sharpening of spears and talk of political secession would have on the British Parliament and Government.[42] Ngei had also by now wound up the African People's Party and returned to KANU.

In his eve-of-independence summation MacDonald said that he had persuaded Kenyatta and Daniel arap Moi, the Kalenjin leader whom he shrewdly picked out as 'easily the most important KADU figure after Ngala and even including Ngala', to get closer together. 'As a result Moi now goes direct to Kenyatta with most of his regional or tribal troubles instead of coming to me and my then having to talk with Kenyatta. Kenyatta has responded in his usual friendly way, with the result that the two of them are now on pretty good terms.' MacDonald went on that the two-party system was unlikely to last long 'because it is not an African concept except insofar as it might be based on tribal rivalries which is [*sic*] the very relic of old Africanism which we most wish to destroy.' Moi, he reckoned, was not averse to joining the Government on reasonably easy terms.[43]

One man, however, was not to enjoy the coming celebrations of *uhuru*. As early as August MacDonald had heard from a confidential source that the Government was talking about making Frederic Bennett a prohibited immigrant.[44] Throughout the life of the colony this had been one of the more dramatic ukases at the disposal of the executive; during the Emergency two future KANU Ministers, Mbiyu Koinange and Joseph Murumbi, had been made PIs. Was the new relationship between Kenya and Britain to be launched under the shadow of a British MP being treated in this way? MacDonald informed Sandys but, because of the source of the report, urged that Bennett not be told.[45] He obviously hoped after the October conference that, in the current euphoria, the idea would be quietly dropped. But in November Bennett's name appeared at the head of the list of Conservative backbenchers who were to be present on Independence Day. The decision to deny him entry was announced on the eve of the Second Reading debate in the House of Commons of the Kenya Independence Bill.

Sandys, desperately worried about the parliamentary impact, cabled MacDonald for an explanation from Kenyatta, adding bitterly that KANU Ministers seemed to be 'planning to establish what amounts to an anti-British attitude'. MacDonald was not going to have any of that. 'I confess I am surprised at your charge,' he replied. 'I have seen no evidence of this here.' On the specific question of Bennett he said he certainly did not agree that he had done nothing improper. He included a list of what he considered to have been 'serious errors in his conduct' which he thought amounted to 'a very improper and dangerous intervention by a British Member of Parliament in Kenya politics'.[46]

The Kenya Independence Bill was introduced as a very low-key affair on a Friday morning by a Parliamentary Under-Secretary, with the Colonial Secretary winding up. Although no statement on Bennett had come from Kenyatta, Sandys's fears were not fulfilled. It was not a difficult debate. Everyone spoke highly of MacDonald and Kenyatta, MPs across the spectrum showed solidarity with Bennett and Bennett himself made a dignified speech, in which he emphasized that he had exerted all his influence against KADU ideas of secession.[47]

UHURU

Days of unseasonable rain preceded Uhuru Day and 1,200 dancers were reduced to rehearsing in the wet. But on 11 December it cleared up and strenuous work was put into pumping the water from the stands in the brand new open-air stadium next to the game park. Outside the New Stanley Hotel workers removed the street sign marked Delamere Avenue and replaced it by one saying Kenyatta Avenue, before repeating the operation for the benefit of Robin Day and a camera crew who emerged from the hotel. The departure of British rule from East Africa was well-orchestrated, the people in charge having already done it twice, for Tanganyika and Uganda. Since the Duke of Edinburgh was anyway planning to spend a holiday at Lake Rudolph (now known as Lake Turkana) in the non-Somali part of the NFD, it had seemed convenient that on the way there he should put an end to British rule in both Zanzibar and Kenya. The weather was still so bad on 10 November, when he arrived from Zanzibar, that his landing at Nairobi was much delayed. On the same day that he landed the Federal Parliament of the Central African Federation died, Sir Roy Welensky remarking, 'I fought and I lost because I did not know that I was taking part in a game of chance.'

The African Heads of State were present in Nairobi in force (but not the President of Somalia), together with Duncan Sandys and the Duke of Devonshire, whom Kenyatta greeted with extra warmth on account of his grandfather, on behalf of the British Government. Altogether 80 foreign governments were represented, including the People's Republic of China in the person of Marshal Chen-yi, the Vice-Premier. The Americans had attempted to put pressure on the Kenyans to prevent him rather than a Nationalist Chinese from being invited. 'I find the presumption of the Americans and their lack of finesse quite astonishing,' Griffith-Jones had said; the trace of *schadenfreude* was not hard to detect.[48] There was quite a long list of individuals whose support the Kenya Government wanted to acknowledge. They included five Labour MPs – Fenner Brockway, Leslie Hale, Barbara Castle, Dingle Foot and John Stonehouse – as well as representatives of organizations on both sides of the Iron Curtain which had offered help when it was needed.

There were 4,000 guests at the garden party given on 11 November by MacDonald in honour of Prince Philip. They included four Mau Mau generals who had been captured in the Aberdare Mountains and had since been released. They wore khaki uniforms without insignia and stood around shyly on the Governor's lawn and shook hands with one or two of the bolder European ladies. Hundreds of forest fighters had never surrendered and now came out to accept pardon and rehabilitation. Field-Marshal Mwariama, who emerged from the forest long-haired and wild-eyed, was embraced by Kenyatta and was the object of much press attention. He was, said the *Manchester Guardian*, 'the ghost of Kenya's past'.[49] Four men from the forest moving towards the Royal Box were politely headed off from addressing the Duke by Kenyatta.

It was the night for the dancers, two and a half hours of them, representing every part of the country. Perhaps the Maasai were the most spectacular, dressed in leopard skins with their bodies decorated with red ochre and their hair plaited in grass. To avoid the traffic jams on the way to the stadium, Kenyatta and the Duke of Edinburgh went by side-roads and got stuck in the mud, arriving half an hour late. Tribal priests poured libations of honey and oil on the earth. As midnight approached a weak radio signal was received from Mount Kenya, up which a flag party of sixteen men (four of them Africans) and one woman were struggling in foul weather to plant Kenya's new flag – black, red and green with a shield and two spears – on the summit. They could not quite make the highest peak, so they settled for Peak Nelian, the second highest of the three.[50]

At midnight Kenya was free. There had been much anxiety on the part of Whitehall about what exactly was going to happen at this point. Press rumours reached Duncan Sandys about what the Kenyans had in store. It was reported that Kenyatta would pull down the Union Jack with his own hands while the floodlights were still on; another rumour was that Mrs Dedan Kimathi, the widow of the Mau Mau commander executed by the British, would do the honours. The British were anxious to avoid any such embarrassment to Royalty.[51] It was avoided. The lights went out as the Union flag was lowered and then two minutes later they triumphantly lit up again to establish the independence flag of Kenya. The following day a delegation of Mau Mau generals, their plaited hair hanging over their shoulders and armed with pangas and knives, met Kenyatta at the Independence Arena. They had come to Nairobi to see for themselves that the British flag was no longer flying in Kenya. The Duke handed over the constitutional instruments to Kenyatta who, discarding the English text of his speech that had been circulated, spoke impromptu in Swahili.[52] At one point in the ceremony, Kenyatta asked a British civil servant what happened next. 'The oath,' was the reply.[53] Previous rumours of intended risings on Independence Day proved ill-founded. The atmosphere was happy and the large crowds good-tempered.[54] Only one man seemed unhappy – Sir Geoffrey de Freitas, the new British High Commissioner. His house was not ready for him, his Rolls had not arrived, the British Prime Minister whom he admired (Macmillan) had been replaced by another (Douglas-Home) whom he did not, the 'challenging and important' country to which he had expected to be accredited (the East African Federation) was not there, and in the lesser country (Kenya) to which he had come he was not to be the No. 1 European, since Kenya, being unable to agree about the powers of a President, had decided to be for the time being a monarchy, and Malcolm MacDonald, who had thoroughly won the trust of Kenyatta, was to carry on as Governor-General.[55]

10 Epilogue

The cliché 'Let history decide' carries with it an implied promise of a clear if deferred verdict. In reality that verdict generally turns out to be muddy and indistinct. In regard to one of the main questions that, with sundry exceptions, divided white from black opinion in Kenya in the period leading up to independence, ~~history~~ for once spoke clearly. Most Europeans (and British opinion at home) thought (until the last few weeks before *Uhuru*) that Jomo Kenyatta was a tribalist and the greatest single menace to the unity of Kenya and to the survival of a white community there; for some his thoughts and motives could properly be described as evil. Most Africans, on the other hand, in Kenya and outside thought and expected that Kenyatta was the one man who could unite the peoples of Kenya and begin the task of creating a nation there. At the time when the succession to Kenyatta was first being feverishly debated Tom Mboya told the author of his hope that *Mzee* would live so long that it would not any more matter to what tribe his successor belonged.

Despite what has happened more recently in Kenya, history has come down decisively on the side of those who believed in Kenyatta. Even a man like Lord Howick (formerly Sir Evelyn Baring) who had wished that Kenya should be forever unpolluted with his name, came to recognize him as a benign and effective ruler. His prestige made a major contribution to Kenya's good reputation in its first decade of independence as being one of the most successful of Britain's ex-colonies in Africa.

In 1959 people in Britain were still asking themselves, as Lord Perth did in the Colonial Office, whether the Africans were ready for self-rule. This proved to have been the wrong question. The question should have been: were the people of Britain ready to spend the money, bear the sacrifice and accept the opprobrium of holding down people determined to be free? How was it possible to train people for government for anything more than two or three years if those people most gifted to the task were unprepared to wait any longer? In any case, the amount of economic investment required in the colonies was far beyond what Britain was in any position to provide.

In the case of Kenya, Iain Macleod achieved and is entitled to the credit for a constitutional breakthrough. But he was later responsible for some backpedalling in regard to the pace of further advance and to the release of Kenyatta. Given the strength of British feelings about Kenyatta personally and of Macmillan's apprehensions of a political backlash, it may not be surprising that Macleod should have waited until August 1961. But the result was that in the meantime a minority party took office, while those most likely to be in the lead at independence remained in opposition.

By the time that KANU, with Kenyatta, Gichuru and Mboya, at last had a share of power the country had been saddled with a novel, untried and perhaps unworkable constitution. The most that could be said for the British conduct of events was said after his dismissal by the penultimate Governor, Sir Patrick Renison. 'It gave the smaller tribes, or at any rate, their leaders a chance of catching up on the political lead of the Kikuyu and Luo and of learning to stand more firmly on their own feet,' he argued, adding, 'They took this chance and learned rapidly.'[1] Fortunately, all parties desisted from carrying out their worst threats and between them Jomo Kenyatta and Malcolm MacDonald brought the country to independence without disaster.

The policy of intense training and rapid promotion of the most promising Africans in the civil service, begun in 1960, ensured that most departments had black Permanent Secretaries at independence, although some expatriates (for instance in the police) were kept on for a while. Despite the confusion caused by the halfway steps towards *majimbo*, the structure of administration held through the perilous transition.[2]

Almost immediately, in January 1964, there was a military mutiny at Nakuru following on a revolution in Zanzibar and outbreaks in the armies of Tanganyika and Uganda.[3] Kenyatta appealed to Sir Geoffrey de Freitas for support from the British army units still in the country and the announcement that this would be forthcoming together with subsequent troop movements were enough to restore order.[4] Clashes with the Somali *shifta*, clearly trained, harboured and armed by the Somali Republic, went on for several years with cumulatively quite heavy casualties involved, including two British administrators killed,[5] until a treaty was arranged between the two countries in the margins of an African Heads of State and Government meeting at Kinshasa in 1967.

Vice-Premier Oginga Odinga was under suspicion from the outset on account of his connections with communist countries and his sponsorship of Field-Marshal Okello, who brought off the military coup in Zanzibar. He further antagonized Kenyatta by refusing to accompany him to a Commonwealth meeting in London in the hope of becoming Acting Prime Minister in his absence. (Kenyatta asked him: 'Are you going to challenge my authority?' When Odinga remained stubborn Kenyatta closed the conversation by saying, 'I accept your challenge.') Interception of Odinga's cables showed that he was under heavy pressure from his Chinese paymasters to show more results. He had for instance felt obliged to inflate the success of a radical candidate in a by-election as 'a great victory for the progressive forces'.[6] There were constant rumours of the training and arming of radical bands.

Duncan Sandys had announced at the end of the last constitutional conference that he had a promise from the Kenya Government to implement the *majimbo* constitution in two stages, with some of the powers going to the Regional authorities on 1 December 1963 and the remainder not later than 1 January 1964.[7] This timetable was soon the subject of slippage. Handover day was first put off until 1 July, then until 31 December 1964. In August Kenyatta announced that, to clear the decks for Federation, Kenya would become a Republic on the first anniversary of independence, with the leader of the majority party becoming executive President. He also said that Kenya would soon become a one-party state, an outcome that had been recommended at the time of Uhuru both by Malcolm MacDonald and by the leader writer of the *Manchester Guardian*.[8]

In November the Constitution Amendment Bill, dismantling the onerously crafted *majimbo* state, received a two-thirds majority in both Houses, thanks to much crossing of the floor. On 10 November Ngala dissolved the Opposition. Kenyatta became President on 12 December 1964. Kenya applied to be and was accepted as a Republic within the Commonwealth, a body to which it attached considerable importance. Indeed it was not long before Tom Mboya could be found vigorously defending the institution of the Commonwealth at a London cocktail party against the arguments for winding it up of a British Cabinet Minister, Richard Crossman.[9]

Sir Geoffrey de Freitas, who had felt increasingly uncomfortable in his diminished role, in which he found himself expected by the white settlers to act as if he were their constituency member, had begun organizing his escape from Nairobi as early as May 1964.

The continued absence of an East African Federation was his excuse for departure and when a Republic was proclaimed and there was no need for a Governor-General, Malcolm MacDonald, described by Mboya as 'a great statesman, diplomat and a real servant of mankind', slipped quite easily into the by now vacant shoes of the British High Commissioner.[10]

Despite periodic anti-British outbursts on the Nairobi backbenches (such as a motion demanding De Freitas's recall because of his 'very hostile and uncompromising attitude'), the policies of Kenyatta's Government, officially non-aligned, possessed a quite definite tilt towards the west. Quite elaborate defence exercises were regularly carried out between the British and Kenyan forces which for a while continued to be led by British senior officers. It was not long after independence before the internal security apparatus began to be used by Africans against radicals and their communist friends.

This became more apparent when in 1964 Daniel arap Moi, formerly of KADU, became Minister for Home Affairs. Although Odinga had duly become Vice-President and presumed heir to Kenyatta when the Republic was inaugurated, he was out of that office eighteen months later. After a succession of expulsions of Communist diplomats and journalists and after an allegation by Moi that £400,000 had been used in an attempt to subvert the Government, there came a decision by the KANU parliamentary group to abolish the party post of deputy president which Odinga filled. He shortly thereafter resigned from the Government, taking Kaggia, Oneko and Waiyaki with him and formed a radical opposition called the Kenya People's Union (KPU). Thirty members of both Houses indicated support and were instantly faced with massive retaliation.

'Those who tried to play with the Government will be trampled on like mud,' said the President. New legislation was rushed through to vacate the thirty seats, which twenty-one members of the new opposition, including Kaggia and Oneko, failed to regain in what was called 'The Little General Election'. Odinga himself was re-elected and all except one of his comrades in Nyanza. But Opposition members were harassed and found their passports withdrawn.[11] After a short interval during which Murumbi was Vice-President,[12] that post was awarded to the strong man of the Government, Daniel arap Moi, who was neutral as between Kikuyu and Luo and had also commended himself to Kenyatta by his acquiescence, being a Kalenjin, in a major movement of landless Kikuyu into the Rift Valley.[13]

Quite harsh criticism of government policy was for several years allowed from within the ranks of KANU and was even for a time effectively articulated by junior Ministers, such as Bildad Kaggia until he resigned and later Josiah Mwangi Kariuki, the Assistant Minister for Tourism and Wildlife, to an extent that would be unthinkable in Westminster. But the system took very unkindly to any attempt to do the same through the medium of another party. Odinga's KPU was banned in 1969 and in 1982, after Kenyatta's death, he was placed under house arrest for a year when he tried to register the Kenya African Socialist Alliance.

The prospect of an East African Federation began fairly rapidly to fade, as Uganda and Tanzania (the union of Tanganyika and Zanzibar founded in April 1964) realized their increasing inability to keep pace with Kenya, where nearly all international companies chose to locate their East African branches. The three independent governments proceeded on their own way, with periodic collisions with each other. The common market having nearly broken down, it was relaunched as the East African Community in 1967 to run common services like the airline, the harbours and the railways and to operate systems of quotas which were supposed to counteract Kenya's in-built advantages, but this never had a chance to work.[14]

In 1975–7 the common services progressively broke down amid harsh mutual reproaches, culminating in the announcement by Nyerere's Government of Tanzania that the frontier with Kenya was permanently closed. From 1971 the Community's Authority never met, because Nyerere would not sit down with Uganda's military ruler, Idi Amin. In Kenya the powerful Attorney-General, Charles Njonjo, told Parliament in June 1975 that the Community had failed for lack of political goodwill, that the idea of political federation should be forgotten and buried and that the Community should be dissolved. In 1977 separate national airlines and railway systems were being formed.

While most of the white settlers who had comparatively small mixed farms sold out within a few years of independence the grander type of European and the managers of large plantations stayed on. One of the early spectacles of independent Kenya was that of Lady Delamere receiving the winner's cup at the Nairobi races from the hands of Jomo Kenyatta. Her stepson, the present Lord Delamere, still in 1998 lives in some splendour on 50,000 acres that Sir Charles Eliot gave his grandfather in the days of the Protectorate.[15] The

European population of Kenya had gone down from 55,000 at the
time of independence to 40,000 when the next census was taken in
1969 and its composition was changing. Far more than before were
representatives of large corporations making Nairobi their regional
headquarters.

The community which suffered most were the hard-working, self-
reliant and self-sufficient Kenya Asians who were the country's most
prominent traders. 'It's still just like a suburb of Bombay,' protested James Beauttah with distaste to the present author when we
were walking through the streets of Fort Hall in 1964. It was a
sentiment that was widely felt.

The essential distinction in the constitution was that between citizen
and non-citizen, regardless of race. Non-Africans domiciled in Kenya
had two years in which to make up their minds whether to register
as citizens.[16] Dual citizenship was not allowed. Overwhelmingly the
Arabs (and many of the whites who stayed) became citizens but
well over half of the Asians did not, preferring to hold on to their
British nationality. Among the business community the proportion
was more like two-thirds.[17] From 1967 onwards non-Kenyan Asians
were confronted by laws which forced them, if they held jobs, to
reapply for temporary permits as if they were fresh immigrants or,
if they ran businesses, to operate in very limited urban areas.[18]
This caused a rush to emigrate to Britain where there was a panicky
reaction, led by Duncan Sandys, now in Opposition, who talked
of 'closing a loophole in the law' whereas, it was pointed out to
great effect by Iain Macleod, the situation arose from a generous
provision of the Kenya constitution which Sandys himself had negotiated. 'Your Kenya constitution is devastatingly clear,' Macleod
wrote in an open letter to his party colleague. 'So is Hansard . . .
And so, therefore, is my position. I gave my word. I meant to give
it. I wish to keep it.'[19] The Labour Government, having carried a
Commonwealth Immigrants Bill to limit such admittances, was then
obliged to concede that Britain could not rebuff Kenya Asians with
British passports if they were expelled from Kenya and had nowhere else to go. They have since proved themselves admirable
immigrants.

An ominous trail of blood from political assassinations either
never explained at all or inadequately cleared up has marred the
political record of independent Kenya. First, there was the left-
wing Asian and ally of the forest fighters and later of Odinga, Pio
Gama Pinto, who was executed very professionally in his driveway

in 1965 by two teenagers. Next, Tom Mboya was assassinated in a Nairobi street on 5 July 1969; so perished, one month before he would have been 39, one of the most gifted leaders modern black Africa has yet produced. Africa could ill afford to squander so rare a resource. A Kikuyu, trained as a sapper in Bulgaria, was tried, condemned on circumstantial evidence and executed for the crime but without his reference to the 'big men' who should have been picked up ever having been elucidated.

The next victim was the charismatic Josiah Mwangi Kariuki, once a favourite of Kenyatta's who, though a junior Minister as late as October 1974, had articulated for some time the growing sense that a small elite group was acquiring great wealth and that, as Kenyatta grew very old, cronyism was becoming the predominant form of government. The seeds of corruption had been sown very early after *uhuru*, though its impact had been masked by the country's initial appearance of prosperity. But Kenya, lacking natural resources, is basically a poor, rural country and great contrasts in wealth, at first tolerated, were increasingly criticized. 'We do not want,' Kariuki said, 'a Kenya of ten millionaires and ten million beggars.' In March 1975 Kariuki was murdered. He had last been seen in the company of members of the paramilitary GSU (Government Services Unit).[20] The most recent, post-Kenyatta, instance of politics leading to death was in 1990 with the assassination of the incumbent Foreign Minister, Robert Ouko, a Luo, a crime which also was never cleared up.[21]

Kenyatta died in 1978. Although there had been over the years tense struggles and intrigues between a section of the Kikuyu elite and the supporters of Vice-President arap Moi, over the succession, the actual passage of power to the Vice-President proceeded surprisingly smoothly.[22] This was a tribute to Moi's immense energy in building up contacts and support above all in the rural areas across the country. Thus in the end a member of the former KADU leadership, which had stood for democracy, pluralism and opposition to big tribe-dominance, acquired the supreme power which twenty years later he still wields, having been re-elected President again in 1997.

The outcome should have been ideal – the fulfilment of Mboya's wish that Kenyatta should live so long that it would not matter what tribe his successor came from – but unhappily the reverse has been the case. The corruption and cronyism which had started eating into Kenyatta's fine record as his term approached its end were many times increased under his successor. The single party which had been an informal loose-reined catch-all under Kenyatta, who had managed the country through the civil service rather than the party, was made a legal reality in 1982 and an altogether more tightly disciplined affair. The scope for criticism and free debate, already limited, was continually narrowed, civil society crippled and human rights infringed until in December 1989 President Moi over-reached himself by proposing to build the tallest building in Africa, with sixty storeys, to house the KANU party offices and to be fronted by a massive statue of himself.

This aroused sufficient opposition, both internally and among Kenya's international creditors, that Moi was obliged not only to cancel the project but to allow in December 1991 the formation of other political parties.[23] There have since been two incompetently (or, as some say, dishonestly) run elections – in 1992 and 1997 – which Moi won against the Kikuyu and the Luo who since the re-introduction of pluralism had been in opposition to his regime but had showed themselves incapable of banding together under one presidential candidate. In a sense one might say that Lord Perth's policy of April 1961 of promoting 'the Rest' at the expense of the Kikuyu and Luo[24] has, through the agency of arap Moi, for the time being prevailed, though at a high price in terms of Kenya's internal stability, economic prospects and international reputation.

But these matters go beyond the scope of this book and tend to subvert its message, which is that Kenya attained independence at the end of 1963 without at that time suffering any of the terrible Congo-like consequences that, only the previous year, had been freely predicted.

Notes and References

1   The Foundation of Kenya Colony

1. P[ublic] R[ecord] O[ffice] Kew CO 533/234 ff 432–44. Kenya was how Johann Krapf, the German missionary who was in 1849 the first white man to see the mountain, transliterated the Kamba pronunciation of the Kikuyu name for it, Kirinyaga. The Kamba substituted glottal stops for intermediate consonants, hence 'Ki-i-ny-a'. T. C. Colchester, 'Origins of Kenya as the Name of the Country', Rhodes House. Mss Afr s.1849.
2. PRO CO 822/3117 Malcolm MacDonald to Duncan Sandys. Secret and Personal. 18 September 1963.
3. The new rail routes in question were the Uasin Gishu line and the Thika extension. M. F. Hill, *Permanent Way. The Story of the Kenya and Uganda Railway* (Nairobi: East African Railways and Harbours, 2nd edn 1961), p. 392.
4. *Daily Sketch*, 5 July 1920, p. 5.
5. *Sekanyolya* ('the crane [or stork] looking out on the world') was first printed in Nairobi in the Luganda language in 1921. From time to time it brought out editions in Swahili and for special occasions in English. Harry Thuku's *Tangazo* was the first Kenya African single-sheet newsletter.
6. Interview with James Beauttah, Fort Hall, 1964. Beauttah was one of the first English-speaking African telephone operators. He claimed to be the first African to have electricity in his house.
7. PRO FO 2/377 A. Gray to FO, 16 February 1900, 'Memo on Report of Law Officers of the Crown re. East Africa and Uganda Protectorates'. 'The effect of the opinion of the law officers is that Her Majesty has, by virtue of her Protectorate, entire control over all lands unappropriated . . . and may, if so pleased, proclaim such land as "Crown lands" . . . The opinion leaves an extremely thin line of demarcation between British dominions and Protectorates.'
8. PRO CO 544/12 pp. 400 *et seq.* Report of Native Affairs Department, 1920–21.
9. CO 533/214 John Sinclair, Acting British Resident, Zanzibar, to Northey. Milner to Curzon, 3 January 1920.
10. *The Times*, 9 July 1920. 'Kenya Colony: The New Rules in East Africa'.
11. Norman Leys, *Kenya* (Hogarth Press, 1926).
12. PRO CAB 134/1560 CPC(61)30, 14 November 1961. Memo to Cabinet from the Colonial Secretary.
13. The 1921 census of Africans was broken down as follows: Nyanza 881,135; Ukamba 274,136; Kikuyu 677,137; Coast 177,692; Naivasha 138,012; Masai 42,000; Jubaland 60,000; Northern Frontier District 80,000; totalling 2,330,112. The figures for the last three provinces were guesses. Jubaland was seceded to Italy in 1924. PRO CO 544/12

205

pp. 400–63. Report of the Native Affairs Dept, 1 Apr. 1920–31 Mar. 1921.

14. See the address presented by the British community in Zanzibar to the Acting Consul-General, Frederic Holmwood, on the occasion of Queen Victoria's Jubilee in 1887: 'Zanzibar which, looking at the important Indian element in its population and trade might almost be called a British colony, ... now ... boasts of most of the appliances of civilization which a progressive trading community requires.' See also N. S. Thakur, *A Brief History of the Development of Indian Settlement in East Africa* (Nairobi, 1961).

15. Most of the indentured labourers who survived the rigours of East African employment returned to India. They were not a principal source of the East African Asian population.

16. U. K. Oza, 'Indian Settlement in East Africa', *Colonial Times*, 1 July 1933. 'On account of our Indian Empire we are compelled to reserve to British control a large portion of East Africa. Indian trade, enterprise and emigration require a suitable outlet. East Africa is, and should be, from every point of view, the America of the Hindu' – Sir Harry Johnston, Commissioner for the Uganda Protectorate, 'Report on Uganda', FO 2/719, 11 July 1901.

17. Colonists' Association, 'Address to Alfred Lyttelton, Colonial Secretary', 1905. Author's archive.

18. For a bizarre example, see Richard Waddington to Frederic Holmwood, Acting Consul-General in Zanzibar, on 6 September 1886, proposing, in defiance of geography, to lay a light railway between Zanzibar and Bombassa [*sic*] to open up the Kimberley goldfields. Holmwood himself wanted to build a line to the uplands around Mount Kilimanjaro, which being 4,000 ft above sea level were suitable for European settlement. Holmwood Papers. Zanzibar Archives.

19. Ronald Robinson and John Gallagher, *Africa and the Victorians. The Official Mind of Imperialism* (Macmillan, 1961), chapter XI 'Uganda, The Route of Liberalism'.

20. Until 1902 the Uganda Protectorate included the Provinces of Kisumu and Naivasha, thereafter in Kenya. For that reason, when for a short while the British lent countenance to a Zionist project to found a Jewish National Home in the East African Highlands, the idea was in some quarters given the *soubriquet* of 'Juganda'.

21. PRO FO 2/447 Eliot to Lord Cranborne, 15 May 1901.

22. PRO FO 2/569 Dr Radford to Dr Macdonald (Principal Medical Officer, EAP). FO 2/571 John Ainsworth to Eliot.

23. Herbert Samuel MP, *Parliamentary Debates (Hansard) House of Commons Vol. 116*, 11 December 1902, col. 938 ff.

24. Quoted by Herbert Samuel MP, 'A Tourist in Uganda' in *East Africa and Uganda Mail*, 10 January 1903.

25. In *East African Protectorate* (Edward Arnold, 1905), Sir Charles Eliot wrote, 'It is a curious confession but I do not know why the Uganda Railway was built and I think many people in East Africa share my ignorance.' (p. 208)

26. Eliot, ibid, p. 220.

27. *The Nineteenth Century*, September 1904.
28. PRO FO 2/843 Marsden (Cape Town) to Eliot, 7 November 1903.
29. A. T. Matson, 'Early Newspapers of East Africa'. A onetime major in the Salvation Army, Olive Gray 'tilted at various personalities and abuses in a flowery style which often degenerated into forthright abuse'. The *East African and Uganda Mail* was founded in August 1899 and expired in August 1904. The 'rat' was Arthur Marsden.
30. PRO FO 2/720 Frederick Jackson to Sir Clement Hill, 25 May 1903.
31. W. S. Churchill, *My African Journey* (The Holland Press, 1962), p. 14.
32. Norman Leys, *Kenya*, p. 171.
33. Margery Perham (later Dame Margery) was at this point at the beginning of her most distinguished career as an africanist.
34. Margery Perham, *East African Journey. Kenya and Tanganyika 1929–30* (Faber & Faber, 1976), p. 140.
35. For example, Sir Evelyn Baring, 'I had always regarded British people on the whole as being calm and reasonable. Of course, the Kenya settlers looked like British people but, probably due to the altitude, calm and reasonable was just what the political leaders were not. They were highly excitable.' Rhodes House, Howick Papers, Mss Afr s.1574.
36. Eliot, *The East African Protectorate*, p. 3.
37. PRO CO 533/41 J. Gosling, Postmaster-General Nairobi to Frederick Jackson, 10 January 1908, forwarded by Jackson to the Earl of Elgin, 27 January 1908.
38. M. P. K. Sorrenson, *Origins of European Settlement in Kenya* (OUP, 1968), chapter XII 'The Masai Treaties'. At the 1961 East African Governors' conference, when the British were beginning to think of leaving, it was argued that the Maasai Agreements would be unlikely to enjoy Treaty status in international law because, by the Agreements themselves, 'the Maasai had conceded so much of whatever sovereignty they originally held as to destroy the legal personality assumed'. PRO CO 879/190, 4 January 1961.
39. John Lonsdale, 'The Moral Economy of Mau Mau. Wealth, Poverty and Civic Virtue in Kikuyu Political Thought', in B. Berman and J. Lonsdale, *Unhappy Valley. Conflict in Kenya and Africa. Books I and II* (James Currey, 1992), pp. 332–4.
40. Jomo Kenyatta, *Facing Mount Kenya* (Secker & Warburg, 1938).
41. In Colonel R. Meinertzhagen's *Kenya Diary* (Oliver & Boyd, 1957) one of the first of the white settlers, Sandbach Baker, tells the author that he had been given 5,000 acres in 1901 provided he supplied Nairobi with meat. Asked if the Kikuyu were compensated he said the land was unoccupied owing to a decrease in the population because of famine and disease (p. 77).
42. Y. P. Ghai and J. P. W. B. McAuslan, *Public Law and Political Change in Kenya* (Nairobi: OUP, 1970), pp. 27–8.
43. This passage owes much to John Spencer, *The Kenya African Union* (KPI/Routledge & Kegan Paul, 1985), pp. 10–12, which brilliantly summarizes the economic background.
44. But see John Lonsdale, 'The Conquest State of Kenya, 1895–1905', in Berman and Lonsdale, *Unhappy Valley I*, pp. 13–44, in which the various

minor operations are added up and shown to amount to a considerable degree of conflict. See especially the chart on pp. 28–9 of 'British military operations in the Kenya highlands, 1893–1911'.

45. 'Memorandum from the Kikuyu Land Board Association to the Joint Select Committee on Closer Union', submitted by J. Kenyatta and P. G. Mockerie. Printed as appendix in Parmenas Mockerie, *An African Speaks for His People* (Hogarth Press, 1934), p. 78.

46. Dagoretti Political Record Book. Entry for 23 May 1908. K[enya] N[ational] A[rchives].

47. Colonel Robert Meinertzhagen, *Kenya Diary 1902–1906* (Oliver & Boyd, 1957) *passim*, but see especially pp. 51–2 and 73–4.

48. John Lonsdale, 'The Politics of Conquest in Western Kenya, 1894–1908', in Bruce Berman and John Lonsdale, *Unhappy Valley. Conflict in Kenya and Africa, Book I, State and Class*, p. 55.

49. Bethwell A. Ogot, 'British Administration in the Central Nyanza District of Kenya, 1900–60', *Journal of African History*, IV, 2 (1963) pp. 249–73. A. T. Matson, *Nandi Resistance to British Rule* (Cambridge African Monographs, 1993). PRO CO 533/6 The Nandi Expedition.

50. CO 533/41 Sir James Hayes Sadler to the Earl of Elgin, 31 January 1908. Minute by Winston Churchill, 3 February 1908.

51. Cynthia Brantley, *The Giriama and Colonial Resistance in Kenya* (University of California Press, 1981), especially chapter 7: 'Rebellion 1914'.

52. Spencer, *Kenya African Union*, p. 18. According to Spencer, the Fort Hall Kikuyu regarded themselves as of pure Kikuyu blood, undiluted by extra-tribal marriages, and were regarded by the others as 'proud and arrogant'. They in turn thought of Nyeri men as 'brave but unsophisticated' and of Kiambu men as 'suspicious and untrustworthy'. Kiambu people's stereotype picture of fellow-tribesmen in Nyeri and Fort Hall was said to be that of 'simple, unsophisticated folk, gullible and hot-tempered'.

53. Ogot, 'British Administration in Central Nyanza', pp. 249–73.

54. Ogot, ibid, pp. 252–3.

55. Keith Kyle, 'White Man's War'. Unpublished paper delivered at Nuffield College, Oxford, 1966.

56. The *East African Standard* (*EAS*) had actually been launched – as the *African Standard* – in 1902 by the leading Indian merchant in Mombasa, A. M. Jeevanjee, but it was taken over by white interests in 1905.

57. *EAS*, 8 August 1914.

58. PRO CO 28/537 Memo by Sir Eyre Crowe (FO), 13 August 1914.

59. Kyle, 'White Man's War'.

60. PRO CO 544/12 Native Affairs Department 1920–1.

61. Mockerie, *An African Speaks for His People*, appendix 'Memorandum from the Kikuyu Land Board Association . .', p. 80.

62. A. M. Jeevanjee, the most prominent and wealthiest Indian businessman in East Africa, was nominated to the Legco in 1909, but he was not reappointed in 1911, leaving the Indian community unrepresented.

63. For the Grogan flogging incident, see PRO CO 533/28 Acting Commissioner Jackson to the Earl of Elgin, 19 March 1907; Sub-Commissioner Hobley to Jackson, 22 March; Jackson to Elgin, 9 April; Governor

Hayes Sadler to Elgin, 19 May. Sadler said that Grogan's only excuse was, 'The Kikuyu had lost their respect for the white man [and] that want of respect was, with natives, generally followed by assault on white women.'

64. Robert M. Maxon, *Struggle for Kenya. The Loss and Reassertion of Imperial Initiative, 1912–1923* (Toronto: Associated University Presses, 1993), pp. 91–2.
65. Harry Thuku, *An Autobiography* (OUP, 1970), p. 18.
66. PRO CO 533/249 ff 245–250 Jeevanjee to Viscount Milner, 2 September 1920.
67. Rhodes House, Mss Afr s.633 Coryndon Papers Box 3. The editor of *The Democrat* was imprisoned 'for his own personal safety'. A judge issued a deportation order, but the Governor ordered him to go free.
68. The Native Affairs Department echoed this opinion and declared in its report for 1920–1 that 'There can be no question that in the future, and the sooner the better for the Colony, the skilled labour must be African'. While acknowledging that 'some [white] employers recognize their duty... to raise the status of the native', the department observed reproachfully that 'others take no interest once the day's task is done'. PRO CO 544/12.
69. Robert M. Maxon, *Struggle for Kenya*, pp. 181, 316n266.
70. According to the Native Affairs Department (Report, 1920–21, PRO CO 544/12) direct tax borne, for example, by the natives in Nyanza Province increased from £72,970 in 1915–16 to £294,730 in 1920–1. Total figures showed native tax up in those years from £182,699 to £658,413.
71. Buganda is the territory, in which a Muganda is a person; the Baganda are the people and Luganda is the language.
72. *EAS*, 21 May 1921, p. 29.
73. Spencer, *The Kenya African Union*, p. 37.
74. 'The crane [or stork] looking out on the world.'
75. Spencer, *Kenya African Union*, pp. 43–4.
76. According to Oginga Odinga, *Not Yet Uhuru. An Autobiography* (Heinemann, 1967), p. 25, James Beauttah visited Kisumu, on Lake Nyanza, for the East Africa Association and addressed large meetings.
77. Keith Kyle, 'Gandhi, Harry Thuku and Early Kenya Nationalism', *Transition* (Kampala) no. 27 (no. 4 of 1966), pp. 16–22.
78. The best account of the Thuku riots is to be found in Carl Rosberg and John Nottingham, *The Myth of Mau Mau. Nationalism in Kenya* (New York: Praeger; and London: Pall Mall Press), pp. 49–55.
79. Luhya (or Baluyia) did not become a universally adopted name for what had been called the Bantu Kavirondo until after the Second World War. It was adopted by the North Kavirondo Central Association in 1935. But the elders at that time rejected the name. B. A. Ogot, *History of the Southern Luo Vol. I*, p. 139n21.
80. John Spencer, *James Beauttah* (Nairobi: Stellascope Publishing Company, 1983).
81. Secretary of the Kavirondo Association to Chief Native Commissioner, in *The Leader*, 14 January 1922, p. 21. The 'mass meeting' was held at

Lundha, North Gem; the attendance was reported with suspect precision as being 8,846. See also the account in Oginga Odinga, *Not Yet Uhuru*, pp. 25–9.

82. *EAS*, 4 February 1922. 'We think this most momentous declaration by the Colonial Secretary at a public function practically settles the political and racial future of Kenya Colony and for this . . . the greatest thanks are due to our statesman-settler, Lord Delamere.' (*The Leader*, 4 February 1922, p. 14)

83. *EAS*, 15 August 1922.

84. The Parliamentary Under-Secretaries concerned were Edward Wood (the future Earl of Halifax)(Colonies) and Earl Winterton (India). It was therefore known as the Wood–Winterton award.

85. Vincent Harlow and E. M. Chilver (eds), *History of East Africa Vol. II*, p. 298. Elspeth Huxley, *White Man's Country. Lord Delamere and the Making of Kenya Vol. II* (Chatto & Windus, 1935 and 1953), pp. 135–7. According to Huxley (p. 136), Governor Coryndon's 'comfort was carefully considered; his place of detention was selected on account of the excellent trout fishing available close by'.

86. Rhodes House, Mss Afr s.633 Coryndon 3/5. 'The Indian Question During the Governorship of Sir Robert Coryndon'. The account given here derives primarily from this source which is amply documented. Maxon, *Struggle for Kenya*, is helpful but rather inclined to think of the Governor as being not so much panicky as a willing tool (because he was South Africa-born) of the settlers.

87. Reading to Earl Peel (Secretary of State for India), 2 May 1923. Reading Collection, India Office Records Mss. Eur.E. 238/6. Cited by T. G. Fraser, 'Imperial Policy and Indian Minorities Overseas', in A. C. Hepburn, *Minorities in History* (Edward Arnold, 1978), p. 163.

88. Rhodes House Mss Afr s.633 Coryndon 3/5, 'The Indian Question'.

89. *The Times*, 28 February 1923.

90. As Leader of the Conservative Opposition Bonar Law had given every support and encouragement to the threats of civil war by which Ulster Unionists opposed Asquith's Irish Home Rule bill in 1912–14.

91. B[ritish] D[ocuments on the] E[nd of] E[mpire], Series A Vol. 3, *The Conservative Government and the End of Empire 1951–1957 Part II* (HMSO, 1994) pp. 234–5. Peter Smithers was PPS to the Minister of State at the Colonial Office. Shortly before the Declaration of Emergency he reported on a trip to seven East and Central African territories.

92. Bodleian Modern Mss Room, Macmillan Diaries dep.d 37 f 33.

93. The mysterious and, in the circumstances, rather sinister one-word message 'Assistance' in fact related to the Kenya budget, but the appropriate Whitehall official was not there during the weekend, so it was not understood. Attempts to check up failed because of the damage to the cable service caused by the flood. Huxley, *White Man's Country Vol. II*, pp. 161–6.

94. Rhodes House Mss. Afr 746 Blundell 29/1 Item 9. 'A Preliminary Survey of the Constitutional History of Kenya', signed 'K. W.' [Kendall Ward] and dated 5 October 1951.

95. Cmnd. 1922 (1923).
96. T. G. Fraser, 'Imperial Policy and Indian Minorities Overseas', p. 164.

2 **The Rise of African Nationalism**

1. John Spencer, *The Kenya African Union* (KPI/Routledge & Kegan Paul, 1985), p. 100.
2. The name Beauttah, by which he was known in adult life, is an anglicized form of Mbutu wa Ruhara. John Spencer, *James Beauttah* (Nairobi: Stellascope Publishing Company, 1983).
3. Jeremy Murray-Brown, *Kenyatta* (George Allen & Unwin, 1972; Fontana, 1974) pp. 103–4.
4. PRO CO 544/18 Colony and Protectorate of Kenya, Administrative Reports and Papers 1925, *Native Affairs Department Annual Review*, pp. 395–448.
5. Spencer, *The Kenya African Union*, p. 100n.25.
6. For example, S. H. La Fontaine, the DC Fort Hall, met with Kang'ethe and sixty other KCA members on 25 July 1927 and subsequently minuted, 'The attitude of the members was most respectful and their behaviour orderly. As I have always maintained there is far more to be gained by allowing the Association to ventilate their opinions than by driving them underground.' K[enya] C[entral] A[ssociation] files, K[enya] N[ational] A[rchives] K 968.17.
7. KNA, K 968.17.
8. Interview with Beauttah, Fort Hall 1964. Also Spencer, *James Beauttah*, p. 14. 'Ever since my days in Uganda when I saw how successfully the Baganda had dealt with the British and how useful the Kabaka was in unifying them, I had urged that we Kikuyu get a Paramount Chief.'
9. KNA K.C.A. file, K 968.17. Joseph Kang'ethe and others to Grigg, 31 Dec 1925. DC Fort Hall to SC Nyeri, 2 January 1926. A 'mass meeting' of 600 Kikuyu sent a telegram to the Chief Native Commissioner asking for a reply to their petition, adding, 'We, the very loyal subjects of the King, beg to say that we have been deprived of [the] only one educated Kikuyu we had in [the] country [presumably James Beauttah]'. The reply was a rebuke for the telegram's 'very needless expense'.
10. For a sensitive examination of the meaning and significance of Kenyatta's journalism, see John Lonsdale in '"Listen While I Read": The Orality of Christian Literacy in the Young Kenyatta's Making of the Kikuyu', in Louise de la Gorgendière *et al.* (eds), *Ethnicity in Africa* (Centre of African Studies, University of Edinburgh, 1996).
11. *Muigwithania*, vol. 1, no. 3, 25 July 1928, included a letter from G. H. M. Kagika, on the theme 'We Kikuyu speak one language from Kabete to Meru. Then what prevents us agreeing together even as our language agrees? . . . Let us put away sneering such as, Who are *they*? Who are *you*? You Kabete folk. You Metumi-ites. You Gaki people . . .'. The editor also calls on chiefs and wealthy men to build houses of stone or brick and have their children sent to Europe 'to be civilized by an

education which is not curtailed'. KNA, K 968.17. Police translations are used in this and subsequent quotations. The translator was A. Ruffel Barlow, a lay missionary with the Church of Scotland Mission.

12. *Muigwithania*, vol. 1, no. 3, KNA, K 968.17.
13. PRO CO 544/25 Native Affairs Department Annual Report 1928 Vol. II.
14. L. S. Amery, *My Political Life Vol. II War and Peace 1914–1929* (Hutchinson, 1953), pp. 360–2.
15. Amery, ibid, p. 362.
16. President, Kikuyu Central Association to Rt. Hon Sir Samuel Wilson, 30 May 1929. KNA. The KCA also asked that Swahili should be allowed in Legco and knowledge of it counted in the civilization test or, if not, that teaching of Swahili should be abolished in Kikuyu schools and only Kikuyu and English taught.
17. Spencer, *The Kenya African Union*.
18. *Correspondence between the Kikuyu Central Association and the Colonial Office 1929–1930* (privately printed, London 1930).
19. *Muigwithania*, vol. 2, no. 2, July–August 1929. KNA.
20. Kenyatta, 'Muigwithania's Journey, 59 Castletown, West Kensington, W. 14, 15 April 1929', in *Muigwithania*, vol. 1, no. 12 (editor Henry Gichuiri), May 1929. KNA.
21. Kenyatta, 'The Voice of the Disseminator of the Work of the Country. The Town of London, England, 26 March 1929', *Muigwithania*, vol. 1, no. 11, April 1929. This was his first report from London. It began, 'I wish first to return thanks to the Almighty for bringing me into this distant country and for taking me past all danger in the Great Sea.' Its thesis was that Kikuyu must take steps to avoid the reproach that 'The Black People have very much land and rich land but they do nothing with it: it remains idle.'
22. KNA Political Situation Report, Kiambu, 12 January 1930.
23. See Minority Rights Group, *Female Circumcision, Excision and Infibulation: Facts and Proposals for Change* (revised 1985 edition).
24. A. Fenner Brockway, *Outside the Right* (George Allen & Unwin, 1963), p. 59.
25. Kenyatta, *Facing Mount Kenya*, pp. 130–54.
26. PRO CO 544/28 Native Affairs Department Annual Report 1929 Vol. II. 'The policy of the Government is not to attempt complete prohibition.'
27. There were 14 missionary societies in Kenya, Protestant and Roman Catholic, British, American, French and Italian. They maintained 67 British mission stations, 34 American, 13 French, 20 Italian and 8 Seventh Day Adventists. Eleven were in townships; the rest in 'native' districts.
28. Spencer, *Kenya African Union*, p. 76.
29. D. C. Kiambu, 'Political Situation Report . . .'.
30. *Kikuyu Crisis*, Church of Scotland Memorandum prepared by the Kikuyu Mission Council on Female Circumcision, 1 December 1931.
31. Sir Edward Grigg to Dr J. W. Arthur, 16 November 1929. 'I could not shut my eyes to the fact impressed upon me by the Provincial

Commissioner that you were generally regarded as an emissary of the Government.' KNA.
32. F. B. Welbourn, *East African Rebels* (SCM Press, 1961). On syncretic teaching in Kavirondo see, for example, John Ainsworth, 'Extract from My Record of Service, Chapter 30', dealing with the case of 'an educated Christian convert known as Johanna Owalo', who preached against the Trinity and in favour of polygamy. Rhodes House. Also C. Makokha, 'The Rise of African Sects among the Baluyia' (Makerere, 1951, unpublished).
33. *Kikuyu Crisis.*
34. 'Translation of the Words of the Muthirigu or Kurururo Ngoma', KNA.
35. Murray-Brown, *Kenyatta*, p. 141.
36. Rhodes House Mss Afr s.233(1) Acting Inspector of Schools to DC Fort Hall, 17 March 1931. 'Dances and Meetings in the Fort Hall Reserve'.
37. *Kikuyu Crisis.* Shortly after he got back Kenyatta 'was interviewed by the Kirk session of the church at Kikuyu of which church at one time he had been a member. He expressed regret at the impasse . . . He then applied to the DC Kiambu for official support in an attempt to bring peace between the malcontents and the mission. This was refused on the ground that there was a recognized authority in the district, namely the chiefs, and that any peace-making necessary should be achieved through them.'
38. Murray-Brown, *Kenyatta*, pp. 146–7.
39. Michael D. Callahan, 'The Failure of "Closer Union" in British East Africa', *Journal of Imperial and Commonwealth History*, vol. 25, no. 2, May 1997, pp. 267–93.
40. Passfield to Beatrice Webb, 30 September 1931 in Webb Papers. Quoted by Gregory, *India and East Africa*, p. 368.
41. George Bennett, *Kenya: A Political History* (OUP, 1963), pp. 81–2.
42. John Lonsdale, 'Jomo, God, and the Modern World', in Lonsdale and Berman, *The House of Custom: Jomo Kenyatta, Louis Leakey and the Making of the Modern Kikuyu*, cites Andrei M. Pegushev, 'The Unknown Jomo Kenyatta', *Egerton Journal*, vol. 1, no. 2 (1993) (Njoro, Kenya), pp. 180 and 191–2.
43. Dr John Lonsdale has developed in his paper 'Listen While I Read: The Orality of Christian Literacy in the Young Kenyatta's Making of the Kikuyu' an illuminating comparison between Kenyatta's earlier forward-looking journalism and the more static, idealized picture he gives in his book.
44. Peter Mbiyu Koinange, 'Jomo, Colleague in the Struggle for Freedom and Independence', in Ambu H. Patel (ed.), *Struggle for Release Jomo and his Colleagues* (New Kenya Publishers, 1963), pp. 21–2.
45. Harry Thuku, *Harry Thuku. An Autobiography.* Thuku renamed his party the Kikuyu Provincial Association. According to its rule book, members 'will be pledged to be loyal to HM the King of Great Britain and the established Government and will be bound to do nothing which . . . is calculated to disturb the peace, good order and government', p. 97.

46. E. S. Atieno-Odhiambo, 'The Formative Years, 1945–55', in B. A. Ogot and W. R. Ochieng', *Decolonization and Independence in Kenya 1940–93* (London: James Currey; Nairobi: East African Educational Publishers, 1995), pp. 27–30. John Lonsdale, 'Constructing Mau Mau', in *Transactions of the Royal Historical Society, 5th Series, Vol. 40* (London, 1990), pp. 248–9.

47. PRO CO 822/3171 Memorandum of European Settlement Board Farmers, 6 September 1963. 'Humble Petition of Chairman and Members of the Association of European Agricultural Settlement Board Farmers in Kenya', 20 September 1963.

48. For example, Alexander (Sandy) Storrar, Assistant Director of the Department of Agriculture, carried out a recruitment campaign in Britain in May–June 1955. He got 25 men with capital of £10,000 upwards to agree to sell up in Britain and become tenant farmers in Kenya. Another 50 were just as keen and would be able to meet the £5,000 minimum required (*Sunday Post*, 3 July 1955). In November 1955 the European Agricultural Settlement Board announced that it planned to spend £1.75 million on a five-year plan to settle 175 to 200 new tenants or assisted owners (*Sunday Post*, 8 November 1955).

49. Rhodes House Mss Afr 746 Blundell 16/1. ff 1–12 Lord Francis Scott, 'Self-Government for Kenya Now, Except for Reserves. Draft Outline', n.d. The Governor for the self-governing section would also be High Commissioner for the reserves. Although Lord Francis's proposed self-governing colony was to be essentially white-led, it would have displayed something of a multiracial character. In the Parliament there would have been 17 Europeans, 4 Hindus, 4 Muslims, 2 Arabs and 3 educated, detribalized Africans.

50. George Bennett, 'From White Man's Country to Kenyatta's State', in D. A. Low and Alison Smith, *History of East Africa Vol. III* (Oxford: Clarendon Press, 1976), p. 115. Sir Wilfrid Woods, *A Report on a Fiscal Survey of Kenya, Uganda and Tanganyika* (Nairobi: Govt. Printer, 1946), pp. 82, 86.

51. Colony and Protectorate of Kenya, *Legislative Council Debates Official Report*, 22 November 1943, speech of A. B. Patel. Also see letter from Zablon Oti (Nairobi) in *EAS*, 6 December 1943: 'An African touring the African districts for his own nomination is as upright and correct as others who tour their non-native constituencies seeking election to the Legco.'

52. Spencer, *Kenya African Union*, p. 126.

53. James Gichuru, shortly after this, became a headmaster and afterwards a government chief. However, he was detained during the Mau Mau Emergency and was thus able to become a leading though moderate politician, a steadying force in nationalist politics.

54. Rhodes House. Mss Brit Emp s.365. James Gichuru and W. W. W. Awori, 'Memorandum of the Economic, Political, Educational and Social Aspects of the Africans in Kenya Colony'. Minutes by British administrators show that they were impressed by the thoroughness of the survey.

55. The Forty Club was so named because in theory all its members were

circumcised in 1940, but other young ex-Servicemen were also included.
56. Bildad Kaggia, *Roots of Freedom, 1921–1963* (Nairobi: East African Publishing House), p. 64.
57. The Forty Group was founded in 1946 by Henry Kahinga and Domenico Gatu. Many years later, after independence, Gatu described the first members as 'hooligans, unemployed youths who wanted to cause trouble to the Government' (Gatu to Spencer, 4 September 1972). In 1947 they founded the Nyeri Kikuyu Education Association but had to disband it for lack of funds. Spencer, *Kenya African Union*.
58. Spencer, *James Beauttah*.
59. How Awori managed to lose so much money is not altogether clear. He told the author that he was cheated by money-changers. Beauttah (Spencer, *James Beauttah*, pp. 64–5) says that he lost his baggage.
60. Interviews with W. W. W. Awori and Francis Khamisi, Nairobi 1961.
61. Beauttah says that Awori lost his baggage again once he got to England. 'If he could not look after his own property, how could he represent our cause as well?' (Spencer, *Beauttah*, pp. 64–5).
62. Ambu Patel is the compiler of *Struggle for Release Jomo and his Colleagues* (Nairobi: New Kenya Publishers, 1963) and has always allowed researchers generous access to his large personal archive on nationalist politics, mainly centring on Kenyatta.
63. Jack Roelker, *Mathu of Kenya. A Political Study* (Hoover Institution Press, Stanford, California, 1976). George Ndegwa, a member of the Kiambu Local Native Council, had openly declared in 1946 that he was the President of the KCA. He was sent to prison.
64. Interview with Sir Walter Coutts, 6 September 1963, Kampala. Also Rhodes House, Walter Coutts, Mss. Afr. s.1621. Spencer, *Kenya African Union*, p. 175.
65. George Bennett, *Kenya. A Political History. The Colonial Period* (OUP The Students' Library 1, 1963), p. 117.
66. Interview with Awori, 1961. He claimed to have made £10,000 in trading crocodile skins.
67. An Awori editorial in *Radio Posta* of 5 November 1947 sets the tone. 'An atmosphere of unrest had raged the country, the confidence in KAU was declining . . . Silence from the premier African political body reigned. Then the great hour of awakening came, . . . another big meeting in Nairobi. The President with all his glory commandeered the platform and for some 125 minutes he spoke. It was fiery with gusto and almost a harangue.'
68. Spencer, *Beauttah*, p. 89.
69. Oginga Odinga says that he first met Kenyatta in Kisumu in 1948, but he did not get out of his car. Odinga, *Not Yet Uhuru* (Heinemann, 1967), p. 98.
70. Odinga, *Not Yet Uhuru*, p. 99. Ogot, *Central Nyanza 1900–60*, pp. 270–1.
71. PRO CO 533/566/7 Kenyatta to Dugdale, 14 August 1950.
72. Jomo Kenyatta, 'A Prayer for the Restoration of Our Land. Memorial to the S. of S. for the Colonies presented on behalf of the African people of Kenya on the occasion of his visit to East Africa, May 1951'. James Beauttah, 'Memorandum on Educational, Agrarian, Social,

Economical and Political Problems of Kenya, submitted by the Kenya African Union, Central Province branch'.

73. 'KAU Central Province. P.C.'s Comment on James Beauttah's Memo, 12 September 1951'. KNA. 'Due regard of African opinion is naturally given but those who have experience of the authors of this memo have had cause to be astonished by their stupidity, hostility to government and ruthless disregard of the general interests of the African.'

74. Blundell, *So Rough A Wind* (Weidenfeld & Nicolson, 1964), p. 83.

3 The Politics of Mau Mau

1. Rhodes House, Howick Papers Mss Afr s.1574 Interview of Evelyn Baring (Lord Howick) by Dame Margery Perham, 19 November 1969. Baring added that he had inherited a constitution that was 'absolutely fatal', with an unofficial majority and only one African member.

2. Information: Colin Legum.

3. About 400 Kikuyu, however, had been convicted before October 1952 for offences relating to Mau Mau, which had been proscribed as an illegal organization in August 1950.

4. B[ritish] D[ocuments on the] E[nd of] E[mpire], Series A Vol. 3, David Goldsworthy (ed.), *The Conservative Government and the End of Empire 1951–1957 Part II Politics and Administration* (London: HMSO, 1994), doc. 286, pp. 234–8 Baring to Lyttelton, 10 October 1952. Lyttelton, 'Situation in Kenya, 13 October'. CAB 129/55, C(52)332, 13 October 1952.

5. J. C. Carothers, *The Psychology of Mau Mau* (Government Printing Office, Nairobi, 1954), p. 16.

6. PRO CO 822/1909 Thirteenth Council of Ministers, 27 April 1960.

7. Rhodes House, Howick Papers.

8. Bildad Kaggia, *Roots of Freedom 1921–1963* (Nairobi: East African Publishing House, 1975), pp. 66–8.

9. *Mau Mau* has no meaning in any of the languages used in Kenya, nor was it used as a password by the conspirators. Kaggia says the word *muhimu*, which is the Swahili for 'important', was employed as a code for oathing ceremonies.

10. Kaggia, *Roots of Freedom, 1921–1963* (East African Publishing House, 1975), p. 115.

11. As with some other Africans, St. Paul's *Epistle to the Galatians* seems to have been Kaggia's favourite text.

12. Interview with Bildad Kaggia, Nairobi 1961.

13. Kaggia, *Roots of Freedom*, p. 66.

14. John Spencer, *Kenya African Union*, pp. 204–6, 239n.3

15. Interview with Kaggia, Nairobi 1961.

16. Carl Rosberg and John Nottingham, *The Myth of Mau Mau* (Praeger/Pall Mall, 1966) pp. 270–1.

17. Interview with Kaggia, Nairobi 1963.

18. Interview with Kaggia, Nairobi, 1963.

19. Bildad Kaggia, *Roots of Freedom*, p. 82.

20. Kaggia interview, 1963.
21. Mbiyu Koinange and Achieng Oneko, *Land Hunger in Kenya* (London: Union of Democratic Control, 1952) sets out in moderate language the full African case against the British treatment of the land question. They demanded 'the real implementation of Britain's declared policy'. Politically they required as an interim measure 22 elected MLCs, equal to the combined non-African representation.
22. The summary which follows of the 'Mau Mau' organization draws heavily on two published sources: Bildad Kaggia, *Roots of Freedom* and Oginga Odinga, *Not Yet Uhuru*.
23. Kaggia in *Drum*, no. 237, January 1971. *Roots of Freedom*, pp. 109–10.
24. Kaggia, *Roots of Freedom*, pp. 113–14.
25. Information: Colin Legum.
26. Kaggia, *Roots of Freedom*, pp. 114–15.
27. Rhodes House, Howick Papers.
28. Goldsworthy (ed.), *BDEE Series A Vol. 3 Part II*, doc. 286, pp. 234–5. CO 822/338 no. 14A, undated manuscript minute by Lyttelton. Dr Lonsdale makes the point that 'hooliganism' was also the word Kenyatta was using in his speeches about Mau Mau.
29. Goldsworthy (ed.), *BDEE Part II*, doc. 287, n. 3. CAB 128/25, CC 85(52)1 14 October 1952.
30. Figures of casualties during the Mau Mau Emergency are analysed by Bennett and Smith in D. A. Low and Alison Smith, *History of East Africa Vol. III*, pp. 132–3.
31. He was a member of the famous Leakey family. Blundell, *So Rough a Wind*, p. 111.
32. *Parliamentary Debates (Hansard) House of Commons Vol. 505*, 21 October 1952, cols 866–9. *Vol. 507*, 7 November 1952 cols 456–553 (Lyttelton 456–67).
33. *Parliamentary Debates Vol. 507*, 7 November 1952, cols 503–14.
34. A. Fenner Brockway, *Outside the Right* (George Allen & Unwin, 1963), pp. 55–62 and 100–13.
35. Brockway, *Outside the Right*, p. 103.
36. *East Africa and Rhodesia*, 23 October 1952.
37. Goldsworthy (ed.), *BDEE Part II*, docs. 192 ['Commonwealth Membership': Cabinet memorandum by Lord Swinton with Appendix, 11 October 1954, pp. 29–42] and 193 ['Commonwealth Membership': brief by Sir N. Brook for Sir W. Churchill, 1 December 1954, p. 43]. CAB 129/71, C(54)307. PREM 11/1726F.
38. Goldsworthy (ed.), *BDEE Part II*, doc. 195, pp. 45–6. CAB 128/27/2, CC 83(54) 7 December 1954.
39. A. J. Hughes, *East Africa: The Search for Unity* (Penguin, 1963), pp. 222–3.
40. Interview with Kaggia, Nairobi 1963.
41. Oliver Lyttelton, *The Memoirs of Lord Chandos* (The Bodley Head, 1962), p. 418.
42. There was also a court ruling against the actions of the British administration in Uganda. In his oral history interview at the Bodleian Lennox-Boyd gives a misleading impression that the Kabaka's return

was agreed upon as soon as he took over. I am grateful to Dr Philip Murphy, author of the forthcoming biography of Lennox-Boyd, for clarifying for me the sequence of events.

43. Goldsworthy (ed.), *BDEE Part II*, doc. 299, p. 274. Minute by W. A. C. Mathieson, 29 November 1956. PRO CO 822/912.
44. Goldsworthy (ed.), *BDEE Part II*, doc. 298, Twining to Gorell Barnes, 12 November 1956.
45. The literature on Mau Mau includes O. W. Furley, 'The Historiography of Mau Mau', in Bethwell A. Ogot, *Politics and Nationalism in Colonial Kenya* (HADATH/East African Publishing House, 1978), pp. 105–33; Carl Rosberg and John Nottingham, *The Myth of 'Mau Mau': Nationalism in Kenya* (Pall Mall Press, 1966); David Throup, *Economic and Social Origins of Mau Mau* (James Currey, 1987); Josiah Mwangi Kariuki, *'Mau Mau' Detainee* (OUP, 1963); Donald Barnett and Karari Njama, *Mau Mau from Within* (Macgibbon & Kee, 1966); Oginga Odinga, *Not Yet Uhuru* (Heinemann, 1967); Bruce Berman and John Lonsdale, *Unhappy Valley: Book II: Violence and Ethnicity* (James Currey, 1992); Malcolm Page, *KAR. A History of the King's African Rifles and East African Forces* (Leo Cooper, 1998).
46. A. J. Hughes, *East Africa: The Search for Unity* (Penguin, 1963), pp. 118–19.
47. Odinga, *Not Yet Uhuru*, pp. 115–17.
48. Josiah Mwangi Kariuki, *'Mau Mau' Detainee*, foreword by Margery Perham (OUP, 1963), pp. 25–7. John Spencer, *Kenya African Union*, pp. 239–40. See also Barnett and Njama, *Mau Mau from Within*, pp. 56–9, and F. D. Corfield, *Historical Survey of the Origins and Growth of Mau Mau* (HMSO, 1960).
49. Barnett and Njama, *Mau Mau from Within*, p. 57.
50. Kariuki, *'Mau Mau' Detainee*, pp. 29–30. Barnett and Njama, *Mau Mau from Within*, pp. 118–19.
51. Odinga, *Not Yet Uhuru*, pp. 113–22.
52. John Lonsdale, 'Constructing Mau Mau', in *Transactions of the Royal Historical Society 5th Series Vol. 40* (London, 1990), especially pp. 242–3. 'If it was enough to say with Blundell, that they included "masturbation in public, the drinking of menstrual blood, unnatural acts with animals and even the penis of dead men", then even a dirty mind must shrink from exploring further.'
53. Barnett and Njama, *Mau Mau from Within*.
54. John Lonsdale, 'Wealth, Poverty and Civic Virtue in Kikuyu Political Thought', in Berman and Lonsdale, *Unhappy Valley II*, pp. 453–4, which challenges an earlier view that this tragedy arose from an entirely separate feud. 'By the end of 1956 the Kikuyu Guard were reckoned to have killed 4,500 Mau Mau, not far off half the total insurgent dead, and to have lost 730 men of their own.'
55. Rosberg and Nottingham, *The Myth of Mau Mau*, p. 333. But the stereotypes so attributed were not only those made by Europeans but also by other African tribes.
56. Bennett and Smith, 'Kenya from "White Man's Country" to Kenyatta's State 1945–1963', in *History of East Africa Vol. III*, pp. 132–3. The exact

total of executions was 1,015. More than a half were for 'possession of firearms' or 'consorting with terrorists'. *House of Commons Vol. 551*, cols 145–6, 25 April 1956. Asian deaths through Mau Mau were three in the security services and 26 civilians.

57. Rhodes House, Young Papers, Mss Brit.Emp. s.486, 5/3 ff 100–7. Macpherson to Young, 23 December 1954; Young to Baring, 28 December 1954.
58. Lennox-Boyd interviewed by Alison Smith, Bodleian Modern Mss Library, Mss Eng c.1433 East Africa, ff 264–5.
59. For example, the report by R. M. A. Hankey, British Chargé d'Affaires in Cairo in FO 371/102721 JE1023/2 of 27 August 1953, that the Egyptian President Neguib had received Joseph Murumbi as Vice-President of KAU and that 'two disgraceful articles' had appeared in the newspaper *Al Tahrir* about Mau Mau's 'gallant resistance', one of them by the editor, Anwar Sadat. Hankey had told Foreign Minister Fawzi that he must see to it that this sort of error did not recur, because otherwise he would find it made his job ten times more difficult.
60. After James Mwangi Kariuki had taken the first 'Mau Mau' oath, he asked if it was all right for him to continue recruiting for KAU. He was told that he could but must not disclose his new allegiance to KAU members (Kariuki, *'Mau Mau' Detainee*, pp. 27–8).
61. Macharia was placed on trial in 1959, when his statement that he had lied at the Kapenguria trial was believed but his allegation that he had been bribed to lie was not.
62. Montagu Slater, *The Trial of Jomo Kenyatta* (Secker & Warburg, 1959); Murray-Brown, *Kenyatta*, pp. 260–76.
63. Murray-Brown, *Kenyatta*, pp. 291 and 294–5.
64. Sir Michael Blundell, *So Rough a Wind* (Weidenfeld & Nicolson), pp. 123–8.
65. Rhodes House, Evelyn Baring, in interview with Margery Perham.
66. Gen. Sir George Erskine, 'Kenya, Mau Mau', 23 November 1955. Text of talk in Imperial War Museum.
67. The Ministers under Baring were: R. G. Turnbull (Chief Secretary), J. Whyatt (Legal Affairs), E. H. Windley (African Affairs), J. W. Cusack (Internal Security and Defence), C. H. Hartwell (Education, Labour and Lands), A. Hope-Jones (Commerce and Industry), E. A. Vasey (Finance and Development), Major F. W. Cavendish-Bentinck (Agriculture), L. R. Maconochie-Welwood (Forest Development, Game and Fisheries), W. B. Havelock (Local Government, Health and Housing), I. E. Nathoo (Works), B. A. Ohanga (Communal Development), M. Blundell and A. B. Patel (without Portfolio). Ohanga was defeated as soon as African MLCs became elected, as was James Jeremiah, who was made the only African Parliamentary Secretary.
68. Blundell, *So Rough a Wind*, p. 178.
69. *EAS*, 15 January 1956. The Muthaiga club was the white settlers' classiest hideout in Nairobi.
70. Goldsworthy (ed.), *BDEE Part II*, doc. 296: W. L. Gorell Barnes for Lennox-Boyd, 'The franchise in East and Central Africa', 15 October 1955, pp. 257–60. PRO CO 822/929 no. 26. The draft was approved

by Lennox-Boyd on 22 October and the policy was accepted by the Cabinet Colonial Policy Committee on 10 November. PRO CAB 134/ 1201, CA5(55)2.
71. It was calculated that 60 per cent of adults were thereby enfranchised instead of, under Coutts, 40 per cent.

4 Tearing Down Lyttelton

1. The Colonial Policy Committee (CPC), which was formed in 1955, was chaired by Lord Salisbury, as Lord President of the Council, until April 1957 and thereafter by the Lord Chancellor, Lord Kilmuir, until November 1958 when Macmillan himself took over. To work to it, an Official CPC was set up in January 1956, with representatives of the Foreign, Commonwealth Relations and Colonial Offices, under the chairmanship of Sir Norman Brook, the Cabinet Secretary. Peter Clarke and Clive Trebilcock, *Understanding Decline* (Cambridge University Press, 1997), p. 239, n. 24. Also see Philip Murphy, *Politics and Decolonization*, pp. 22–3.
2. PRO PREM 11/2617 Macmillan to Lord Salisbury. PM's Personal Minute M19/57, 28 January 1957.
3. Bodleian Modern Mss Room, Ms Eng c. 3433 East Africa f 94. Alan Lennox-Boyd (Lord Boyd of Merton), interviewed by Alison Smith, 13 December 1974.
4. PRO CO 1032/144 f 4 Lennox-Boyd to Salisbury, 13 February 1957.
5. PRO CO 1032/146 Ian Watt to Sir Hylton Poynton, 1 August 1957.
6. There were in fact three reports: the Colonial Office print of May 1957 on 'Future Constitutional Development in the Colonies'; the print of July 1957 on 'Economic and Financial Considerations'; and the 'Report of Officials' of September 1957. There is a good discussion of this exercise in Tony Hopkins, 'Macmillan's Audit of Empire, 1957', in Clarke and Trebilcock (eds), *Understanding Decline*. Hopkins uses an outdated classification of his main source as CO Confidential Print GEN 174/012 instead of the current PRO listing which is CO 1032/ 144–147.
7. PRO CO 1032/146 The Treasury note also said, 'Although damage could certainly be done by the premature grant of independence, the economic damage to Great Britain in deferring the grant of independence for her own selfish interests after the country is politically and economically ripe for independence would be far greater than any danger resulting from an act of independence negotiated in an atmosphere of goodwill.'
8. PRO CAB 134/1556 CPC(57) 30(Revise), 6 September 1957. Brook, 'Future Constitutional Development in the Colonies'. Also CO 1032/ 146 f 75 'Report of the Chairman of the Official Committee on Colonial Policy', 12 July 1957.
9. *Politica*, vol. 1, no. 2, June 1953. J. P. Mathenge, 'The Kenya African Union – Catastrophe Ahead?'
10. *Sunday Post*, 25 December 1955.
11. *SP*, ibid.

12. Information: Colin Legum.
13. Interview with Luke Obok, Nairobi 1961. *The Colonial Times*, 22 December 1955. *Sunday Post*, 25 December 1955.
14. *Colonial Times*, 3 January 1956.
15. *Colonial Times*, 26 March 1956.
16. *EAS*, 3 November 1956. G. F. Engholm, 'The African Elections in Kenya, March 1957', in W. J. M. Mackenzie and Kenneth Robinson, *Five Elections in Africa* (Oxford: Clarendon Press, 1960), p. 440.
17. Interview with Argwings-Kodhek, Nairobi 1961. *EAS*, 14 May 1956.
18. Interviews with Luke Obok and Omolo Agar, Nairobi, 1961.
19. B. A. Ogot, *History of the Southern Luo Vol. 1 Migration and Settlement* (East African Publishing House, 1967), pp. 198n. 31, 203. David Goldsworthy, *Tom Mboya. The Man Kenya Wanted to Forget* (Heinemann, 1982), p. 4.
20. Goldsworthy, *Tom Mboya*, pp. 10–23.
21. Alan Rake, *Tom Mboya. Young Man of New Africa* (New York: Doubleday, 1962), pp. 91–2.
22. Theodore Draper, *American Communism and Soviet Russia* (New York: Viking Press, 1960), pp. 405–41.
23. Interview with Chief Justice Ralph Windham of Tangyanika, Dar-es-Salaam, 1962. See also Goldsworthy, *Tom Mboya*, pp. 41–3.
24. Interview with Sir Walter Coutts, Kampala, 1963. Also Coutts interview, Rhodes House Mss Afr s.1621.
25. PRO DO 168/45 MacDonald to Duncan Sandys, 15 September 1963.
26. Information from Argwings-Kodhek, Nairobi 1961.
27. G. F. Engholm, 'African Elections in Kenya, March 1957', p. 450. The lady in question was Jean Wacira (later Cliffe).
28. PRO CO 822/1819 Minute by Sir J. Macpherson, 2 January 1959.
29. Roelker, *Mathu of Kenya*, pp. 135–7.
30. Interview with Daniel arap Moi, Nairobi 1962. Engholm, 'African Elections in Kenya, March 1957', pp. 453–4. A. J. Hughes, *East Africa: The Search for Unity*, pp. 14–15, 124.
31. *Sunday Post*, 'Young Man on a Tiger', 31 August 1958.
32. Odinga, *Not Yet Uhuru*, pp. 1–140. Keith Kyle, 'The Role of Mr Odinga', in *Spectator*, 25 December 1964.
33. Personal impressions.
34. Tom Mboya, *The Observer*, 29 July 1957.
35. PRO CO 822/1252 Secret and Personal Correspondence of Sir E. Baring. Baring to Lennox-Boyd, 10 April 1957.
36. PRO CO 822/1430 Notes by W. A. C. Mathieson of conversation at the Colonial Office between Sir James Macpherson and himself with Michael Blundell, Walter Havelock and Llewellyn Briggs, 24 July 1957.
37. PRO CO 822/1430 P. J. Rogers, 'The Common Roll Principles', 10 June 1957.
38. Lennox-Boyd interview, Bodleian, ff 239–40.
39. *Parliamentary Report, House of Commons Vol. 577*, 14 November 1957 cols 1112 ff.
40. Mboya Papers. Author's archive.
41. Interview with O. Odinga, Nairobi 1963.

42. Goldsworthy, *Tom Mboya*, pp. 94–8.
43. Mboya Papers. Mboya to Nkrumah, 18 April 1958.
44. Mboya Papers. Mboya to Nkrumah, 9 May 1958.
45. Mboya Papers. Tettegah to Mboya, 3 February 1958; Mboya to Tettegah, 11 February 1958.
46. *Sunday Post*, 31 August 1958. 'Young Man on a Tiger: Mboya Faces a Crisis'.
47. Personal information. The individual was Abraham Muigai, who called himself 'Lumumba' after the Congolese nationalist icon.
48. Odinga, *Not Yet Uhuru*, p. 167.
49. Odinga, ibid, pp. 156–7.
50. Odinga, ibid, pp. 158–61.
51. Mboya Papers.
52. Racial segregation was eased but not yet abolished. In January 1957 Tom Damerell, a Government Industrial Relations officer, tried to take three African labour officials, including Mboya, into a restaurant and was told, 'We don't serve Africans.' *Sunday Post*, 27 January 1957. Housing segregation, though incomplete, existed as late as 1961.
53. For the Swynnerton Plan and related questions of land consolidation see M. R. K. Sorrenson, *Land Reform in the Kikuyu Country* (OUP, 1967), pp. 113–252.
54. PRO CO 822/1303 Tom Mboya, 'What Next in Kenya?', *West African Worker*, January 1957.
55. See leading article in *EAS*, 29 June 1956. Also letter to *EAS* from E. D. Jakeyo Ang'ina, 4 August 1956: 'Having assessed the opinions here [Nairobi] and in the Luo Reserve I can say that hardly anybody in the Luo country is in favour of land consolidation . . . Women seem to be most active in opposing it in the reserves.' According to Sorrenson, *Land Reform in the Kikuyu Country*, the Luo refused to have anything to do with it because they considered it a punishment inflicted on the Kikuyu for rebellion (p. 194). See also *Uhuru*, 12 August 1958, 'The Riddle of Land Consolidation. The view of Uhuru Economist' for a balanced African discussion of the issue.
56. Interview with the Earl of Perth, London 1997. At the time of his political preferment Lord Perth was about to take up the chairmanship of Schroder's.
57. Mboya Papers. Letter to *The Times*, 10 November 1958.
58. PRO CO 822/1765 Briefing note for Lennox-Boyd for conversation with Ernest Vasey 1 October 1958. Argwings-Kodhek was said to be in financial difficulties. He had saved himself from imprisonment for civil debt by paying over £5,000 in income tax. 'Where he got the money is unknown. He survives to embarrass Mboya.'
59. *Legislative Council Debates*, Vol. 78 col. 9, 4 November 1958. Cited by Goldsworthy, *Tom Mboya*, p. 104.
60. PRO CO 822/1819 Minute by Gorell Barnes, 31 December 1958.
61. PRO CO 822/1819 Minute by the Earl of Perth, 3 January 1959.
62. PRO CO 822/1819 Minute by Sir John Macpherson, 2 January 1959.
63. PRO CO 822/1819 f 47 Chequers Conference (24–5 January 1959).

64. Charles Douglas-Home, *Evelyn Baring: The Last Proconsul* (Collins, 1978), pp. 283–4.
65. PRO CAB 134/1558 CPC(59)2. Memorandum by Lennox-Boyd, 10 April 1959.

5 The Bridge Player

1. Mboya Papers.
2. PRO CO 822/1252 Lennox-Boyd conversation with Baring, 20 January 1959.
3. A. A. J. Van Bilsen, *Plan de trente ans pour l'émancipation de l'Afrique belge* (Brussels, 1955); *Vers l'Indépendance du Congo et du Ruanda-Urundi* (Brussels, 1958).
4. Josef Mathenge's first name went through several versions. His father, mother, one of his brothers and himself were all baptized on the same day by a Roman Catholic missionary, who being Italian, gave them Italian Christian names. Mathenge was therefore Giuseppe. He anglicized it on confirmation as Joseph, but changed it to Josef after Stalin as a nationalist gesture in 1957. One of his uncles was a fellow-politician Mwai Kibaki who was baptized Emilio.
5. Interview with Omolo Agar, Nairobi, 1961.
6. John Stonehouse, who later became notorious because of his faked drowning 'accident', did good work for the co-operative movement in Uganda before his election to the House and maintained his interest in East Africa afterwards.
7. George M. Houser, 'Whirlwind Tour. Tom Mboya Visits the US', *Africa Today*, May–June 1959 issue. 'By any account Tom Mboya's tour of the US made a tremendous impression . . . It brought to American educators a new sense of the importance of helping African students to study in the United States.' Also, PRO CO 822/1303 Confidential report by L. C. Glass, Director-General of British Information Services on Mboya's performance at the annual World Affairs Conference in Boulder, Colorado, 16 April 1959. 'Mboya spoke eloquently and modestly. He has a dignified appearance and a fine voice. He made a deep and visible impression.'
8. Interview with Argwings-Kodhek, Nairobi 1961.
9. Rhodes House Mss Afr s.1681 Africa Bureau Box 291 File 10. Masinde Muliro to Jane Symonds, 10 August 1959 ff 1–3.
10. Muliro to Scott, 18 July 1959. Rhodes House, ff 6–7.
11. Odinga, *Not Yet Uhuru*, p. 168.
12. There is an excellent detailed account of the series of meetings behind the split in Goldsworthy, *Tom Mboya*, pp. 122–5.
13. Mboya Papers
14. *EAS*, 29 June, 1 July, 2 July 1959.
15. J. M. Kariuki, *'Mau Mau' Detainee*.
16. Kariuki, ibid, p. 87.
17. Sir Michael Blundell, *So Rough a Wind*, pp. 197–200.
18. PRO CO 822/1252 Baring to Lennox-Boyd, 8 April 1958.

Notes and References

Terence Gavaghan, *Corridors of Wire: A Saga of Colonial Power and Preventive Detention in Kenya* (privately printed, 1994). The writer says of Kariuki's *'Mau Mau' Detainee*, 'The tone was passionate yet rational, harsh yet mainly magnanimous, the best that might have been expected from anyone deprived of liberty in such conditions for any reason.' (p. 164)

20. PRO CO 822/1252 Baring to Lennox-Boyd 8 April 1958.
21. Gavaghan, *Corridors of Wire*, pp. iii–iv, 138–44. Colonial Office, *Record of Proceedings and Evidence in the Inquiry into the deaths of eleven Mau Mau detainees at Hola Camp in Kenya* (HMSO: Cmnd 795, July 1959); *Further documents relating to the deaths of eleven Mau Mau detainees at Hola Camp in Kenya* (HMSO: Cmnd 816, July 1959).
22. Bodleian Modern Mss Library. Macmillan Diary dep d.36, entries for 4, 10, 15, 16, 17 June 1959.
23. Harold Macmillan, *Riding the Storm 1956–1959* (Macmillan, 1971) pp. 735–6.
24. Mr Justice Devlin had chaired an enquiry into disturbances in the colony of Nyasaland. His report which categorized Nyasaland as a 'police state' was described by Macmillan in his diary as 'dynamite'. On 13 July 1959 Macmillan wrote, 'It may well blow this Government out of office' (Mss Macmillan dep.d.35 Bodleian Library, Oxford).
25. MS Macmillan Diary dep d. 35 ff 119–20, entry for 4 June 1959.
26. PRO CO 822/1303 Baring to Lennox-Boyd, 18 May 1957.
27. MS Macmillan Diary dep d.37 ff 22–3 entry for 18 September 1959. 'I feel that the sooner Evelyn Baring gets away now the better. He has done a fine job. But he can achieve no more.'
28. Bodleian Modern Mss Room MS Eng c.3433 East Africa. Lennox-Boyd (Lord Boyd of Merton) interviewed by Alison Smith, 13 December 1974.
29. PR0 PREM 11/3413 Minute to Macmillan, 6 January 1960.
30. Rhodes House Mss Afr s. 1627 Sir Walter Coutts interviewed by George Bennett.
31. Odinga, *Not Yet Uhuru*, p. 179.
32. Robert Shepherd, *Iain Macleod* (Hutchinson, 1994) and personal impressions.
33. Rhodes House, interview with Lennox-Boyd, ff 159–60.
34. Rhodes House, Mss Afr s. 2179 Interview with Iain Macleod by W. P. Kirkman, ff 31–2.
35. Macleod to author and others at editorial dining room of *The Economist*, 1960. To a half-serious suggestion that on the Nkrumah model he should lock up some Ugandan nationalist and thus create a hero, he replied gloomily that this had been tried already in Uganda [presumably with Ignatius Musazi] and it had not worked.
36. Shepherd, *Iain Macleod*, p. 173.
37. PRO CO 822/2100 Meeting of Secretary of State with African leaders, Nairobi, 16 December 1959.
38. PRO CO 822/2100 Record of meeting of S. of S. and African Elected Members of KIM, 23 December 1959.
39. PRO CAB 134/1558 CPC(59)18 Macleod to Cabinet: 'Security Powers in Kenya'.

40. PREM 11/3030 'The Lancaster House Conference, 1960'. De Zulueta to Bligh, 20 January 1960.
41. PREM 11/3030 ibid Butler's minute to Macleod. 26 January 1960. Minute by J. T. A. Howard-Drake, 8 February 1960.
42. Philip Murphy, *Party Politics and Decolonization* (Oxford: Clarendon Press, 1995), pp. 60–8.
43. Odinga, *Not Yet Uhuru*, pp. 179–80.
44. Impressions of Sir David Hunt, 1997.
45. [Keith Kyle], 'Africans in Congress' in *The Economist*, 6 and 20 February 1960.
46. Rhodes House, Mss Afr s.2179 Iain Macleod interviewed by W. P. Kirkman, ff 13–18.
47. Cited by George Bennett and Carl Rosberg, *The Kenyatta Election: Kenya 1960–1961* (OUP, 1961), p. 22.
48. Paul Peatling to Michael Blundell, 2 February 1960 in Blundell, *A Love Affair with the Sun*, p. 199.
49. Rhodes House, Mss Afr s.746 Blundell 25/3 Item 3 (1960).
50. PRO PREM 11/3031 Philip de Zulueta (No. 10) to Derek Pearson (CO), 25 February 1960. PM(60)7 Macleod to Macmillan 17 February.
51. Sir Michael Blundell, *So Rough a Wind*, p. 276.
52. MS Macmillan dep d.37, entry for 21 February 1960.
53. Interview with Lord Perth, London 1997. Perth was particularly impressed by this advice coming from a non-Kikuyu.
54. Perth, ibid.
55. Yash Tandom, 'A Political Survey', in Dharam Ghai (ed.), *Portrait of a Minority. Asians in East Africa*, pp. 81–8. Yash Ghai and Dharam Ghai, *The Asian Minorities of East and Central Africa* (Minority Rights Group, 1971), pp. 4–7.
56. Rhodes House, Mss Afr s. 746 Blundell 5/5 Blundell to Macleod, 28 April 1960.
57. Blundell to Welensky, 29 February 1960 in Blundell, *A Love Affair with the Sun*, Appdx C., p. 207.
58. *Parliamentary Debates (Hansard) House of Lords Vol. 229*, 7 March 1961, cols. 305–12.
59. Macleod to author and others at *The Economist* editorial lunch, Bagehot Club, 1960.
60. Robert L. Tignor, *Capitalism and Nationalism at the End of Empire* (Princeton University Press, 1998), pp. 356–9 and 370. Relevant correspondence in PRO CO 822/2187 and 822/2624.
61. Personal impressions. The author conducted the Mboya interview on ITV.
62. Richard Lamb, *The Macmillan Years 1957–1963. The Emerging Truth* (John Murray, 1987), p. 225. Lamb is likewise mistaken in describing Mboya as the 'leader of KANU' in 1961 (p. 226).
63. [Keith Kyle], 'Africans in Congress – II' in *The Economist*, 20 February 1960.
64. Rhodes House, Blundell Correspondence, Markham to Blundell, 2 March 1961.

6 Kenyatta Released

1. Julius Kiano became Minister of Commerce and Industry, J. N. Muimi Minister of Health and Welfare and Ronald Ngala Minister of Labour, Social Security and Adult Education. Musa Amalemba remained Minister of Housing and Taita Towett became Assistant Minister of Agriculture.
2. *Sunday Post*, 27 March 1960.
3. Mboya Papers.
4. *SP*, 3 April 1960.
5. *SP*, 24 April 1960. Mboya also was reported as having said in private conversation that his call for civil disobedience had been made in order to counter a statement by Odinga in Accra that he was not genuinely in favour of Kenyatta's release. PRO CO 822/2220. Special Branch Summary No. 5/60.
6. The British had been fearing that 'a campaign of positive action is almost inevitable' as early as the previous November and had studied precedents in India and Ghana to see how it might develop. Rhodes House Mss Afr s.2159 Manby Papers Box 2 M. C. Manby, 'Memo from Special Branch. Positive Action in Kenya', 12 November 1958.
7. Bodleian Modern Mss: Macmillan dep d.37 f.35, entry for 23 February 1960.
8. PRO PREM 11/3413 PM's Personal Minute M113/60, 20 April 1960.
9. PRO PREM 11/3413 PM's Personal Minute to Macleod, M113/60, 20 April 1960. Macleod to Macmillan, PM(60)22 21 April.
10. PRO CO 822/1909 Minute by Macleod, 13 April 1960.
11. PRO CO 822/1909 Renison to Macleod, 20 April 1960.
12. Colonial Office, *Historical Survey of the Origins and Growth of Mau Mau* (Cmnd. 1030, HMSO, May 1960).
13. PRO CO 822/1909 Minute by J. L. F. (Ian) Buist, 9 May 1960.
14. PRO CO 822/1909 Renison to Macleod, 20 April 1960.
15. Rhodes House, Macleod interview, ff 23–4.
16. PRO CO 822/1909 Renison to Macleod, 24 April 1960.
17. PRO CO 822/1909 Thirteenth Council of Ministers, 27 April 1960.
18. PRO CO 822/1909 Macleod to Renison, 29 April 1960. Renison to Macleod, 30 April. Macleod to Renison, 1 May. Renison to Macleod 2 May.
19. Rhodes House, Macleod interview, ff 23–5.
20. PRO CO 822/1909 Memo on Corfield Report by J. L. F. (Ian) Buist, 9 May 1960.
21. Mboya Papers. Mboya to J. H. Oldenbroek, Brussels, 2 May 1960. 'Ghana is going all out to fight the ICFTU and already there is evidence of money being made available to splinter groups in West Africa and now this is being extended to East Africa through Arthur Ochwada.'
22. PRO CO 822/2109 Special Branch, 'The Formation of KANU'.
23. PRO CO 822/2109 Special Branch, 'The Formation of KANU' and Summary No. 5/60.
24. PRO CO 822/2109 'KANU. Special Branch Summary No. 5/60.
25. PRO CO 822/2109 D. W. Manby, Director of Intelligence and Security

to Chief Secretary's Office and Ministry of Defence, 16 July 1960.

26. PRO CO 822/2109 T. Neil (Chief Secretary's Office) to Ian Buist (CO), 'KANU. Formation and Early Development, prepared by Special Branch'.
27. PRO CO 822/2109 Neil to Buist, ibid.
28. *Sunday Post*, 22 May, 11 June and 25 June 1960.
29. PRO CO 822/2058 Special Branch Reviews and Reports.
30. Rhodes House Mss Afr s. 2159 Manby Papers Box 2 file 2 Misc. 1958–63, 14 November 1960.
31. Rhodes House Blundell Papers 5/5. Blundell to Edward Thompson (Ind Coope), 14 December 1960.
32. Rhodes House Mss. Afr. s.2159 Manby Papers Box 2 file 2 Misc. 1958–63. Special Branch note on the GAG (Ginger Action Group), 14 November 1960. According to this, Odinga had paid for the defence costs of two GAG members and had just given Sh/-3,000 each to Akumu, Mathenge and one other.
33. Kasavubu had been for a short while the Burgomaster of a district of Léopoldville.
34. Kiano to author, Nairobi, 1961.
35. PRO CO 822/1910 Minute by Martin, 29 December 1960. Renison to Macleod, 12 December.
36. Macmillan Diary, 20 January 1961. Quoted in Macmillan, *At the End of the Day 1961–1963* (Macmillan, 1973), p. 290.
37. PRO CO 822/1910 Renison to Macleod, 12 December 1960. Minutes by F. D. (Max) Webber, W. B. L. Monson, and Sir John Martin.
38. PRO CO 822/1911 Note of discussion at Chequers, 8 January 1961. Macleod to Macmillan, PM(61)5, 9 January 1961.
39. For these circumstances see Keith Kyle, *Suez* (Weidenfeld & Nicolson, 1991).
40. PRO CO 822/2892 Watkinson to Macleod, 6 December 1960.
41. PRO CO 879/190 Conference of East African Governors at Colonial Office, 4–9 January 1961. CO 822/2892 Macleod to Watkinson, 12 January 1961. 'If KANU is successful in the elections, the Governor believes there is every chance of their being brought to see in time the advantages to Kenya of having British troops stationed there. The Governor therefore believes that there is a reasonable chance that we should be able to remain in Kenya perhaps indefinitely.'
42. George Bennett and Carl Rosberg, *The Kenyatta Election 1960–1961* (OUP, 1961) pp. 87–110.
43. This figure includes the related Embu and Meru tribes in the Kikuyu total.
44. Manby Papers, 14 November 1960.
45. PRO CO 822/2110 Extracts from Kenya Intelligence Committee Monthly Appreciation No 1/61, 10 February 1961.
46. Mboya Papers, KANU press statement, 30 January 1961.
47. Mboya Papers, Mboya, 'Statement on Present KANU Crisis', 3 February 1961.
48. PRO CO 822/1911 Renison to Macleod, 4 March 1961.
49. Mboya Papers. 'Lodwar Meeting, 23 March 1961'. Those present were

Kenyatta (in the chair), Ngei, Kaggia, Kigondu; for KANU: Gichuru, Odinga, Mboya, Nyagah and Mwendwe; for KADU: Moi, Tipis, Matano, Murgor, Kilelu, Khamisi. Moi did not want the KADU group to commit itself until they had reported back to their Supreme Council.

50. Keith Kyle, 'Kenyatta – as diplomat', *Time and Tide*, 20 April 1961, p. 644.
51. PRO CO 822/2235 f 53 Renison to Macleod, 12 April 1961.
52. PRO CO 822/1911 Macleod to Chief Secretary Coutts, 11 April 1961.
53. *Parliamentary Debates (Hansard) House of Lords, Vol. 229*, 7 March 1961, cols. 305–61; 8 March, cols 363–508.
54. PRO CAB 134/1560 CPC(61)7 Memo by Macleod to Colonial Policy Committee, 11 April 1961.
55. PRO CO 822/1911 Coutts to Granville Sharp (Kenya Office, London), 30 March 1961.
56. Interview with Sir Walter Coutts, Kampala 1963. Also Rhodes House, Coutts interview with George Bennett.
57. Personal impressions.
58. PRO CO 822/2110 'Record of Meetings at RAF station Eastleigh on 3 April 1961 between political groups and the S. of S. with Governor of Kenya'.
59. PRO CO 822/2235 f 55 Perth to Macleod, 13 April 1961.
60. Personal information. Nathoo had personal as well as public reasons for his reluctance to resign.
61. PRO PREM 11/3413 PM/61/42 Home to Macmillan, 18 April 1961.
62. PRO PREM 11/3413 PM's Personal Minute M117/61, Macmillan to Macleod, 18 April 1961.
63. PRO PREM 11/3413 Macleod to Renison, 19 April 1961.
64. PRO CO 822/2235 f 63 Macleod to Renison, 25 April 1961.
65. PRO CO 822/2235 Renison to Macleod, 11 June 1961.
66. PRO CO 822/2236 Macleod to Renison, 26 July 1961.
67. PRO CO 822/1912 f 306 Macleod to Renison, 8 June 1961. Minute by Macmillan, f 311.
68. Rhodes House Blundell Papers 13/4 f 103. Blundell to Edward Thompson, 5 July 1961.
69. PRO CO 822/1912 Renison to Macleod, 9 July 1961.
70. PRO PREM 11/3413 PM(61)64 Macleod to Macmillan, 26 July 1961.
71. Personal impressions.

7 Majimbo

1. Macmillan Diaries, dep d.43 ff 69–70 entry for 18 September 1961. 'He could help me to recreate a sense of purpose – almost a crusade.'
2. Alistair Horne, *Macmillan Vol. II 1957–86* (Macmillan, 1989), pp. 183–4. Macleod's emotionalism mainly showed over Central Africa and his principal antagonist was Duncan Sandys, whom Macmillan was resolved to keep as Commonwealth Secretary.
3. Macmillan, *At the End of the Day*, pp. 40–1, 314. Shepherd, *Iain Macleod*, pp. 259–61.

4. Horne, *Macmillan II*, p. 408.
5. Interview with Sir Peter Kitcatt, London, 1995, and other impressions.
6. The calibre of the Minister of Finance was critical to a colony on the verge of independence. Until a late stage in Kenya the portfolio continued to be held by a civil servant. In terms of gaining ministerial experience, the post of Parliamentary Secretary to that Ministry was therefore considered of special importance.
7. Interview with Peter Okondo, Nairobi 1961.
8. District Commissioner, Central Nyanza to Chief Native Commissioner 11 May 1951, with minute by Provincial Commissioner, Nyanza. 'Rehabilitation of Students Returning to Kenya'. Kenya National Archives.
9. Interview with Okondo.
10. PRO CO 822/2242 Minute by Leslie Monson, 6 October 1961.
11. PRO DO 168/45 Patrick Wall, MP, 'Political Affairs in Kenya', December 1961.
12. Keith Kyle, *Time and Tide*, November 1961.
13. Rhodes House, Mss Afr 746 Blundell Papers 19/5 f 17, Blundell to Havelock, 1 February 1962.
14. Goldsworthy, *Tom Mboya*, p. 189. PRO DO 168/45 Renison to Maudling: Kenya Intelligence Summary of 6 February – 'Documentary evidence has come to light of disbursement of bloc funds by Odinga to, amongst others, Kenyatta, his secretary Oneko, Ngei, Kubai and the widow of the late Mau Mau leader, Dedan Kimathi.' Personal impressions.
15. Rhodes House, Blundell Papers 19/5, ff 41–2. Jock Leslie-Melville (Nairobi) to R. E. Simms (London), 4 November 1961.
16. Interview with Sir Derek Erskine, Nairobi, 1963.
17. The option of Kenyatta forming his own party was, not surprisingly, the most unpalatable for Europeans. Blundell wrote on 13 September that, 'If this force does emerge, I would hazard the opinion that we should go back ten years and be faced with the old challenge of Mau Mau in a less evil and possibly more constitutional form.' Blundell Papers 19/5 ff 47–51.
18. Mboya Papers. Mboya, Press Statement, 26 January 1961. Odinga, *Not Yet Uhuru*, pp. 221–2.
19. Rhodes House, Leslie-Melville to Simms. Blundell Papers 19/5 Blundell to Macleod, 13 Sept 1961. '[Renison] has not played a decisive role in these talks.' Also see A. J. Hughes, *East Africa: The Search for Unity*, pp. 143–4.
20. PRO CAB 134/1560 CPC(61)30 14 November 1961. Memo by Maudling.
21. The 11th Duke's father was also the Colonial Under-Secretary under Malcolm MacDonald as Secretary of State, 1938–40.
22. PRO CAB 134/1560 CPC(61) 12th Meeting, 15 November 1961.
23. PRO CO 822/2244 KANU memorandum to Secretary of State, 8 November 1961.
24. 'Jomo Kenyatta "Face to Face"; An Interview with John Freeman', *The Listener*, 7 December 1961.
25. Personal impressions in Nairobi, including interview with Odinga. Interview with Maudling, London, 1962.

26. PRO CAB 134/1561 CPC(62)3 Memorandum by Maudling.
27. PRO PREM 11/3856 Memo to Prime Minister on report to the Colonial Policy Committee on Kenya finances, 1 February 1962.
28. PRO CAB 134/1560 Colonial Policy Committee CPC(61)30 12th Meeting, 15 November 1961. Memo by Maudling, 14 November.
29. PRO FO 371/165292 V1015/14G Maudling Memo for Cabinet, 6 February 1962.
30. PRO CAB 128/36 Part 1. CC(62)12th Conclusions, Item 5, 8 February 1962. FO 371/165292 V1015/29G Sir R. Stevens (FO) to Sir Hilton Poynton (CO), 23 February 1962.
31. Impressions of former civil servants.
32. KADU Papers. Ngala to Maudling, 23 February 1962.
33. KADU Papers. Ngala to Maudling, 12 March 1962.
34. For example, Jason Sendwe who was the Congolese Government's representative in the Province of Katanga was not even able to enter Elisabethville, the Katangese capital, where secessionists were in command.
35. *Kenya Constitutional Conference 1962*, Committee on the Structure of Government, 5th and 6th Meetings (Private archive).
36. Reginald Maudling, *Memoirs* (Sidgwick & Jackson, 1978), p. 93.
37. *Kenya Constitutional Conference*, 16th meeting. Private archive.
38. Odinga, *Not Yet Uhuru*, pp. 223–6.
39. Mboya Papers.
40. Odinga, *Not Yet Uhuru*, p. 229.
41. KADU Papers, R. Macleod to I. Macleod, 25 May 1962.
42. Maudling, *Memoirs*, p. 93.
43. PRO CO 822/2390 Maudling to Kenyatta (Urgent and Personal), 6 April 1962.
44. Maudling, *Memoirs*, p. 93.
45. Rhodes House. Mss Afr 746 Blundell Papers 5/6 ff 34–39 and 29/2.
46. Interviews with Henry Steel and Sir Peter Kitcatt, 1995.
47. Rhodes House, Mss Afr 746 Blundell Papers 5/6. Blundell to Bennett, 15 June 1962.
48. Rhodes House, Blundell Papers, Delamere to Blundell, 20 March 1962. Blundell to Delamere, 30 March 1962. Cited by Gary Wasserman, *Politics of Decolonization. Kenya Europeans and the Land Issue 1960–1965* (Cambridge University Press, 1976), p. 99.
49. When Macmillan asked Lord Perth to join the Government in 1957, despite his not being a member of the Conservative Party, he had just been made chairman-designate of Schroder's (Interview with Lord Perth, London, 1997).
50. But this contention by Kanu was challenged by the Ministry of Agriculture, whose surveys showed that of the 3,661 farms, plantation and ranches in the White Highlands, totalling 7,280,000 acres, only 101 farms, amounting to 193,208 acres, could be considered un- or underdeveloped. Tignor, *Capitalism and Nationalism at the End of Empire*, pp. 367–8.
51. Rhodes House, Mss Afr s.1797. Christopher Leo, 'Who Benefited from the Million-Acre Scheme?'

52. KNA. Office of Director of Intelligence, 'Subversive Tendencies Among the Kikuyu. A Review of the Period 1 February–22 September 1962', 27 September 1962.
53. PRO FO 371/165292 Home to Maudling, 13 February 1962.
54. PRO CO 822/3088 Lansdowne to MacDonald, 8 March 1963. For an account of the continuing exchanges with the IBRD (World Bank) about the various settlement schemes, see Wasserman, *Politics of Decolonization*, pp. 158–63, and Tignor, *Capitalism and Nationalism at the End of Empire*, pp. 373–80. In total there were 2.1 million acres in European mixed farming divided into 2,680 units (out of the 7.7 million acres and 3,600 units of European farming). The million-acre scheme, therefore, covered half the potential problem (Tignor, p. 365).
55. Such claims were supported by research undertaken by the Canadian scholar, Christopher Leo (Leo, 'The Future of the "Progressive Farmer" in Kenya's Million-Acre Settlement Scheme', *Journal of Modern African Studies*, 16, 4, 1978, pp. 619–38). 'From the beginning the experts were unanimous that high density settlement could not hope to meet its economic target. One scheme was programmed for economic failure and the other was given every opportunity for success. The evidence of outcomes contradicts these expectations completely.' Leo holds that this was due to the superior incentive of the desperately poor being given a once-in-a-lifetime break.
56. Rhodes House Mss Afr s.1717 XIII Sandy Storrar interviewed by Oxford Development Records Project.
57. Odinga, *Not Yet Uhuru*, pp. 257–69.
58. The Somalis, being Muslims, have sometimes described themselves as Arabs. As late as 1998 it was possible to find in the streets of Damascus posters displaying the Syrian President bestriding the entire Arab world, of which the Horn of Africa was coloured in as a part. See also Rhodes House Mss Afr s 2159 Manby Papers Box 1 file 3, for lecture at Middle East Command Intelligence Conference, Nairobi, August 1963.
59. Rhodes House Mss. Afr s.996. P. Fullerton, Wajir District Hand-Over Notes, 1 June 1961.
60. Keith Kyle, 'How Many Stars in Somalia?', *Christian Science Monitor* (1963).
61. Fullerton, 'Wajir District Annual Report, 1960'. Rhodes House Mss Afr. s.996.
62. *Kenya Constitutional Conference 1962 No. 40*: 'Memorandum by the Northern Frontier District Delegation' (Private archive) See also PRO CO 822/2826 'Petition by five political parties, fifteen chiefs, one ex-MLC and one MLC on N.F.D', November 1961.
63. PRO CO 822/2826 Record of Meeting of Maudling with N.F.D. Somalis, 28 November 1961.
64. *Kenya Constitutional Conference 1962* No. 37: 'The Northern Province of Kenya. Observations by KANU', 22 March 1962. No. 42: 'Memorandum by KADU on the N.F.D. Delegation', 26 March 1962.
65. *Kenya Constitutional Conference* Nos 34 & 41: 'The Maasai Delegation'; No. 39 John Keen, MLC, 'Memorandum on Maasai Treaties of

1904 and 1911'; Keith Kyle, 'Noah of the Famine Lands' in *Reynolds News*, 19 November 1961.

66. Obituary of Sultan Seid bin Abdullah, *Kenya Weekly News*, 5 July 1963.
67. Colonial Office, *Report of the Kenya Coastal Strip Conference, 1962* (HMSO Cmnd. 1701, April 1962).

8 KANU Triumphant

1. Keith Kyle, 'Power Scramble', *Time and Tide*, pp. 12–13, 14 June 1962.
2. PRO CO 822/2910 Griffith-Jones to Maudling, 18 April 1962.
3. PRO CO 822/2910 Griffith-Jones to Maudling, 30 April 1962. Minute of P. J. Kitcatt, 1 May.
4. KADU Papers. Bennett to R. Macleod, 29 May 1962.
5. KADU Papers. Bennett to R. Macleod, 1 June 1962. Bennett to R. Macleod, 6 June 1962.
6. Rhodes House. Mss Afr 746 Blundell Papers 5/6 Blundell to Bennett, ff 47–9.
7. PRO CO 822/2835 Ngala, Address to Secretary of State on visit to Kenya, 7 July 1962.
8. PRO CO 822/2835 Secretary of State's Visit.
9. KADU Papers. Ngala to Renison, 9 July 1962.
10. Interview with the Duke of Devonshire, Chatsworth, 1997.
11. Rhodes House. Mss Brit.Emp.s.452(2) Part II. Interview with Nigel Fisher. Also information from retired civil servants, 1995.
12. Interview with the Duke of Devonshire, Chatsworth, 1997.
13. Alistair Horne, *Macmillan Vol. II*, p. 48
14. Fisher, interview. Interviews with retired civil servants, 1995.
15. Personal information.
16. The Australian diplomat, Sir Walter Crocker, had some reservations about the quality of his performance in India. See Clyde Sanger, *Malcolm MacDonald* (Liverpool University Press, 1995), p. 364.
17. PRO CO 822/3206 Sir David Hunt (Kampala), 'Despatch No. 1 Mr Obote and Kenya', 8 January 1963.
18. Odinga, *Not Yet Uhuru*, pp. 273–5.
19. Because Tanganyika had been a United Nations Trusteeship, independence meant that it acquired a Great White Queen for the first time. The most noticeable impact of the change of status was the instant dropping of the *The Archers* by the radio service.
20. Joseph S. Nye, *Pan-Africanism and East African Integration* (Harvard University Press and OUP, 1966), pp. 130–8. A. J. Hughes, *East Africa: The Search for Unity* (Penguin, 1963), pp. 224–6.
21. Nye, ibid, p. 147. Interviews with former civil servants.
22. PRO DO 160/73 'Prospects for East African Federation'. Duke of Devonshire's minute on Tanganyika's and Uganda's relations with Kenya, 12 December 1962.
23. Interview with John Kakonge, Kampala 1963.
24. PRO CO 822/3206 Sir David Hunt (Kampala), Despatch No. 1, 'Mr. Obote and Kenya', 8 January 1963.
25. PRO CO 822/3206 Hunt to Chadwick (CRO), 2 January 1963.
26. PRO CO 822/3206 Hunt, Despatch No. 1.

27. Bodleian Modern Mss Room, Macmillan Diaries dep. 48, entry for 28 January 1963, ff 62–3.
28. PRO CO 833/3206 Sandys Minute, 23 January 1963.
29. PRO CO 822/3206 Prime Minister's Questions, 31 January 1963. Brockway spoke of 'the great urgency of establishing an East African Federation'; Harris enquired more tentatively about 'the possibility for the eventual federation'.
30. PRO CO 822/3099 Sandys, 'Points for Discussion with the Governor of Kenya', 28 January 1963.
31. Rhodes House Mss Brit Emp s.533/1. Perham's interview with Malcolm MacDonald.
32. PRO CO 822/3099 MacDonald to Sandys, 14 January 1963 f 3. Sandys, 'Points for Discussion with the Governor of Kenya', n.d. f 20.
33. PRO DO 168/45 MacDonald to Sandys, 15 September 1963.
34. Rhodes House, Malcolm MacDonald Interview. The problem of alcohol was, however, a serious one among some of independent Kenya's founding fathers. The career of Josef Mathenge, one of the most promising of the younger politicians, ended prematurely on account of it. Argwings-Kodhek's propensity has been noted. The otherwise admirable James Gichuru was later known to be sometimes incapable of public business.
35. KADU Papers. Macleod to Bennett, 28 February 1963.
36. PRO PREM 11/4328 Sandys (Nairobi) to Macmillan, Butler (Central Africa), Thorneycroft (Defence) and Lansdowne (CO), PM's Personal Tel. 4 112/63, 4 March 1963.
37. M. F. Hill, *Permanent Way*, pp. 448, 462. There are presently no passenger services on the Kitale branch.
38. *Kenya Regional Boundaries Commission 1962. Record of the Oral Representations*, 'A Meeting with a delegation from the Elgeyo-Marakwet African District Council in Eldoret, 3 September 1962'. Views of Chief Chemweno Cheboi (Personal Archive).
39. PRO PREM 11/4328 Sandys to Macmillan, 8 March 1963, PM's Tel. T116/63.
40. PRO CO 822/3099 Sandys, 'Points for Discussion'. See note 32. The 'Queen's Chinese' were Chinese residents of Malaya who had strongly but ineffectively opposed their losing their British citizenship on the creation of the Malaysian Federation. I owe this information to Professor Peter Lyon.
41. PRO CO 822/2540 Kenyatta to Sandys, 6 March 1963.
42. Malcolm MacDonald and Christina Loke, *Treasure of Kenya*, p. 21. Cited in Sanger, *MacDonald*, p. 401.
43. PRO CO 822/3060 Kenya Intelligence Committee. KIC MA (62)12(TS), 'External Influences Other than Communism', 3 December 1962 to 7 January 1963.
44. PRO CO 822/3027 Note for the Record, 'Israeli Interest in Kenya', 15 January 1963.
45. PRO DO 168/45 MacDonald and Griffith-Jones to Sandys, 28 January 1963.
46. PRO CO 822/3059 Kenya Intelligence Committee KIC MA(62)12. Monthly Appreciation 13 December 1962–7 January 1963.
47. Clyde Sanger and John Nottingham, 'The Kenya General Election of

1963', *Journal of Modern African Studies*, vol. 2, no. 1, p. 6. Keith Kyle, 'Who's Who in East Africa', *Time and Tide*, 27 July 1961. '. . . the near-bankruptcy of KANU's national party headquarters (which has twice had its telephone cut off)'.

48. PRO CO 822/3166 'Kenya Elections 1963'. M. C. Manby, Director of Intelligence to Office of the Governor, 6 May 1963.
49. Manby, ibid.
50. Personal information.
51. Manby, ibid.
52. PRO CO 822/3059 Kenya Intelligence Committee KIC MA(62)12, 13 December 1962–7 January 1963.
53. PRO CO 822/3166 'Kenya Digest 25 April 1963'. Elections for the Regional Assembly came first (18–19 May); then for the Senate (22–3 May); and finally for the House of Representatives (25–6 May). It says much for the stamina of the Kenyan voters that there was very little difference in turnout between the three. In several pastoral areas where the voters had to travel long distances to the poll they were allowed to cast all three votes in one visit.
54. Keith Kyle, 'Kenya on the Eve', *Spectator*, 17 May 1963.
55. Personal experience.
56. *Kenya Regional Boundaries Commission 1962. Record of the Oral Representations Part I*. Evidence of G. W. Nthenge, Kamba MLC, 9 August 1962. 'The one thing which we mainly object to is the fact that the Kikuyu do not treat the Kamba as equals. Then we feel embarrassed and say, "Why should we mix with them?"' The present author, on enquiring of a Kikuyu about the Kamba language, was told it was like listening to her six-year-old daughter talk.
57. Personal information and commentary on BBC General Overseas Service.
58. Kyle, 'Kenya on the Eve'.
59. Information: Colin Legum.
60. Kyle, 'Kenya on the Eve'.
61. *Daily Nation*, 6 May 1963. Quoted by Sanger and Nottingham, 'The Kenya General Election of 1963', p. 16.
62. Kyle, 'Kenya on the Eve'.
63. Keith Kyle, 'Kenyatta Takes Over; Self-Government for Kenya', *Forum Service*, 8 June 1963.
64. Personal information.
65. PRO CO 822/3166 Kenya Elections 1963. 1,910,031 votes were cast for the Lower House, of which 6,704 were spoilt. KANU and APP between them took 1,159,527 (60%) to KADU's 476,105 (25%). 267,795 votes (15%) were cast for Independents. Eighteen Members – 9 KANU, 8 KADU and 1 Independent – were returned unopposed.
66. PRO CO 822/3103 'Internal Self-Government in Kenya', MacDonald to Sandys, 30 May 1963.
67. PRO CO 822/3103 Sandys (Malta) to Sir Hylton Poynton, 3 June 1963.
68. PRO CO 22/3103 MacDonald to Sandys, 5 June 1963.
69. PRO CO 822/3103 Sir John Martin to Sandys, 6 June 1963. Minute by Sandys.

9 Uhuru na Harambee

1. Personal information.
2. Kenyatta's British biographer Jeremy Murray-Brown examines the evidence about his age in Appdx A 'When Was Kenyatta Born?' of his *Kenyatta*, pp. 323–5 and comes down, on balance, in favour of 1897, which would have made him sixty-six at independence. At the time most of the press referred to him as a seventy-three-year-old.
3. PRO DO 168/45 MacDonald to Sandys, 15 September 1963.
4. Rhodes House, Mss Brit Emp s.533/1–2. MacDonald interviewed by Dame Margery Perham.
5. PRO DO 168/45 MacDonald to Sandys, 29 November 1963.
6. PRO DO 168/73 MacDonald to Sandys, 7 June 1963.
7. Rhodes House, Mss Brit Emp. s.452(2) Part II. Interview with Nigel Fisher.
8. PRO CO 822/3100 Max Webber to Griffith-Jones, 23 May 1963. Griffith-Jones to Webber, 24 May.
9. PRO DO 168/73 *Parliamentary Debates, House of Commons,* 2 July 1963, cols 201–4.
10. PRO DO 168/73 Nyerere to Macmillan, 7 June 1963.
11. PRO CO 822/3144 Memorandum by W. B. L. Monson, 24 June 1963.
12. PRO DO 168/73 Sandys to MacDonald, 10 June 1963. 'I wonder if it is really necessary for Mboya to come to London now'.
13. PRO DO 168/73 f 86a Max Webber (CO) to MacDonald, 15 June 1963; f 87 Sandys to MacDonald, 17 June; f 97 W. B. L. Monson to Sandys, minute, 20 June; f 97c Webber to MacDonald, 20 June; CO 822/3144 Ngala to Sandys, 20 June; CAB 129/114 C(63)105 Sandys, Memo to Cabinet, 20 June 1963.
14. PRO CO 822/2826 Meeting between S. of S. and the Governor of Kenya, 12 November 1962.
15. F[oreign] R[elations of the] U[nited] S[tates] 1961–1963 Vol. XXI Africa, Doc. 292, 21 March 1963, pp. 460–1 Komer to Kennedy. But see also *FRUS XXI* Doc. 275, 21 November 1961, pp. 432–5 in which British officials tell their US opposite numbers that 'The British definitely did not intend to alter territorial boundaries prior to independence.'
16. Clyde Sanger, *Malcolm MacDonald*, pp. 398–400. The Wajir rebuff was almost immediately followed by MacDonald's medical breakdown.
17. Information from P.A.R. (later Lord) Blaker, then Private Secretary to the Minister of State at the Foreign Office, Peter Thomas.
18. *Parliamentary Debates House of Commons* 30 April 1963, col. 885.
19. PRO PREM 11/4328 Fisher to Redmayne, 2 May 1963. Redmayne to Macmillan, 5 May.
20. Macmillan's main evidence for this was a letter to *The Times* from the settler-Earl of Enniskillen and strong language in a thank-you note from a dinner companion who served on the party's Commonwealth Affairs Committee. PRO PREM 11/4338.
21. PRO PREM 11/4328 Macmillan to Boyd-Carpenter, PM's Personal Minute M182/63, 7 May 1963. Boyd-Carpenter to Macmillan, 9 May. Boyd-Carpenter to Macmillan, 17 May.

22. PRO DO 168/73 Hunt to Chadwick (CRO), 1 July 1963.
23. Andrew Boyd of *The Economist* invented the expression 'uncwth' (pronounced, as if in Welsh, 'uncouth') – and its opposite 'cwth' to describe this phenomenon.
24. PRO CO 833/3195 Le Tocq to Chadwick, 12 July 1963. Le Tocq wrote of one contribution to the Uganda debate on federation, 'Busumtwi Sam has clearly been at work for Mwangi's speech is straight from Osagyefo's [the Redeemer's, i.e. Nkrumah's] heart'.
25. Nekyon was usually referred to as Obote's brother but they looked very unalike (Nekyon being tall and robust, Obote small and weedy). Obote explained that they were in fact cousins but known as brothers by tribal custom.
26. PRO CO 833/3195 Eric Le Tocq (Kampala) to Chadwick (CRO), enclosing Martin Reith's account of Uganda National Assembly debate, 12 July 1963.
27. Bodleian Modern Mss Room: De Freitas Papers. Sandys to De Freitas, 9 July 1963. Sir Saville Garner to De Freitas, 9 July.
28. PRO CO 822/3195 CAB(63)81 Mboya and Murumbi, 'Talks on the Establishment of the Federal Republic of East Africa'.
29. PRO CO 822/3062 M. C. Manby, Director of Intelligence, Weekly Personal Report, 26 August, 2 September, 7 September 1963.
30. Manby, ibid, 2 September 1963.
31. PRO CO 822/3144 Anthony Webb (Nairobi) to Peter Kitcatt (CO), 21 August 1963. Alternatively, according to British Intelligence, Nyerere, who was to be Federal Prime Minister, would accept Obote as Finance Minister and Nekyon as Minister for Internal Security.
32. PRO DO 168/75 David Hunt (Kampala) to Chadwick.
33. PRO CAB 128/37 f 383. CC(63)58th Conclusions, 3 October 1953, item 2.
34. PRO CAB 128/37 ff 400–1. CC(63)60th Conclusions, item 3.
35. Interview with Sir Peter Kitcatt, 1995.
36. PRO DO 168/49 Sandys to Griffith-Jones, 13 October 1963.
37. PRO DO 168/49 f 135 Griffith-Jones to Sandys, 17 October 1963.
38. PRO CAB 128/38 Part I ff 6–7 CM(63)1st Conclusions 22 October 1963, item 5.
39. PRO DO 168/45 Malcolm MacDonald to Duncan Sandys, 15 September 1963.
40. Rhodes House, Mss Brit Emp s.452(2) Part II. Interview with Nigel Fisher.
41. PRO DO 168/49 f 138 MacDonald (London) to Griffith-Jones, 18 October 1963.
42. PRO CO 822/3275 MacDonald to Sandys, 22 November 1963.
43. PRO CO 822/3101 MacDonald to Sandys, 29 November 1993.
44. PRO CO 822/3144 MacDonald to Sandys, 8 August 1963.
45. PRO CO 822/3144 MacDonald to Sandys, 10 August 1963.
46. PRO CO 822/3275 MacDonald to Sandys, 22 November 1963.
47. *Parliamentary Debates House of Commons Vol. 684*, 22 November 1963 cols 1329–1400.
48. PRO CO 820/3100 Griffith-Jones to Max Webber, 27 August 1963.

49. Leader, *Manchester Guardian*, 12 December 1963.
50. Clyde Sanger in the *Manchester Guardian*, 12 December 1963; Richard Beeston in the *Daily Telegraph*, 12–13 December; Peter Younghusband in the *Daily Mail*, 11–12 December. Personal impressions.
51. PRO CO 822/3237 Sandys to MacDonald. 'If there is any question of turning the independence celebrations into a demonstration of anti-British sentiment I would feel it my duty to warn The Queen and possibly to advise that it would be inappropriate for the Duke of Edinburgh to be present in circumstances which would be regarded as insulting and humiliating'.
52. *The Times*, 12 and 13 December 1963, and personal impressions.
53. Evidence of a civil servant.
54. Personal impressions and PRO DO 168/52 Fortnightly Summaries, 12–21 December 1963 Part I.
55. Bodleian: De Freitas Papers. Sir Saville Garner to De Freitas, 3 October 1963; De Freitas to Sandys, 5 November; Garner to De Freitas, 20 December 1963.

10 Epilogue

1. Patrick Renison, 'The Challenge in Kenya', *Optima*, March 1963, p. 10.
2. The history of the Kenyanization of the civil service and the phasing out of the expatriate administrators is a subject that deserves extended treatment for which there is no room here.
3. For the Zanzibar revolution and the military mutinies, see series in the *Spectator* by Keith Kyle on 24 January, 31 January, 7 February and 14 February 1963.
4. The British Government afterwards unwisely pressed Kenyatta to make his gratitude public in the manner already adopted by Nyerere. Kenyatta, being politically unable to do this, told De Freitas that he would have to be satisfied with his personal and private expression of thanks. PRO PREM 11/4889 De Freitas to CRO, 29 January 1964. 'Saw Kenyatta in presence of Mboya. We had a long and chilly talk'.
5. The Britons killed were Herbert Judge, a Regional Government Agent, at Wajir on 4 February 1964 and Henry Kenneth Arnold, an Assistant Agent, caught in an ambush of three lorries between Wajir and Mandera on 8 April 1964.
6. Information from Senator Josef Mathenge, Leader of Government Business in the Senate, 1964.
7. Sandys, 'Statement at the Final Plenary Session', Annex A to *Kenya Independence Conference, Cmnd 2156* (HMSO, October 1963).
8. 'The best thing that could happen to Kenya now would be for tensions to diminish to the point where it could become, by consent, a one-party system.' – *Manchester Guardian* leader, 12 December 1963.
9. Personal information.
10. Sir Geoffrey de Freitas had been skilful in arranging his re-entry to the British House of Commons in the election of October 1964.
11. Cherry Gertzel, *The Politics of Independent Kenya* (Nairobi: East African Publishing House, 1970), pp. 73–94. George Bennett, 'Kenya's "Little

General Election"', *The World Today* (RIIA, August 1966).

12. Murumbi, part-Goan and part-Masai was a very capable and trusted figure, much relied on by Kenyatta, who had meant at one time to make him his successor. His main drawback, according to Josef Mathenge, was that 'he still doesn't speak any African language efficiently – he can stumble through just a few words of Swahili at a public meeting' (Mathenge to author, 12 July 1964). After a few months as Vice-President, Murumbi decided he wanted a business career and accepted a senior post with Rothman's (the cigarette firm).

13. I owe this last point to Andrew Morton, author of a forthcoming biography of arap Moi.

14. R. M. A. van Zwanenberg and Anne King, *An Economic History of Kenya and Uganda 1800–1970* (Macmillan, 1975), pp. 247–50.

15. Rupert Wright, 'The Kennedys of Kenya', *Spectator*, 11 April 1998, pp. 14–15. The Delamere estate was originally even larger – 115,627 acres.

16. If one was born in Kenya to at least one parent also born in Kenya, citizenship (regardless of race) was automatic. It was those who did not meet this test who were given two years' grace.

17. According to the *Kenya Population Census 1969 Vol. I*, p. 69, 60,994 Asians were Kenya citizens and 78,043 were not. By this time a number of Kenya Asians had already left.

18. Donald Rothchild, *Racial Bargaining in Independent Kenya* (OUP, 1973), esp. pp. 186–203 and 316–35.

19. Robert Shepherd, *Iain Macleod*, pp. 490–8. Macleod, who was a member of the Shadow Cabinet, published his refutation of Sandys's views in an open letter to him in the 23 February 1968 issue of the *Spectator*, which he had formerly edited.

20. Jennifer A.Widner, *The Rise of a Party-State in Kenya. From Harambee! to Nyayo!* (University of California Press, 1992), pp. 86–7, 90, 105.

21. Widner, ibid, p. 193.

22. Joseph Karimi and Philip Ochieng, *The Kenyatta Succession* (Nairobi: Transafrica, 1980), *passim*.

23. Widner, *The Rise of a Party-State in Kenya* (University of California, 1992), *passim*.

24. PRO CO 822/2235 Perth to Macleod, 13 April 1961.

Bibliography

In addition to the unpublished sources on which this book is primarily based I have consulted the following books and articles:

(a) Books

AMERY, L. S., *My Political Life Vol. II 1914–1929* (Hutchinson, 1953).

ARNOLD, G., *Kenyatta and the Politics of Kenya* (J. M. Dent, 1974).

BARNETT, D. L. and NJAMA, K., *Mau Mau from Within. Autobiography and Analysis of Kenya's Peasant Revolt* (MacGibbon & Kee, 1966).

BENNETT, G., *Kenya. A Political History. The Colonial Period* (OUP, 1963).

BENNETT, G. and ROSBERG, C., *The Kenyatta Election: Kenya 1960–1961* (OUP, 1961).

BERMAN, B. and LONSDALE, J., *Unhappy Valley. Conflict in Kenya and Africa. Books I and II* (James Currey, 1992).

BLUNDELL, Sir M., *So Rough a Wind* (Weidenfeld & Nicolson, 1964).

BLUNDELL, Sir M., *A Love Affair with the Sun* (Nairobi: Keystone Publishing, 1994).

BRANTLEY, C., *The Giriama and Colonial Resistance in Kenya* (University of California Press, 1981).

BROCKWAY, A. F., *Outside the Right* (George Allen & Unwin, 1963).

CAROTHERS, J. C., *The Psychology of Mau Mau* (Government Printing Office, Nairobi, 1954).

CHURCHILL, W. S., *My African Journey* (Holland Press/Neville Spearman, 1962).

CLARKE, P. and TREBILCOCK, C. (eds), *Understanding Decline: Perceptions and Realities of British Economic Performance* (Cambridge University Press, 1997).

CORFIELD, F. D., *Historical Survey of the Origins and Growth of Mau Mau* (HMSO, 1960).

COX, R., *Pan-Africanism in Practice. PAFMECSA 1958–1964* (OUP, 1964).

DE LA GORGENDIÈRE, L. *et al.* (eds), *Ethnicity in Africa* (Edinburgh: Centre of African Studies, 1996).

DELF, G., *Jomo Kenyatta* (Victor Gollancz, 1961).

DELF, G., *Asians in East Africa* (OUP, 1963).

DOUGLAS-HOME, C., *Evelyn Baring: The Last Proconsul* (Collins, 1978).

ELIOT, Sir C., *The East Africa Protectorate* (Edward Arnold, 1905).

GAVAGHAN, T., *Corridors of Wire. A Saga of Colonial Power and Preventive Detention* (privately printed, 1994).

GERTZEL, C., *The Politics of Independent Kenya 1963–8* (Heinemann, 1970).

GHAI, D. (ed.), *Portrait of a Minority. Asians in East Africa* (OUP, 1965).

GHAI, Y. and D., *The Asian Minorities of East and Central Africa* (Minority Rights Group, 1971).

GHAI, Y. P. and McAUSLAN, J. P. W. B., *Public Law and Political Change in Kenya* (Nairobi: East African Publishing House, 1970).

GOLDSWORTHY, D., *Tom Mboya. The Man Kenya Wanted to Forget* (Heinemann, 1982).

GOLDSWORTHY, D. (ed.), *British Documents on the End of Empire Series A Vol. 3. The Conservative Government and the End of Empire 1951–1957 Part II* (HMSO, 1994).

GREGORY, R. G., *India and East Africa. A History of Race Relations within the British Empire 1890–1939* (Oxford: Clarendon Press, 1971).

HARLOW, V. and CHILVER, E. M. (eds), *History of East Africa Vol. II* (Oxford: Clarendon Press, 1965).

HEPBURN, A. C., *Minorities in History* (Edward Arnold, 1978).

HILL, M. F., *Permanent Way. The Story of the Kenya and Uganda Railway* (Nairobi: East African Railways and Harbours, 2nd edn, 1961).

HORNE, A., *Macmillan Vol. II 1957–86* (Macmillan, 1989).

HUGHES, A. J., *East Africa: The Search for Unity* (Penguin, 1963).

HUXLEY, E., *White Man's Country. Lord Delamere and the Making of Kenya Vols I–II* (Chatto & Windus, 1935).

HUXLEY, E. and PERHAM, M., *Race and Politics in Kenya* (Faber & Faber, 1956).

KAGGIA, B., *Roots of Freedom, 1921–1963* (Nairobi: East African Publishing House, 1975).

KARIMI, J. and OCHIENG, P., *The Kenyatta Succession* (Nairobi: Transafrica, 1980).

KARIUKI, J. M., *'Mau Mau' Detainee* (OUP, 1963).

KENYATTA, J., *Facing Mount Kenya* (Martin Secker & Warburg, 1938).

KENYATTA, J. *Suffering without Bitterness* (Nairobi: East Africa Publishing House, 1968).

LAMB, R., *The Macmillan Years 1957–1963. The Emerging Truth* (John Murray, 1995).

LEYS, N., *Kenya* (Hogarth Press, 1926).

LOW, D. A. and SMITH, A., *History of East Africa Vol. III* (Oxford: Clarendon Press, 1976).

LYTTELTON, O., *The Memoirs of Lord Chandos* (The Bodley Head, 1962).

MACDONALD, M. and LOKE, C., *Treasure of Kenya* (Glasgow: Collins, 1965).

MACKENZIE, W. J. M. and ROBINSON, K. (eds), *Five Elections in Africa* (Oxford: Clarendon Press, 1960).

MACMILLAN, H., *Riding the Storm 1956–1959* (Macmillan, 1971).

MACMILLAN, H., *At the End of the Day 1961–1963* (Macmillan, 1973).

MANGAT, J. S., *A History of the Asians in East Africa 1886–1945* (Oxford: Clarendon Press, 1969).

MATSON, A. T., *Nandi Resistance to British Rule* (Cambridge African Monographs, 1993).

MAUDLING, R., *Memoirs* (Sidgwick & Jackson, 1970).

MAXON, R. M., *Struggle for Kenya. The Loss and Reassertion of Imperial Initiative, 1912–1923* (Associated University Presses, 1993).

MBOYA, T. J., *Freedom and After* (Andre Deutsch, 1963).

MEINERTZHAGEN, R., *Kenya Diary 1902–1906* (Oliver & Boyd, 1957).

MOCKERIE, P. G., *An African Speaks for his People* (Hogarth Press, 1934).

MUNGEAM, G. H., *British Rule in Kenya 1895–1912. The Establishment of Administration in the East Africa Protectorate* (Oxford: Clarendon Press, 1966).

MURPHY, P., *Party Politics and Decolonization. The Conservative Party and British Colonial Policy in Tropical Africa 1951–1964* (Oxford: Clarendon Press, 1995).

MURRAY-BROWN, J., *Kenyatta* (Fontana/Collins, 1972).

NYE, J. S., *Pan-Africanism and East African Integration* (OUP, 1966).

ODINGA, A. O., *Not Yet Uhuru* (Heinemann, 1967).

OGOT, B. A., *History of the Southern Luo. Vol. 1 Migration and Settlement 1500–1900* (Nairobi: East African Publishing House, 1967).

OGOT, B. A. (ed.), *Politics and Nationalism in Colonial Kenya* (Nairobi: HADATH/East African Publishing House, 1978)

OGOT, B. A. and OCHIENG', W. R., *Decolonization and Independence in Kenya, 1940–93* (James Currey, 1995).

OLIVER, R. and MATHEW, G. (eds), *History of East Africa Vol. I* (Oxford: Clarendon Press, 1963).

PAGE, M., *A History of the King's African Rifles and East African Forces* (Leo Cooper, 1998).

PATEL, A. H., *Struggle to Release Jomo and His Colleagues* (Nairobi: New Kenya Publishers, 1963)

PERHAM, M., *East African Journey. Kenya and Tanganyika 1929–30* (Faber & Faber, 1976).

RAKE, A., *Tom Mboya. Young Man of New Africa* (New York: Doubleday, 1962).

ROBINSON, R. and GALLAGHER, J., *Africa and the Victorians. The Official Mind of Imperialism* (Macmillan, 1961).

ROSBERG, C. G. and NOTTINGHAM, J., *The Myth of 'Mau Mau'. Nationalism in Kenya* (Pall Mall Press, 1966).

ROSS, W. McG., *Kenya from Within. A Short Political History* (George Allen & Unwin, 1927).

ROTHCHILD, D., *Racial Bargaining in Independent Kenya. A Study of Minorities and Decolonization* (OUP, 1973).

SANGER, C., *Malcolm MacDonald. Bringing an End to Empire* (Liverpool University Press, 1995).

SHEPHERD, R., *Iain Macleod* (Hutchinson, 1994).

SLATER, M., *The Trial of Jomo Kenyatta* (Secker & Warburg, 1959).

SORRENSON, M. P. K., *Land Reform in the Kikuyu Country* (OUP, 1967).

SORRENSON, M. P. K., *Origins of European Settlement in Kenya* (OUP, 1968).

SPENCER, J., *James Beauttah* (Nairobi: Stellascope Publishing Company, 1983).

SPENCER, J., *The Kenya African Union* (KPI/Routledge & Kegan Paul, 1985).

THROUP, D., *Economic and Social Origins of Mau Mau* (James Currey, 1987)

THUKU, H. and KING, K., *Harry Thuku. An Autobiography* (Nairobi: OUP, 1970).

TIGNOR, R. L., *Capitalism and Nationalism at the End of Empire: State and Business in Decolonizing Egypt, Nigeria and Kenya 1945–1963* (Princeton University Press, 1998).

TRENCH, C. C., *Men Who Ruled Kenya. The Kenya Administration 1892–1963* (The Radcliffe Press, 1993).
VAN ZWANENBERG, R. M. A. and KING, A., *An Economic History of Kenya and Uganda 1800–1970* (Macmillan, 1975).
WASSERMAN, G., *Politics of Decolonization. Kenya Europeans and the Land Issue 1960–1965* (Cambridge University Press, 1976).
WELBOURN, F. B., *East African Rebels* (SCM Press, 1961).
WELBOURN, F. B., *East African Christians* (OUP, 1965).
WIDNER, J. A., *The Rise of a Party-State in Kenya. From Harambee! to Nyayo!* (Berkeley: University of California Press, 1992).

(b) Articles and Pamphlets

Atieno-Odhiambo, E. S., 'The Formative Years, 1945–55', in Ogot and Ochieng, *Decolonization and Independence in Kenya 1940–93* (James Currey, 1995).
Bennett, George, 'The Development of Political Organizations in Kenya', *Political Studies* 5, 2 (June 1967).
Bennett, George, 'Kenya's "Little General Election"', *The World Today* (RIIA, August 1966).
Callahan, Michael D., 'The Failure of "Closer Union" in British East Africa', *Journal of Imperial and Commonwealth History*, vol. 25, no. 2, May 1997.
Chesire, Wesley, 'What Part shall the Kalenjin People Play in an Independent Kenya? *Nee Rubei? Kalenjin Makerere Students Magazine*, November 1958.
Convention of Associations, *Kenya Today* (1960).
Engholm, G. F., 'African Elections in Kenya, March 1957', in Mackenzie and Robinson, *Five Elections in Kenya* (Clarendon Press, 1960).
Erskine, General Sir George, 'Kenya, Mau Mau', 23 November 1955, Imperial War Museum.
Fraser, T. G., 'Imperial Policy and Indian Minorities Overseas', in A. C. Hepburn, *Minorities in History* (Edward Arnold, 1978).
Furley, O. W., 'The Historiography of Mau Mau', in *Politics and Nationalism in Colonial Kenya*, ed. Ogot (Nairobi, 1972).
Hopkins, Tony, 'Macmillan's Audit of Empire, 1957', in Clarke and Trebilcock, *Understanding Decline* (Cambridge University Press, 1997).
Kenya Constitutional Conferences 1960, 1962, 1963 (private archive).
Kenyatta, J., 'The Voice of the Disseminator of the Work of the Country', *Muigwithania*, vol. 1, no. 11, April 1929.
Kenyatta, J., 'Muigwithania's Journey', *Muigwithania*, vol. 1, no. 12, May 1929.
Kibaki, Mwai, 'The Use for Hope', *Politica* (Makerere College Political Society) vol. 1, no. 1, May 1953.
Kikuyu Mission Council, 'Kikuyu Crisis. Church of Scotland Memorandum on Female Circumcision', 1 December 1931.
Koinange, P. M. and Oneko, A., 'Land Hunger in Kenya', *New Times and Ethiopian News*, 2 and 12 April 1952.
K. W. [Kendall Ward], 'A Preliminary Survey of the Constitutional History of Kenya', 5 October 1951, Blundell Papers, Rhodes House.

Kyle, Keith, 'White Man's War' (unpublished).

Kyle, Keith, 'Gandhi, Harry Thuku and Early Kenya Nationalism', *Transition*, 27 (Kampala, 1966).

Kyle, Keith, 'The Politics of the Independence of Kenya', *Contemporary British History*, vol. 11, no. 4, Winter 1997.

Leys, Colin, 'Politics in Kenya: The Development of Peasant Society', *British Journal of Political Science*, 1 (1971).

Lonsdale, John, 'Constructing Mau Mau', in *Transactions of the Royal Historical Society, 5th Series Vol. 40* (1990).

Lonsdale, John, 'The Politics of Conquest in Western Kenya', in Berman and Lonsdale, *Unhappy Valley Book I* (Oxford: James Currey, 1992).

Lonsdale, John, 'Jomo, God, and the Modern World', in Lonsdale and Berman, *The House of Custom: Jomo Kenyatta, Louis Leakey and the Making of the Modern Kikuyu* (forthcoming).

Makokha, C., 'The Rise of African Sects among the Baluhya', Makerere College prize essay (1951, unpublished).

Mathenge, J. P., 'The Kenya African Union – Catastrophe Ahead?', *Politica*, vol. 1, no. 2, June 1953.

Matson, A. T., 'Early Newspapers of East Africa' (private archive).

Matson, A. T., 'The Pacification of Kenya' (private archive).

Mboya, T. J., 'The Kenya Question: An African Answer' (Fabian Society, 1956).

Mboya, T. J., 'What Next in Kenya?', *West African Worker*, January 1957.

McWilliam, M. D., 'Economic Policy and the Kenya Settlers 1945–1948', in *Essays in Imperial Government*, ed. K. E. Robinson and A. F. Madden (Oxford, 1963).

Ogot, Bethwell A., 'British Administration in the Central Nyanza District of Kenya 1900–60', *Journal of African History*, IV, 2(1963).

Oyangi, J. M. 'A Nationalist Challenge to African Elected Members' Organization', in *Uhuru*, 9 December 1958.

Oza, U. K. 'Indian Settlement in East Africa', *Colonial Times*, 1 July 1933.

Pankhurst, Sylvia, 'Tom Mboya and the PCP', *Ethiopian Observer*, vols 11–12, November 1958. *Special Issue on Kenya*.

Pegushev, Andrei, 'The Unknown Jomo Kenyatta', *Egerton Journal*, vol. 1, no. 2, 1993.

Renison, Sir Patrick, 'The Challenge in Kenya', *Optima*, March 1963.

Renison, Sir Patrick, 'Kenya in Transition', *African Affairs*, 62, 249 (October 1963).

Samuel, Herbert, 'A Tourist in Uganda', *East Africa and Uganda Mail*, 10 January 1903.

Sanger, Clyde and Nottingham, John, 'The Kenya General Election of 1963', *Journal of Modern African Studies*, vol. 2, no. 1.

Index

Abdi, Yusuf Haji, 157
Africa Bureau, 88, 93
African People's Party, 173, 176–7
Aga Khan, Prince Karim, 132, 175
Agar, Omolo, 92, 173
Akech, A. M., 149
Akumu, Denis, at Tunis 104, 108;
    and GAG, 120; receives
    money from Odinga, 227n.32
Alexander, Reginald, 162
All-Africa People's Conferences,
    Accra 88–9; Tunis 104, 108–9,
    192
Alport, Cuthbert (Lord), 105
Amalemba, Musa, 83–4, 111
Ambitho, Were, 92, 119
Amery, L. S., Colonial Secretary,
    and 'closer union', 27–8, 34
Amin, Idi, 201
Andrews, Rev. C. F., 18
Argwings-Kodhek, Clement,
    personality, 71–2; president of
    Nairobi District African
    Congress, 72; launches slogan
    'Africa for the Africans', 72;
    nominated for Nairobi seat,
    73; and 'A–K Plan', 75;
    challenged by Mboya, 75; and
    implosion of NDAC, 75–6;
    attacks flies in Obote's
    mother's eyes, 76; defeated by
    Mboya, 76; proposes
    Convention of Associations,
    88; in financial difficulties, 88,
    222n.58; organizes despatch of
    students to Eastern Europe,
    92, 109; visits Nkrumah, 109;
    contests Nyanza seat, 125;
    made junior Minister, 177
Arthur, Dr J. W., 18–19, 31–2, 33
Asians, Kenya (*see also* Indians),
    82, 90, 104–5, 106, 135, 138,
    202, 218– 219n.56

Astor, David, 80
Awori, W. W. W., and KASU
    survey, 39; personality, 40;
    sent to London, 40; loses
    money, 40; editor, *Radio
    Posta*, 40; on Kenyatta's
    oratory, 215n.67; 73

Banda, Dr Hastings Kamuzu, 95,
    112
Baring, Sir Evelyn (Lord Howick),
    Governor of Kenya, 45; on
    excitability of white settlers,
    207n.35; opinion of Kenyatta,
    46–7; declares Emergency, 52;
    confrontation with white
    settlers, 63; and Lyttelton
    constitution, 64; holds Mboya
    as 'by far the most intelligent'
    African politician, 79; on
    further changes in
    constitution, 79–81; 83–4;
    restricts Kenyatta to Lodwar,
    88; not committed to
    independence by 1975, 90;
    impressed by Gavaghan, 96;
    recalled to London over Hola,
    97; Macmillan thinks can
    achieve no more, 224n.27;
    replaced by Renison, 98
Baringo District Independent
    Party, 77
Basudde, Daudi, 19
Beamish, Sir Tufton, MP (Lord
    Chelwood), 160
Bennett, (Sir) Frederic, MP, 53;
    KADU constitutional adviser,
    146; creates pro-KADU lobby,
    160–1; fears KADU losing
    ground in Whitehall, 161, 169;
    tries to pin Sandys down by
    parliamentary question, 180–1;
    blamed for giving KADU